IRMA THOMAS

American Made Music Series

IRMA THOMAS

Soul Queen of New Orleans

Johnette Downing and Scott Billington

With Irma Thomas

Foreword by Gwen Thompkins

University Press of Mississippi / Jackson

The University Press of Mississippi is the scholarly publishing agency of the Mississippi Institutions of Higher Learning: Alcorn State University, Delta State University, Jackson State University, Mississippi State University, Mississippi University for Women, Mississippi Valley State University, University of Mississippi, and University of Southern Mississippi.

www.upress.state.ms.us

The University Press of Mississippi is a member of the Association of University Presses.

Any discriminatory or derogatory language or hate speech regarding race, ethnicity, religion, sex, gender, class, national origin, age, or disability that has been retained or appears in elided form is in no way an endorsement of the use of such language outside a scholarly context.

Manufactured in the United States of America
∞

Publisher: University Press of Mississippi, Jackson, USA
Authorised GPSR Safety Representative: Easy Access System Europe - Mustamäe tee 50, 10621 Tallinn, Estonia, gpsr.requests@easproject.com

Library of Congress Cataloging-in-Publication Data

Names: Downing, Johnette author | Billington, Scott author | Thomas, Irma contributor | Thompkins, Gwen writer of foreword
Title: Irma Thomas : Soul Queen of New Orleans / Johnette Downing and Scott Billington ; with Irma Thomas.
Other titles: American made music series
Description: Jackson : University Press of Mississippi, 2026. | Series: American made music series | Includes bibliographical references and index.
Identifiers: LCCN 2026029960 (print) | LCCN 2026029961 (ebook) | ISBN 9781496865038 hardback | ISBN 9781496865045 trade paperback | ISBN 9781496865052 epub | ISBN 9781496865069 epub | ISBN 9781496865076 pdf | ISBN 9781496865083 pdf
Subjects: LCSH: Thomas, Irma | Soul musicians--United States | Rhythm and blues musicians--United States | Singers--United States | Soul music--History and criticism | Rhythm and blues music--History and criticism | LCGFT: Biographies | Interviews
Classification: LCC ML420.T456 D69 2026 (print) | LCC ML420.T456 (ebook) | DDC 782.421644092 [B]--dc23/eng/20260709
LC record available at https://lccn.loc.gov/2026029960
LC ebook record available at https://lccn.loc.gov/2026029961

British Library Cataloging-in-Publication Data available

Contents

Foreword

Irma Thomas has told her life story time and again. That's what happens over a more than sixty-year singing and recording career. The listeners get curious—fans, journalists, Dick Clark. They ask questions. But every great storyteller knows that the facts are only the beginning. They establish the basis of a plot, the all-important rhythm that the New Orleans band leader and producer Dave Bartholomew called the foundation of any song. Without that foundation, he'd say, "you ain't got nothing." What makes the facts of Thomas's life from childhood onward worth telling and retelling is that they establish why this little girl in the strawberry patch, this youngster playing with china balls, this 'tween kissing boys, this teenage divorcée and mother, this irrepressible singing waitress, this lonely woman-child, this award-winning vocalist, and now this fortunate wife and great-great-grandmother with a college degree has something substantive to say.

And yet, rarely has Thomas's story unfolded as it does in these pages. Aside from the facts, this biography shares what's true about Thomas, and that is infinitely more interesting. In biography, truth is a clear-eyed view of what happened, along with how the protagonist feels about what happened and why. That's what this book manages to capture so well. Authors Johnette Downing and Scott Billington understand great storytelling. And they have delivered Thomas's voice in ways that bring additional meaning to her discography, surprising even her deepest fans with emotional, artistic, and professional context. Try making a playlist of the recordings mentioned in each chapter of this book, then listen while reading and feel your ears expand.

The color in Thomas's voice—that tender, rich, chocolaty darkness that has grown more capacious over time—not only evokes her personal history but US history writ large for a black child of segregation. The details of Jim Crow are too many to describe in a single, albeit fascinating, biography. But the experience, no doubt, shaped her as a human being and as an artist.

And in Thomas's story, the line between state-sanctioned indifference to the needs of black people and the active efforts of many to destroy the lives of black people can be too thin to measure. "I wasn't even given anesthesia for any of my children's births, except one stillborn," Thomas says of her coming of age in New Orleans. "Only the white women got anesthetics for childbirth. This was the segregated south in the 50s."[1]

It's one thing to choose natural birth, but quite another to have that reality foisted upon you by a system inured to your pain. Hence the most revolutionary act for Thomas has been to make it through, a sage plant peeping through a crack in the pavement. And, if the act of surviving was revolutionary for someone like her, then imagine how world-changing the act of growing must have been. Thomas has done that also—time and again. Her 1992 song "True Believer,"[2] she once told me, is a favorite, in part because it reflects the life force that has sustained her over the years. And, perhaps more explicitly, Thomas's Christian faith appears to have been the deepest well from which she has drawn strength—as a daughter, a woman, a mother, a wife, and an artist. Clearly, gospel music—emanating from those childhood Sundays at rural churches in Louisiana, from her abiding love of Mahalia Jackson, and from her longtime membership in the choir of the First African Baptist Church of New Orleans—has helped Thomas find a way when there seemed to be no way forward.

To some, the foundation of Thomas's experiences—the rhythmic facts of her life—may sound like any number of American success stories, the kind that fill podcasts and graduation ceremony remarks. And yet, the melody of her life—how she has voiced her interior landscape, how she has understood, put words to, and phrased her singular memories and emotions—is also what great storytelling is all about. The songwriting producer Allen Toussaint said as much when he described writing "It's Raining," for her—one of their many collaborations. "I just wrote that song, then handed it over to her and sung a little bit of it, just to show her the melody, and it fit like a gown," he said of the 1962 release. "Like an evening gown made and tailored for her."[3] Thomas's gift as a singer is to make her own words or those of others sound like heart-speak. But that's not the end of the story.

Thomas's discography is an epic tale crowded with a never-ending cast of characters—people of nearly every culture, race, gender, economic stratum, and artistic ability have contributed to her recordings and many of them are mentioned in this book. That's because the act of creation in popular music more often than not comes from collaboration—a kind of artistic and professional harmony that may seem fraught at times, but frequently adds dimension to the storytelling. The combined ideas in Thomas's most memorable recordings help the music take flight, refining and elevating each song to become more true, universal, and, hopefully, lasting. Each collaborator brought wings to her best work, helping to make it feel essential.

The New Orleans bandleader Tommy Ridgley gave Thomas her first singing job. Joe Ruffino of Ron Records, produced her first hit single "Don't Mess with My Man." And Toussaint? Well, Toussaint gave Thomas her first taste of being artistic muse to a multifaceted creative power whose respect and friendship were evergreen. They were just kids at the beginning, but still. Then came Eddie Ray and H. B. Barnum in California, who produced and arranged Thomas's *Billboard* hits "Wish Someone Would Care" and "Anyone Who Knows What Love Is (Will Understand)." The list goes on and on and on, featuring top-drawer songwriting talent such as Randy Newman, Jerry Ragovoy, Doc Pomus, David Egan, and Dan Penn, and doesn't stop until it picks up members of the New Orleans–based funk band Galactic, who wrote and produced her late-career anthem "Heart of Steel" and then wrote and produced her first funk album, which she recorded at age eighty-three. Stories about these people and more, including background singers Darlene Love and the Blossoms and Thomas's ever-loyal backing band The Professionals, with whom she has performed for decades, are right here in this book.

Meanwhile, Thomas's fans have made it possible for her professional wingspan to exceed expectation. The concertgoers, record buyers, radio listeners and television viewers have been, to paraphrase the composer Henry Mancini, her "huckleberry friends," without whom this extraordinary career would not have been possible. Count among them the folks running the New Orleans Jazz and Heritage Festival, who have featured her, by popular demand, on their biggest stages for more than half a century. Count the award-winning documentarians who've broadcast her story across public television and radio. And count me, too. As a New Orleanian, I have long loved Thomas's music. And when Rounder Records released her 2006 album *After the Rain* I insisted she come to Washington, DC, and appear on NPR's *Weekend Edition*, where I was then senior editor. The moment Thomas began singing, everyone in the studio stopped what they were doing—spellbound. Months later, she called me out at a dry cleaner in New Orleans, saying "I know you're not leaving here without saying hello!" And I've been her huckleberry ever since. Later, I interviewed her over two episodes of my public radio program *Music Inside Out* and they were among the most popular shows we ever produced.

Downing, a multiple award-winning poet, children's book writer, children's music performer and recording artist, is yet another ardent Thomas fan and the lead author of this biography. She and Thomas have recorded together and sung live at the New Orleans Jazz Fest. Their duet, called "Poor Worry Anna," is featured on an album of folk songs for children that Downing released in 2019—an album that also includes Billington playing harmonica.

It was a good day for music when Billington and Thomas met. For thirty years, he produced her albums on Rounder Records. Their collaboration resulted in ten albums and more accolades than even Thomas can name. Most notably, she earned a 2006 Grammy Award®, induction into the Louisiana Blues Hall of Fame, and inclusion in NPR's 50 Voices of the 20th Century series. The news organization honored Thomas as the "Soul Queen of New Orleans," alongside Enrico Caruso, Billie Holiday, Nat "King" Cole, Howlin' Wolf, and Nusrat Fateh Ali Khan, among others.

No one spends three decades working with Thomas and then embarks on cowriting a biography as deeply researched and insightful as this one without himself being a fan and a friend. Billington, who also produced nine albums with the R&B, gospel, and jazz singer Johnny Adams as well as pivotal releases from Clarence "Gatemouth" Brown, Charlie Rich, the piano virtuoso James Booker, and Bobby Rush, among others, placed Thomas in sonic spheres that best revealed her to listeners. Musically speaking, his ears are huge. And just as she recorded as a young singer with members of the Wrecking Crew in California (a term that not all of those masterful session players appreciated), Billington placed her with members of New Orleans's own Wrecking Crew—David Torkanowsky on piano (who also accompanied Thomas that day at NPR in Washington, DC), James Singleton on bass, and other founders of the jazz band Astral Project, as well as drummer Herman "Roscoe" Ernest III, and session musicians from the Toussaint hit factory, Sea-Saint Studios. Some of the Thomas-Billington releases were orchestrated and electric, while others framed her within a more acoustic setting. At least one album was recorded live with The Professionals. But they all show varying facets of a performer who is capable of conveying the full spectrum of emotion, bringing humanity, humor when possible, and good common sense to each song.

Billington writes about what came together easily for Thomas in the studio and what required extra work. He describes their process—the cutting and stitching of musical takes, as well as how they went about choosing and recording songs in such a way that an album playlist could roll out seamlessly, like a bolt of damask, never hitting the floor. Billington cops to mistakes that he or they may have made over the years—the kinds of stumbles that are inevitable when people try to bring something into the world that has never before existed and get paid for doing so. In fact, the frankness with which Thomas and the authors handle the business side of her career adds a refreshing layer of truth to the book.

There are few clichés here—no romantic descriptions of success as mere luck, or hidden nepotism shyly revealed. Nor are Thomas's tribulations presented as stereotype, intimating that being born poor and black meant that only a white savior could have catapulted her to success. Being prepared, punctual, good at math, and a saver of money have always mattered most for people who work in music and this book explains exactly why.

Downing and Billington demonstrate a real talent for unearthing the corresponding research to support this magisterial rendering of Thomas's life. New Orleanians will be reminded of the much-loved Central City clubs that were popular in the golden era of R&B, as well as the Lion's Den, near Orleans Parish Prison, that Thomas and her husband-manager Emile Jackson once owned. That's where they sold dinners that Thomas had prepared herself and where she sang a full set of songs to rooms packed with customers and even to an audience as tiny as two. What a pro. But for all readers, this book bears witness to one of the most exciting eras of American popular music, and a woman's invaluable contributions to it, in song. The strawberries Thomas picked, the boys she kissed, the babies she bore, the men she married, the dresses she sewed, the fish she caught, the loneliness she felt, and the education she longed for and eventually earned helped give her the voice she needed in those many years and in the ensuing decades.

"I don't scream," Thomas famously told a producer in Los Angeles. She doesn't need to. Her feelings are there in the songs. And in these pages. Thomas prefers to tell the truth.

Gwen Thompkins
Executive Producer and Host,
Music Inside Out

IRMA THOMAS

Introduction

The music of New Orleans is different. In no other American city did so many musical elements simultaneously come together. Blues, Afro-Cuban rhythms, traditional jazz, barrelhouse piano, ragtime, military bands, marching brass bands, Dixieland jazz, gospel music, and French opera all flourished side by side, each shaping the evolution of the other. From a cultural standpoint, New Orleans is perhaps the most Creolized city in the United States. As Eric Seiferth and Alfred Lemmon wrote, "New Orleans music is not one type of music, nor one type of rhythm, and its origin cannot be attributed to one kind of New Orleanian. Interrelated in a thousand small ways, some predictable, others less so, the sounds of the city are a result of our unique cultural and social history."[1] Music is central to life in the Crescent City, where children learn the cadences and body rhythms of their culture as a birthright, through their early exposure to brass bands at jazz funerals and Sunday afternoon second line parades, Mardi Gras Indians, traditional jazz, gospel choirs, and Mardi Gras anthems such as Al Johnson's "Carnival Time" and Stop, Incorporated's "Second Line." Music is inescapable.

Rhythm and blues evolved as a distinctive new genre in the years following World War II, when swing, blues, and jazz were melding across the nation into a hybrid sound that was more muscular and immediate than any of its antecedents. However, New Orleans rhythm and blues had an edge, and in many ways it led the charge. The confluence of a street sensibility with tight musical arrangements, the pronounced Caribbean influence, the syncopated snare and bass drum patterns, the horn ensembles, the piano triplets, and the casual ebullience of the singers are all trademarks. New Orleans musicians had a deep well from which to draw. Then, as now, they often crossed genres in a way that gave the music an accomplished virtuosity, with the result that New Orleans rhythm and blues had an idiosyncratic depth of local character. Smiley Lewis, Ernie K-Doe, Fats Domino, The Meters, and Professor Longhair could come from nowhere else.

From the late 1940s to the early 1970s—the golden era of New Orleans rhythm and blues—music assumed a place of elevated importance in the community. There were a great number of employment opportunities for rhythm and blues musicians and ensembles, in clubs such as the Club Delise, The Pimlico Club, The Blue Eagle, The Autocrat Club, The Hi-Hat, and the Dew Drop Inn; at concerts at Lincoln Beach on Lake Pontchartrain; at high school dances and proms; and at college fraternity parties. Radio stations played local records and could make a local hit, giving artists publicity and a big enough audience to work at nightclubs and other venues across the Gulf Coast, where clubs such as the 100 Men Hall in Bay St. Louis, Mississippi, and the Sugar Bowl in Thibodaux, Louisiana, resonated with the sounds of New Orleans. It was an era in which a determined, charismatic, and creative singer could make a name for herself.

Although a music business infrastructure never coalesced in New Orleans in the way that it did in Los Angeles, New York, or Nashville, national record labels occasionally sent their artists to New Orleans to record because the musicians and the groove there were not easily duplicated elsewhere. In the 1950s, the recording destination was Cosimo Matassa's J&M Studio, where the house band played on hits such as Roy Brown's "Good Rocking Tonight" and Little Richard's "Tutti Frutti." New Orleans–born Antoine "Fats" Domino Jr., whose piano and lilting vocals were abetted by the arrangements of cowriter and producer Dave Bartholomew, was one of the best-selling artists of the 1950s, with songs such as "Blueberry Hill," "I'm Walkin'," and "Blue Monday." Domino is considered to be one of the pioneers of rock and roll music.

In the late 1950s and early 1960s, many local entrepreneurs realized that they could turn a modest profit by recording, releasing, and promoting local rhythm and blues. Occasionally, one of them would hit the jackpot with a national hit. Thus, it was small, independent record labels such as Ace, Ric/Ron, Minit, Scram, Bo-Sound, and Sansu that introduced artists such as Johnny Adams, Shirley and Lee, Aaron Neville, and Ernie K-Doe. There was often a sure-footed quirkiness in these records: the syncopation of Professor Longhair's piano playing, the deep grooves and downright goofiness of Huey "Piano" Smith and the Clowns, and the raw, proto-funk of Eddie Bo. By the early 1970s, international artists were again traveling to New Orleans to record with pianist, songwriter, and arranger Allen Toussaint at his Sea-Saint Studios, where he hosted Paul McCartney and produced the best-selling LaBelle hit "Lady Marmalade."

Yet, perhaps no artist in the New Orleans rhythm and blues pantheon is as beloved as Irma Thomas, whose story is a lesson in steadiness, perseverance, and trusting her gut instinct when it came to controlling her destiny and career. Her voice, her ability to communicate the story in the lyrics of a song, and the warmth of her presence exemplify the complete and enduring joy of New Orleans music.

Irma was part of the "second wave" of New Orleans R&B in the 1960s, and the twenty songs she recorded with Allen Toussaint embody the essence of the era. Their records such as "It's Raining," "Ruler of My Heart," "Cry On," and "Take a Look" tap into the full spectrum of the city's musical roots, while simultaneously revealing Allen's wholly original compositional mind. It was one of the great songwriter/singer partnerships of the twentieth century, despite their modest output. Her recordings made in Los Angeles for Imperial Records with producer Eddie Ray and arranger H. B. Barnum, including "Wish Someone Would Care" (her biggest national hit), "Anyone Who Knows What Love Is (Will Understand)" and "Time Is on My Side," are among the most powerful rhythm and blues–influenced pop records of the era, and her most enduring work.

Irma went on to record in many of the greatest hit-making studios of the 1960s and 1970s, including FAME Studios in Muscle Shoals, Alabama; Sigma Sound in Philadelphia; Criteria in Miami; and Malaco Studios in Jackson, Mississippi. Seeking stability for her family, she moved to Los Angeles and then to Oakland, but eventually found that her greatest opportunities remained at home in New Orleans. Her performances at the New Orleans Jazz and Heritage Festival brought her new acclaim. In 1986, she signed with Rounder Records, working with producer Scott Billington on a series of recordings that would result in their four Grammy® nominations and a 2006 Grammy® win.

However, there is more to Irma. Her career has endured for nearly sixty years, with her voice virtually undiminished at the age of eighty-five. In fact, Irma believes her voice is better now, with the rich tone of a seasoned performer. Her discography reflects the sensibility of an artist who has never lost touch with her deep connection to her city and her fans. After Irma graduated from Delgado University, the Irma Thomas Center for W.I.S.E. Women (Women in Search of Excellence) at the university was founded in her honor to help young women pursue their educational goals. She has toured the world, but she remains, as she often says, "just Irma."

In this book, we will follow Irma's life within the context of the period of cultural blossoming in which she was reared. Despite setbacks along the way, this is a story of optimism and long-term success: of "doing what needed to be done" to make it to the next day or the next concert stage, with a sureness rooted in faith. Above all, Irma simply wanted to sing, and the joy she found in doing so, and in communicating that joy to her audiences, sustained her from her first talent show performance as a girl to her new projects in her ninth decade. This book tells the story of her remarkably durable career in the music business.

CHAPTER ONE

Country Girl

(1941–1946)

"You're lucky to be here at all," Irma Lee was told by her mother, Vader Todd. From Anacoco, Louisiana, Todd was the eldest of eighteen children, and she had done her share of child-rearing and caring for her siblings. She was not especially interested in starting a family of her own, especially a large one.

Irma's parents learned they were pregnant with Irma just before her father, Percy Lee, left to serve in World War II. With the help of a midwife, Irma Lee was born at home on February 18, 1941, in the small city of Ponchatoula, the strawberry capital of Louisiana, located in Tangipahoa Parish about an hour northwest of New Orleans on Highway 51. A few months later, Todd moved with her newborn to a home on Franklin Street in the Central City section of New Orleans (the neighborhood would later be demolished as part of New Orleans's "urban renewal" in the 1960s).

Irma did not know her biological father until she was three or four years old. She said, "The man I thought was my father, L. J. Milton, actually was not. Being unmarried and not wanting her child to be labeled illegitimate, my mother chose to marry L. J. My biological father returned home from the Army. I'm certain it was still during wartime because I remember my mother scolding me for playing with ration tokens, which were very valuable items, not toys. She later explained that we needed them to buy food. As an only child, I often amused myself with things around the house, not realizing their true value. Once my real father returned, L. J. Milton was no longer in the picture."

Nonetheless, Irma kept the last name of Milton until she started school. It wasn't until many years later, when she applied for a passport as Irma Lee

Irma's mother, Vader Todd. (Photograph courtesy of Irma Thomas)

Milton that she discovered that her real father's name was not on her birth certificate. Percy Lee was able to hire a lawyer to remedy the situation, and as a result, according to Irma, she has two birth certificates.

Vader Todd took a job at the Southern Bell Telephone Company office at Poydras and Carondelet Streets, while her father worked at the Dibert, Bancroft and Ross Company, a steel rolling mill located between Jefferson Davis Parkway (renamed Norman C. Francis Parkway in 2020) and Tulane Avenue. They never actually married because Lee's previous marriage had not been legally dissolved. Still, their bond was strong and enduring, and the family moved into a small upstairs apartment—one room and a kitchen—in a rooming house in the back of the Vogue Hotel at 2231 Thalia Street, in Central City. The Vogue Hotel, listed in the *The Negro Motorist Green*

Book as a recommended place to stay in New Orleans, was a popular resting spot for touring musicians. The *Green Book*, published by Victor Hugo Green beginning in 1936, helped Black motorists and travelers find welcoming accommodations, food, gas stations, and other services.

"The Vogue Hotel had an entertainment lounge or club on the ground floor, where I used to play," Irma recalled. "Neighborhoods were much safer then, so I could wander around at will without fear of harm. I got to meet some performers that my mother told me were well-known in the Black community, such as Louis Jordan, Cecil Gant, and Nellie Lutcher."

These stylish musical giants were among the most popular jukebox artists and touring attractions of their day, each playing music that could be described as early rhythm and blues. The quick-witted entertainer Louis Jordan, known as the "King of the Jukebox," was a key figure in the development of this emerging music style, with numerous hits including "Caledonia," "Choo Choo Ch-Boogie," and "Let the Good Times Roll." Pianist Cecil Gant's 1944 hit "I Wonder" became a blues ballad standard, while the clear-voiced Lake Charles, Louisiana–born singer and pianist Nellie Lutcher had major hits with "Hurry on Down," "He's a Real Gone Guy," and "Fine Brown Frame." While Irma does not recall specifics, the presence of these artists in her childhood playground made an impression, if only for the glamor they exuded.

In the 1930s and 1940s, many radio stations and networks featured broadcasts of live music (such as Nashville's Grand Ole Opry, and Artie Shaw's big band broadcasts from New York on the CBS network), but radio airplay for records in most genres of music—country, modern jazz, blues, and early rhythm and blues—did not become common until after World War II, and it did not happen in New Orleans until the late 1940s. Still, hit songs could be made on the jukebox. The Rock-Ola jukebox company posits that jukeboxes once consumed up to three quarters of the records pressed in the country.[1] The word itself was coined, with initial resistance from the companies that manufactured them, to describe the record-playing machines that were especially popular in barrooms—in vernacular "jukes" or juke joints. In fact, the music trade magazine *Cash Box* was initially published to serve the jukebox industry, with a chart of top jukebox plays. It initiated its Top 100 record sales chart only in 1959, after radio had fully replaced jukeboxes as the most important means of exposure and promotion for record companies.

Irma had always been drawn to music. When she could not be found, her mother knew to look in the corner barroom since Irma was fascinated with the jukebox there. Irma said, "One of my favorite places to wander was a barroom called Del P's around the corner that had an autophone [likely the Panoram, made by the Mills Novelty Company], which was a jukebox with a picture screen. When customers played a record, a little movie would play on the screen. Although I was only about three or four years old, I played the autophone a lot, with nickels and dimes that people, even entertainers, gave me to play records. My favorite was 'Paper Doll' ('I'm going to buy a paper doll to call my own') by the Mills Brothers. And, of course, I danced a lot. I have always been a little ham. Back then it wasn't strange for children to go into a barroom. Lots of times, parents brought their kids with them when they went out for fun. My parents took me with them rather than pay a babysitter. The result is that I learned to love music at a very young age." She also recalled "The Honeydripper" by Oklahoma-born Joe Liggins, a swinging record that was a bridge between jazz and rhythm and blues, as one of her jukebox favorites. Anyone who knows Irma today would find it easy to imagine the charismatic, pretty girl charming the bar's patrons with her dancing.

Although young Irma could be brought along with her parents during recreation hours, there was the issue of childcare while her parents worked. Irma was enrolled in Sarah Allen Daycare in the Union Bethel African Methodist Episcopal (AME) Church, where she graduated from kindergarten, and subsequently at the rigorous Mount Zion Lutheran School, at the intersection Thalia and Franklin Streets, where she began acquiring the fundamentals of her education. However, finding an after-school babysitter remained a challenge for her parents.

Irma said, "My father was very protective of me and refused to hire just anybody. They finally found a lady they thought was reliable who lived in our rooming house. How mistaken they were. She wound up causing one of my most serious childhood illnesses: food poisoning. I don't think the lady did it intentionally. She was trying to feed me something, and whatever she fed me made me sick."

Irma remembered another accident that occurred when she was staying with her mother's sister, Aunt Rose, in New Orleans. She was playing near a toy factory around the corner on Clio Street when she stepped on a sharp object which pierced her foot and cut her ankle. The factory stamped parts out of sheet metal during the manufacturing process, and the discarded shards were thrown behind the building. Irma said, "I still have the scar. Aunt Rose didn't take me to the hospital; instead, she treated the wound with turpentine and cobwebs. [In traditional Southern healing, the application of turpentine to wounds was believed to stop bleeding, while spider webs were believed to be an antifungal and antiseptic to minimize infection.] Then they wrapped my foot. There weren't many doctors who would treat Black people. You could go to Charity Hospital and you might get waited on or you might not. Although the treatment was unorthodox, it obviously worked. I survived to tell about it."

In 1946, the family moved again, this time to 4126 Laurel Street in uptown New Orleans, the home of her father's cousin, Juanita White. They lived on one side of a typical New Orleans home called a shotgun double, a raised rectangular structure with all the rooms and doors aligned, so called because if a gun were theoretically fired through the front door, the bullet would exit through the back door. Actually, the structural design was intentional to help ventilate the home through cross breezes before the time of air-conditioning. Irma recalled, "My mother, father, and I all slept in one of the rooms. Several cousins also lived in that house: Juanita, her mother Aunt Queenie; Juanita's daughters, Deedee and Joann; and her son, Billy. While living on Laurel Street, I went to Blessed Sacrament Catholic School, which was five or six blocks away off Laurel. The nuns made us go to confession, but I would just sit there. I mean, what does a little kid have to confess? You ate one cookie? Two cookies instead of one?"

Between June 13–17, 1946, Tropical Storm One would give Irma her first hurricane season experience. Irma said, "This was long before hurricanes had names. To get out of harm's way, my dad decided that we should seek refuge at the Municipal Auditorium in downtown New Orleans. This was many, many miles away from Laurel Street. We left home before the weather got too severe; it was only raining. My parents carried umbrellas, and I wore a raincoat, but no galoshes. My shoes were soaked by the time we reached our destination. It's funny how I remember stuff like that, insignificant occurrences that seem to have no real bearing on life. On the other hand, it's things like that that helped to toughen me up for the problems and hardships that most of us eventually have to face in life." The inevitable hurricanes in New Orleans may also have a more subtle effect on the *laissez faire* attitude that pervades the city's culture, because in a place where everything can be blown away or washed away during any hurricane season, the earthly pleasures of life, music among them, assume a place of elevated importance.

Irma's father was becoming increasingly concerned about his daughter's wellbeing. The babysitter who had accidentally poisoned Irma had passed away, and the logistics of caring for his young child in New Orleans, while he and Irma's mother worked full-time jobs, became overwhelming for him. As a result, in 1946, when Irma was five years old, he sent her to live with his mother, Emma Miles, and his sister, Caretha Cryer, in Greensburg,

Irma's father, Percy Lee (left) and his brother (whose name cannot be recalled). (Photograph courtesy of Irma Thomas)

Louisiana, a rural town north of New Orleans near the Mississippi border, where he had been born. After her grandmother, Ms. Miles, died that same year, Irma stayed with Ms. Cryer and her children until 1950. In summer months, she often lived with her great aunt and great uncle, Pauline and Ernest Doughty, in Hammond, Louisiana, and she occasionally stayed with other family members in the area. Her Aunt Pauline and Uncle Ernest, whom Irma remembered as humorous and always joking around, each lived to be over a hundred years old.

Irma felt like a city girl living in the country and, although she found her situation strange and difficult, she said, ". . . as a child, you adjust to your surroundings because you don't have much choice. You either live it or you don't. My parents decided that's where they wanted me to be at that time, so I gleaned what I could from living out there."[2]

"Greensburg is really in the country. My grandmother owned thirty to thirty-four acres of land there. I vividly recall the unpainted house—which is still there, by the way—as a typical square building with four posts across the front porch. The house seemed huge to me. I was only five. What did I know? The front door was right in the middle of the house with windows on each side. Instead of window panes, all the windows had double-hinged shutters. My grandmother's room, also the living room, was the first room to the left. It had a fireplace and a large black pot-bellied stove that fascinated me.

"The next room towards the back of the house was that of my Aunt Caretha, who had three children of her own. Also at the back of the house was the kitchen. To the right of the house was the children's room, where I slept with all of my cousins. We had a wrought iron bed with a mattress made of cotton and corn shucks. It made a lot of noise when we got in it. I loved the tin roof that made sleep very comfortable. The rhythmic tapping of raindrops lulled me into a sound sleep. Listening to the radio was a welcomed diversion from the boredom of sitting out on the porch, looking at nothing, watching the flies buzz by and the birds take wing during the day, and listening to the crickets at night. Life was peaceful, typically country. Our nearest neighbors were at least a quarter of a mile away. Children played simple games like hopscotch, on roughly drawn squares in the dirt. We jumped rope, talked about much of nothing, or made up stories. Occasionally we visited a neighbor."

Country life was not all fun and games. There was work to be done. "Everybody in the family was a strawberry picker. From the time you could barely walk, they would take you in the fields with them. You carried your baby wherever you were working at that time. Wearing rubber boots was necessary to keep the snakes from biting. Even though I was quite young, I had to go with them to the strawberry patch and they showed me how to pick strawberries. Workers were paid fifty cents per 'carry'—a basket that contained twelve smaller baskets. I don't remember ever making more than two dollars on any given day. But I was still quite young, not more than six or seven years old. They just had me join them in the field to keep me busy. They used to tease me about how I ate more strawberries than I picked."

In her interviews for her *My Life in Music* WYES/PBS television special, Irma told Cilista Eberle, "John Lee Hooker had a record out called 'Boogie Chillen,' and my uncle used to play the radio all the time. And so I would be out in the strawberry field in my rubber boots doing what I called boogie chillen dancing, and singing 'Boogie Chillen.' And they would tell my Dad when he would come to visit me, 'That girl ain't gonna be nothing. She is just out there singing and she won't pick any strawberries.'"[3] She was discovering, however playfully, that she enjoyed singing and entertaining much more than what might be the more practical job at hand. It would be a pattern that she repeated several times before realizing her true career path.

In Greensburg, she was enrolled in the one-room New Star School. Sometimes, the fancy city clothes Irma's father brought her on visits provoked a rivalry with her cousins. Thus, her great aunt sent Irma to school in overalls so that she would fit in with her cousins and the other students. Irma remembers that she was reading by the age of four, before she attended New Star School. She said, "Reading came easy to me because I've always been fascinated with words. I loved to look at the printed word, reading whatever I could pick up or stumble through.

"New Star had impressive floors that were always waxed to a high shine, and we kids would take off our shoes and slide across the floor in our socks. When I was about seven, I stuck a huge splinter across the fleshy part of my big toe. Removing it was nothing nice. The teachers took out the splinter and patched me up. The school day continued. I didn't go home. Instead, I just hobbled around for the rest of the day."

It was at New Star that her teacher, Miss Clovis Hearse, discovered that Irma had a talent for singing, and told Irma that her voice was something special. Miss Hearse gave Irma her first opportunity to perform on stage in a school production of *Cinderella*. Irma remembered being asked to sing the "Tennessee Waltz," even though, looking back, she had no idea what that song had to do with *Cinderella*.

Irma remembered her teacher, "Miss Hearse was a tall, stout, fair-skinned woman with beautiful long hair. She was always well-dressed, very proper, and very kind. Miss Hearse taught the lower grades, first through third. Another teacher taught fourth and fifth grades."

The musical influences of her childhood were broad, and like many singers of the time, Irma drew inspiration from the church. Her mother belonged to the Sanctified church and her father was a Methodist.[4] A core tenet of the Sanctified church is that believers were put on Earth for an express purpose, as vessels for the Holy Spirit. This principle stayed with Irma for her entire life, as she believed her voice was a gift from God for the purpose of making others happy.

Her life in rural Louisiana centered on church. "Every Sunday, my whole family had to go to church, and we all had to sing. Even though we didn't have any special solos, we sat together and sang as a group. On special holidays like Christmas and Easter, children recited little poems or performed small parts in short plays. At the same time I realized I could sing, I became aware of my acting or performing talent. I was fearless when I performed in front of an audience. I truly enjoyed it. I was a natural born ham from the beginning."

Expanding upon this idea, Irma told journalist Meg Pier, "All children were given things to do on various Sundays—either you read a little piece or you sang a little song, you did something in the church as an upfront person. All the kids were given an opportunity to do something, so I was accustomed to being in front of an audience. It became a natural thing for me to be in front of people because I've been doing it practically all my life. I learned to read by going to Sunday school—they gave us these little cards that had little synopses of scriptures on them with a picture explaining what the scriptures were about."[5]

The radio would also serve as a source of inspiration for Irma as it introduced her to a variety of musical genres and artists in Louisiana and beyond. "On Sundays, I also enjoyed listening to the radio. This was a special treat because my aunt's radio was battery operated, so she didn't play it much. We listened to the gospel music of Mahalia Jackson, The Five Blind Boys, Sister Rosetta Tharpe, The Clara Ward Singers, and others. When not listening to gospel, we tuned in to hillbilly music. At night, we listened to John R and his rhythm and blues music show."

Beginning in the late 1940s, Gallatin, Tennessee's "clear channel" AM radio station WLAC aired disc jockey John "John R" Richbourg's influential program, which could be heard throughout the South and, on clear nights, as far away as the island of Jamaica, where the sounds of American rhythm and blues, and New Orleans music in particular, excited listeners and wielded a strong influence on the development of ska music. Similarly, Nashville's broadcast of the Grand Ole Opry on WSM was a major factor in the popularization of country music. These and other powerful clear channel radio stations were licensed by the FCC to ensure that rural listeners had access to information broadcast on the radio (and later for national defense purposes), but their influence on the promulgation of popular music cannot be underestimated, especially for a budding singer in rural Louisiana.

While attending New Star, young Irma suddenly announced to her family that she wanted to go to "the big school," St. Helena High, a first through twelfth grade school in Greensburg. She said, "I very much wanted to ride the school bus with the rest of my older cousins who went to school there. I was supposed to register for the second grade, but I was placed in the third grade instead. However, my days at St. Helena were short lived. Because I was so little, the bigger kids picked on me on the school bus. My older cousins rode the same bus, but they were little to no help. They were part of my problem as far as harassment goes. It seems that's what a lot of older kids, even relatives, do: pick on the younger kids. For my own safety, Aunt Caretha put me back in New Star with Miss Hearse for third and fourth grades."

Irma's father had four sisters and one brother. His oldest sister, Lorena, lived about twenty-five minutes from Caretha, which made it easy for regular visits. "My Aunt Caretha had what we called a truck garden, meaning that we grew all our vegetables, and we ate from the field—snap beans or butter beans or turnip greens. There was no supermarket. We literally lived off the land. We would go fishing occasionally just to have something different to eat. When we would go up by Aunt Lorena's house, she had older children who would go fishing, and I would tag along. That's how I learned how to fish."

In the country, the cooking detail was given to the eldest child in the family, who, in the case of Irma's extended family, was her cousin Luberta. The family had meat once or twice per week—usually products such as ham that could be smoked or cured and kept without refrigeration. With fresh produce from the garden, Irma recalled not being sick during her time in the country. She attributes some of the well-being to a monthly dose of castor oil, with an orange chaser to help the taste. As a result, Irma would not eat oranges for many years afterward.[6]

Irma also lived with her Aunt Maybelle, another one of her father's sisters. "My Aunt Maybelle had one daughter named Viney May Johnson, but everybody called her Stella for some reason. Don't even ask where that came from. For about a year, Viney and I lived with Aunt Maybelle in her house up on a hill. To me, the house always looked like it had holes in it because it leaked a lot. It wasn't very well kept either. Naturally, I was not too happy living there. Still, Aunt Maybelle was a loving person. I stayed with all of my father's sisters except Aunt Lorena. She had too many children and there wasn't room for an extra child. Yet from time to time I did spend a couple of nights with her and her children."

In her extended family environment, Irma was well cared for by the women who always saw that she had a secure place to stay. She developed the confidence to stand up for herself as she moved from one family setting to the next, and learned the people and survival skills that would help her throughout life.

CHAPTER TWO

Surrounded by Music

(1947–1953)

Irma's middle childhood years were spent in constant motion. In 1950, at the age of nine, she decided that she had experienced enough of country life, and told her father that she was going to return to New Orleans, one way or another. She was persuasive enough that he relented, and she was soon living again with her parents, even as they moved frequently from one inner city neighborhood to another. Nonetheless, these were happy years. Irma remembered New Orleans as a gentle place, at that time, with neighborhoods that were safe, where a girl could enjoy the pastimes of childhood.

Musically, it was a dynamic time to be in New Orleans, as the rhythm and blues sound began to emerge as a driving musical and cultural force, both locally and nationally. In January 1950, the pianist and sunny-voiced New Orleans singer Fats Domino had released his first record, "The Fat Man," which reached #2 on the *Billboard* rhythm and blues singles chart. It is a reworking of the traditional "Junker's Blues," an explicitly drug-related song that was first recorded by New Orleans pianist Champion Jack Dupree in 1940, and which would also resurface as Lloyd Price's "Lawdy Miss Clawdy" and Professor Longhair's "Tipitina." With its driving backbeat, played by drummer Earl Palmer, and propulsive piano part, it has come to be regarded as one of the first rock and roll records, and as a harbinger of the New Orleans rhythm and blues to come. It was recorded at J&M Studio on North Rampart Street, where recording engineer Cosimo Matassa, with whom Irma would later work, made innumerable hit records with a rotating cast of musicians who created a distinctive New Orleans rhythm and blues sound.

There were other New Orleans records on the national rhythm and blues sales chart, including Professor Longhair's "Bald Head" (as Roy Byrd [an approximation of his real name, Henry Roeland Byrd] and His Blues Jumpers), Dave Bartholomew's "My Fool," and Jewel King's "3 x 7 = 21," but Irma was initially drawn to the smooth vocals of Nat "King" Cole, while maintaining her affinity for her father's blues and gospel records by artists such as Percy Mayfield, Mahalia Jackson, John Lee Hooker, Lightnin' Hopkins, and Nellie Lutcher, and by records she heard on local jukeboxes by artists such as the Virginia-born singer Ruth Brown, who is often referred to as the "Queen of R&B."

At the same time, Bourbon Street, in the heart of the French Quarter, had become a tourist destination, offering music, burlesque shows, dancing, and an atmosphere of general hedonism, the likes of which could not be found elsewhere in the United States. It was a tamped-down version of Storyville, the notorious red-light district at the edge of the French Quarter, which had been shut down in 1917, and which had served as an important incubator of early jazz music.

The primary style of music on the Bourbon strip was the traditional jazz variant called Dixieland, with star attractions such as clarinetist Pete Fountain and trumpet player Al Hirt. However, there was also work for musicians in other genres. Pianists such as Isidore "Tuts" Washington, John Leon "Archibald" Gross, Kid Stormy Weather, and Walter "Fats" Pichon worked on Bourbon Street and in the French Quarter as early as the 1930s, playing barrelhouse (so called for the liquor that was served straight from the barrel in rough barrooms), blues, jazz, standards, and boogie-woogie. By the 1950s, rhythm and blues artists such as Tommy Ridgley and Smiley Lewis were playing on the strip, while Clarence "Frogman" Henry (who sang in a croaky frog voice on his 1956 hit, "Ain't Got No Home") worked in various Bourbon Street clubs until the early 1980s.[1] Tuba player and traditional jazz enthusiast Alan Jaffe would found Preservation Hall in the French Quarter in 1961, with the objective of providing a home for older jazz styles that were being replaced on the strip by rock and roll, rhythm and blues, and burlesque, but it would not be until many years later, after his son Ben took over operations, that the Hall would figure into Irma's career.

New Orleans rhythm and blues was gradually making its way not only onto neighborhood jukeboxes, but also onto local radio stations. At first, as listener demand grew, only white disc jockeys were allowed to be the on-air personalities who played the music, but that would soon change. Vernon Winslow, a University of Chicago–trained advertising designer, had first aspired to be a jazz disc jockey while he was employed at Dillard University, but his initial job in New Orleans radio had been to write on-air copy in an approximation of Black hipster dialect for Duke "Poppa Stoppa" Thiele, a white disc jockey on WJMR. After reading one of his own scripts on the air, he was fired, but in 1949, he broke new ground when he was hired by WWEZ.[2] As "Dr. Daddy-O," Winslow became the first Black disc jockey in New Orleans. His Sunday evening program "Jivin' With Jax" (sponsored by the local Jax beer brewery) included local music and on-air interviews with both regional and national artists such as Duke Ellington and Ivory Joe Hunter, and the show became a sensation.[3] He proved himself an adept scat singer as he introduced his news segment: "'Ooo-ee! There you go. It's blues dawn [Winslow scat sings]. It's our theme song bringing you news and blues. That's right, news and blues. First we give you the latest batch of headlines from the wires of the United Press, then we come right smack dab back at you, knock 'em down dead, you heard it Fred, with the block-hoppin', tree toppin', beboppin' blues.'"[4]

In many ways, he was a prototypical rapper (a tradition exemplified by the ribald poetic "toasts" that were a deep part of Black American culture, and popularized in the work of comedians such as Rudy Ray "Dolemite" Moore). Winslow also wrote a weekly column for *Louisiana Weekly* called "Boogie Beat." More disc jockeys such as Walter "Okey Dokey" Boatner on WBOK and Ken "Jack the Cat" Elliot on WNOE soon entered the field, each dedicated to playing rhythm and blues and especially the locally produced records that their audiences demanded. A new New Orleans's musical identity, apart from the second line parade music and traditional jazz ensembles, but influenced by both, was literally in the air, helping to shape Irma's emerging musical consciousness.

Irma recalled her trip back to the city the summer of 1950: "I told my daddy that if he didn't bring me back to New Orleans, I was going to go home by myself. He knew I was serious because I had already pulled a similar stunt with my mother. I didn't know what being afraid was, because I'd never been in a situation where I needed to be afraid.

"One summer while I was living with my Aunt Caretha, my mother came to take me to visit her mother and father [Aria and Will Todd] in Leesville, Louisiana. We traveled by bus. Her plan was to spend about two weeks with them. But, I got a little bored because the only person I had to play with was

Irma's grandparents, Aria and Will Todd, and her Uncle Morgan. (Photograph courtesy of Irma Thomas)

my Aunt Martha, my mother's teenaged baby sister. Girls this age are not interested in playing with a young child of eight years old like me. However, to her credit, she did teach me how to ride a bike. Still, I decided I wanted to go home, but my mother wasn't ready. Then she made the mistake of giving me my ticket and telling me to go home, if that's what I wanted to do. So, I proceeded to pack my little suitcase, and Aunt Martha brought me to the station, where I got on the bus for New Orleans. First, I rode the bus from Leesville to Alexandria, and then transferred to a bus that took me to New Orleans. I really went home by myself. Remembering this bold and brave behavior of mine, my father knew that if he didn't come and get me from the country, I would most assuredly find some way to get home without his help. He decided to come and get me."

Irma knew it was time to go back to New Orleans when members of her extended family wanted to teach her how to plow. She said, "I was adamant I was not going to walk behind the mule. I did not want to learn how to plow is bad enough. I had to pick beans and pick whatever vegetables were in season at that time. Picked cotton, too. I didn't really enjoy country life."[5]

Upon returning to New Orleans, she lived with her parents in an apartment in one of two adjacent two-story rooming houses at 1718 Felicity Street. Irma said, "Like all the rest of the apartments, ours was only one room and a kitchen with a community bath. I would dare say that living within those two houses must have been at least twenty families. Each duplex had up to four apartments downstairs and four upstairs. After all these years, I am still friends with several of the tenants." And there was often music coming out of each door. "My dad would play his blues, the neighbor had on gospel, the other one had on jazz."[6]

"I slept on a fold-away bed/cot in the same room with my parents. During the day when I wasn't using the cot, my mother folded it up and draped a large bedspread over it. She kept it right in front of the chifforobe in the bedroom. Sometimes during winter I would roll my bed into the kitchen because I liked the warmth of the kitchen. However, there were two problems with that. One, it didn't fit very well in the kitchen. Two, it blocked my dad from raiding the refrigerator during the night, raids my mother always seemed to sleep through, by the way. So he made me move it back into the front room with them."

According to Irma, in the 1950s it was common for a child of nine to be left at home alone. Her parents, like many others at the time, taught her skills that enabled her to take care of herself, as a self-sufficient only child. "I started cooking as a kid. Nine years old, my father put me on a Coke crate. We used them for stools, and my father put the crate to the stove. That's where I stood and learned how to cook. He started me off with frying eggs and bacon and cooking grits, and from there I graduated to cooking beans, and from there to greens, and from then I'd cook anything that I want. My mom was not the big cook in the house. I was."[7]

A quick study in self-sufficiency, Irma was trusted to stay at home alone in the evenings while her parents were out. "My dad bought our first black and white Silvertone television set from Sears and Roebuck. It was my number one company keeper. Whenever they went out at night or on the weekends, I had permission to watch TV until I fell asleep. When they returned home, they had to turn it off. Back in those days, television did not stay on all night. During the week, my dad, of course, watched the boxing or wrestling matches, if they were on. My favorites were Joe Louis and Gorgeous George." She enjoyed watching variety shows as well such as *The Milton Berle Show* and *The Red Skelton Show*, but her favorite was *The Ed Sullivan Show*, on which she first saw one of her early musical influences, Pearl Bailey, the Tony and Emmy Award–winning singer, actress, and comedian.

Apartment life offered young Irma many new friends and joyful childhood experiences. "There wasn't any dirt or grass around my two apartment buildings, only concrete pavement, so we kids played in the alley. Behind the buildings was a wash shed with an overhang, where tenants set up their wash tubs.

No one had a washing machine back then; everyone used a number three tub and rubboard instead. Clothes lines were strung underneath this shaded area, and we girls used to sit in the shade and play doll house. We made our little dolls out of Coke bottles with a clothes pin pushed down into the top of the bottle to hold in their rope hair. We were very creative, dressing up our dolls in outfits we made out of rags or scraps of clothes. When we weren't playing with our dolls, we jumped rope or played hopscotch, typical children's games.

"A favorite with both girls and boys was making China ball guns. First, we carved out a cane reed. Then we whittled a stick down to fit the inside of the reed, leaving a larger end for the handle. For the other end, we either beat the stick with a hammer or chewed it to make a rope-like plunger. This we used to push the China balls through the cane reed, which made a pop sound when they exited the reed. We called these handmade toys pop guns. The boys taught us girls how to make them and also how to make slingshots." China balls are the fruit of the Chinaberry tree, a type of mahogany, which provided the children with an endless supply of ammunition.

"On my block, I was the biggest tomboy. I could climb most trees and posts. My parents bought me my own little cowgirl outfit, which included a holster, six shooter, and cowgirl hat. On Mardi Gras, I dressed up as a cowgirl. That was my favorite costume. After Mardi Gras, we kids used our costumes for playtime.

"When just the girls got together, we played jacks. That's a game children don't play too much these days. Modern technology and high tech games have now replaced many of children's simpler games. In jacks, there were ten metal jacks, shaped like little stars that we picked up one at a time while bouncing a small ball. If we picked up all the jacks without missing, we would go on to the twosies in which we picked up two jacks at a time and then on to the threesies, and so on. When we missed, the next player would get a chance until she missed. This would go around to each player until the person who picked up all the jacks was declared the winner. Playing jacks was a lot of fun. Even as an adult, I played every now and then just to see if I could still do it. I taught my girls how to play."

While living on Felicity Street, Irma was enrolled in the fifth grade at John W. Hoffman Elementary on South Claiborne Avenue. She remembered there was a canal that ran down the middle of the avenue, and she caught the Freret Street bus for seven cents and transferred to the Claiborne Avenue streetcar, which stopped right across the street from the school. She said, "During that time many schools had what was called the platoon or half day system. I attended from seven o'clock in the morning to twelve o'clock noon. This meant waking up really early in the morning to catch the bus. My parents insisted that I take morning classes, so I would return home before dark."

Within eight blocks of their apartment was the Ritz Theater, a 400-seat movie theater at 1807 LaSalle Street, which featured children's movies and live shows on Saturdays. Irma said, "In those days the movies were only twenty-five cents. Sometimes, there were specials; for example, if we bought a Brock candy bar and kept three wrappers, we could get into the movies for a nickel. On special occasions we could get in free. The Ritz Theater also had vaudeville shows. It was at one of those shows that I saw the Coasters, who starred as the main attraction. The shows also featured a dancer and a comedian. Of course, on those days, admission was a little higher, fifty cents. Neighborhood kids went to the Ritz a lot because it was within walking distance."

Although the fifth grade did not afford Irma much opportunity to practice her newly realized singing talent, it did give her a chance to participate in sports, and to further hone her skill at reciting assigned speeches and poems, something she had enjoyed in the country. She represented her school in track and field events in running and broad jump. Even though admittedly she never won a medal in sports, she felt the experience was positive because she was able to visit different schools and playgrounds.

Irma said, "Attending Hoffman was fun. Once a month and on special occasions, students were treated to an after-school movie. I have to laugh now when I remember how terrified I was of a movie called *The Hand*. As a ten-year-old, that movie used to scare me to death! But, I enjoyed it every time despite the fact that I couldn't sleep at night after seeing it. I suppose this movie had the greatest influence on my love for science fiction, a fascination that lasts even now."

Her year at Hoffman Elementary proved successful. Irma said, "I must have been doing all right because I never got whippings for doing anything wrong in school. I did have one interesting episode, though. It occurred in September, the early part of the school year. I fainted, probably because I hadn't eaten. My dad had to come and take me home. I spent the rest of the day by myself." She became adept at amusing herself when left alone at home.

Irma was a curious child. When she saw tap dancing shoes on sale in the window of a store around the corner, she had to have them. "My mama wouldn't buy them for me, so when she told me to go buy new shoes I bought black patent leather tap dancing shoes. She made me wear them. I couldn't wait to outgrow those shoes. Everybody knew I was coming."

In the sixth grade, Irma was enrolled at McDonough No. 38 in the 1300 block of Dryades St., where she began performing in school choral groups.

She was also taking piano lessons, but her teacher told Irma's mother that her money for the lessons was being wasted because all Irma wanted to do was sing, and that she would not learn the piano parts. Irma said, "Finally, they just gave up and said, 'Let her sing!' But I wish I would have stuck with the piano, too."[8] Although Irma had initially set her sights on becoming a teacher, her calling as a singer was slowly coming into focus.[9]

Her teacher, Miss Fern Glapion, was the first person to fully recognize and encourage Irma's talent. Irma said, "I suppose she discovered my performance talent as I practiced the poem 'Twas the Night Before Christmas' for the Christmas pageant, or danced an Irish jig for St. Patrick's Day, or wrapped the Maypole for May Day. Miss Glapion taught the class all these things, and she noticed my vocal ability when she had me sing 'The Christmas Song,' made famous by Nat 'King' Cole. She felt I had a good voice, so I was the one called on to sing for school events."

Miss Glapion also provided a tipping point for her student. Irma's first formal stage would be the newly built Carver Theater, located at 2101 Orleans Avenue. Opened on September 29, 1950, in the Tremé neighborhood, bordering the French Quarter, and named after famed educator and scientist George Washington Carver, it was hailed as America's first theater built expressly for Black patrons. Listed on the National Register of Historic Places, this state-of-the-art performing arts venue hosted films, concerts, plays, off-Broadway shows, Mardi Gras balls, community events, and, for Irma, a very important weekly talent contest.

Irma remembered her teacher and the contest: "The first time she entered me, I placed third, winning two dollars and some free passes to the Carver Theater. They wanted you to come back and patronize the theater and buy popcorn. But what was far more important than the meager winnings, considered a big deal then, was the experience. It cemented my desire to enter show business. I was thrilled to be on stage in front of a live audience. It felt electrifying, even at that young age. The more the audience responded to my voice, the more I connected to them. The second time she took me, I won second place. The third time I went by myself, and I sang 'Too Young' by Nat 'King' Cole.' At the time I was a big Nat 'King' Cole fan, and his songs were easy to learn. Performing well in these talent shows helped Miss Glapion to convince me that I did have talent. I thought I was a big shot!" Cole's songs, with their often intricate melodies and chord changes, would not seem like easy choices for a young singer, but Irma's ears were taking everything in.

The world of music was opening to her, and she could not have been in a better place to be inspired and to develop as a singer. She said, "That was the year the teen couple Shirley and Lee was very popular with their hit 'I'm Gone.'" The squeaky-voiced and endearingly off-pitch Shirley Goodman and her high school friend Leonard Lee would become known as the "Sweethearts of the Blues" as they pioneered a teen-oriented New Orleans rhythm and blues sound that was immensely popular with local kids. Their streak of hits continued with "Feel So Good," "Let the Good Times Roll," and "Shirley, Come Back to Me," each one a kind of episode in an ongoing teenaged soap opera. Goodman, who was five years older than Irma, would become Irma's lifelong friend and supporter.

Irma continued: "Of course, everybody listened to the radio a lot. My parents, for example, kept the radio on when they were off from work. During the summer, when I was home from school, I played it all day for company. On Felicity Street, I could hear music coming out of all the apartments in my building. It seemed like I was surrounded by music. At school during lunch break, some students and I would sing all the popular songs while we stood around the schoolyard."

Irma often purchased *Hit Parader* and other magazines, which published lyrics to the songs currently on the charts. She practiced singing them whenever she could. "My number-one listener was my friend and classmate, Anthony Gould. Anthony and I exchanged phone numbers, and I would sing to him on the telephone. That was our conversation. Singing to Anthony became my favorite summer pastime when my mother was at work. I've long lost track of Anthony, but I would wager that if he is still alive, he probably tells people that I used to sing to him on the phone, which probably makes people laugh. There was always some sort of celebratory band going through the area. I liked music so I would stand out there and watch them."

Second line parades, held either for funerals or as yearly social events for the various organizations that sponsored them, were a fixture in the neighborhoods where she lived. The parades were often staged, as they are today, by social, aid, and pleasure clubs: Black benevolent organizations that first appeared in New Orleans in the nineteenth century. If a member suffered hard times, the club would offer assistance, and when a member died, the member was assured of a proper send-off, complete with a brass band. Today, organizations such as The Money Wasters, Young Men Olympian, Original Lady Buckjumpers, Old & Nu Style, and dozens of others stage yearly parades on Sunday afternoons, during the cooler months of the year. The club members dance down the street in front of the band, decked out in coordinated outfits that change each year, while everyone else follows behind—the "second line." Musician, historian, and author Danny Barker wrote:

This Ralston Crawford photograph from 1958 depicts a typical second line parade, in this case held for a funeral. (Ralston Crawford Collection of Jazz Photography, Hogan Archive of New Orleans Music and New Orleans Jazz, Tulane University Special Collections—used by permission)

> First, it's the sound of the brass bands, the booming sounds of the big bass horn and the big bass drum. The sad wailing notes of the horns always hit you deep inside. If that soul music don't get to you, something's wrong with you. Then there is always the large crowd of many hundreds of ordinary people who follow the funeral procession from start to finish, because after the deceased brother has been taken to the cemetery and interred pandemonium breaks loose—from silent, respectful, slow marching to the cemetery in a sudden burst of approval, 'A job well done,' 'He was put away nicely,' 'He's in God's hands.' And as the Bible states, 'Cry when you enter the world and rejoice when you leave trials, troubles, tribulations behind.' . . . Outside the cemetery the bands walk a half block and strike up one of the familiar popular jazz songs, and all hell breaks loose. Surprised tourists will witness this large group of black folks dancing, many under multi-colored umbrellas. People of all sizes and ages, and each dancing his or her thing as the exciting parade marches on. No inhibitions: everybody lets his self go out to his full physical extent.[10]

Irma said, "New Orleans kind of oozes music. I think that had a lot to do with my being thrust into it. I can't remember a given week where there was never a parade that was celebrating something one way. Either going out or coming in, some organization was celebrating something. The neighborhood where I lived, for every church there was a bar on the opposite corner so I was always surrounded by music in some form or another."[11]

In addition to her father's radio creating a steady soundscape, there was also singing in her home. "My mom would sing around the house to keep herself company while she was doing other things, and my dad could sing, although he was more of a whistler than a singer. Both of them had voices so I guess I was destined to have some kind of a voice. My dad loved to dance. My mom wasn't much of a dancer, so he would dance with me."

When school was out for summer break, the elders in the neighborhood kept a watchful eye for her and other children on the block. Irma said, "They did not literally babysit us, but they did look out for us while our parents were at work. Truthfully, we kids kind of kept ourselves."

In the summer between Irma's sixth and seventh grades, her parents were not getting along, and after a big argument they separated. Irma and her mother moved downtown into a one-room apartment with a kitchenette at 1515 North Claiborne Avenue. She was now living on a thriving main street that was lined with shops, nightclubs, and other businesses, with a broad "neutral ground" that was shaded by massive live oak trees. ("Neutral ground" is an archaic term that was coined to designate the Canal Street median that separated the French- and Creole-speaking municipality on the downriver side of the street from the English-speaking municipality on the uptown side.)[12] The term is still used in New Orleans to describe the grassy median on any street. Irma said, "There were lots and lots of trees along North Claiborne Avenue back then. The only thing you had to be afraid of were the worms [buck moth caterpillars] coming out of the trees. You had to bring an umbrella with you. That was a beautiful neighborhood. You could go out there and put a picnic blanket down. Air conditioning was not something that a lot of people had. So a lot of times during the summer we would spend our days out on the neutral ground."

Irma remembered, "The Black musicians' union was right down the street on the corner from where I lived. In the middle of the block was a place where customers selected live chickens and watched as the necks were wrung, the feathers plucked, and the chickens cleaned. Naturally, the chickens were very fresh, and customers could also buy fresh eggs. In the vicinity there was also a record shop or a music school. I remember going to Mr. Harold Battiste, one of the people who ran the business, and telling him that I wanted to audition for a record. I simply thought it was a good thing to try to do. I was a bold young lady. He let me sing for him, but he only laughed and told me I was too young to be singing. Of course, no record was made, and that marked the beginning and end of an early record career. Big mistake for him, though. He himself admitted this years later when he told me, 'I should have recorded you back then.' Obviously, that was not my fate at that particular time. Other powers that be must have seen a different future for me."

In the mid-1950s, the Los Angeles record label Specialty Records opened an office at 1463 N. Claiborne Avenue, above the Houston's for Music store. Houston's sold musical instruments and offered lessons for aspiring young musicians who wanted to learn how to play an instrument or how to read music. Producer, saxophonist, and record executive Harold Battiste Jr. was tapped by Specialty owner Art Rupe to manage the label's New Orleans office and recording activities. Battiste was a key figure in New Orleans music who learned not only the workings of the record business, but who was also at the vanguard of the city's modern jazz sound. His American Jazz Quintet (which included, at various times, clarinetist Alvin Batiste, saxophonist Earl Turbinton, drummer Ed Blackwell, bassist Richard Payne, and pianist Ellis Marsalis Jr.) created a new template for modern New Orleans music.

In the early 1960s, when it was clear to Battiste that he and his musical associates were creating hit after hit for other artists while receiving only union scale wages, he founded the AFO (All For One) record label, in which the musicians were essentially shareholders. In addition to producing many wonderful jazz records, the label scored a national hit with Barbara George's "I Know (You Don't Love Me No More)," which reached #1 on the *Billboard* R&B chart, and #3 on the Hot 100. However, AFO was not able to sustain the steady flow of hits that would have prompted distributors to pay their outstanding bills, and the company foundered. Later in the decade, after Battiste relocated to Los Angeles, he became the musical director and arranger for Sonny and Cher (the oboe on "I Got You Babe" was his idea). In later years, when Irma moved to Los Angeles, he hired her as a background vocalist on a Sonny and Cher session. He would eventually return home to teach at the University of New Orleans.

Irma held Battiste in high esteem: "I would run across him often. He was in a different field than I was. He was into jazz and I was into rhythm and blues. But of course, that didn't matter in New Orleans because oftentimes you played them both, no matter where you were. He [was] very inspirational as a teacher. His stature as a man in the business, he's very respected and he demands that respect not by word of mouth, but by the way he carries himself. I, who never took a lesson from him, learned from him from a distance, just watching his demeanor and how he carried himself."[13]

Long after Irma had left her North Claiborne Avenue neighborhood, in 1972, the boulevard was chosen as the path of the new Interstate 10, when the overpass that stands today was built over the wide neutral ground, after the old live oak trees that lined the thoroughfare were cut down. "A large mistake," said Irma. While Mardi Gras Indians continue to gather beneath the overpass on each Mardi Gras day, and while various efforts have been made to create murals and other art in the shade of the concrete, the bustling energy of the area never recovered, and today many abandoned buildings line the avenue. One artifact from the area's earlier and more prosperous era survives. The Club Delise at 1500 North Claiborne subsequently became singer Ernie K-Doe's Mother in Law Lounge. After K-Doe's death, it was bought by trumpeter Kermit Ruffins and reopened in 2011 as Kermit's Tremé Mother in Law Lounge. With dwindling attendance in the post-COVID era, the club's hours became sporadic. However, it remains open as the home base for Ruffins, a beloved New Orleans entertainer who can often be found preparing his trademark barbeque on the grill outside the club. As it has for decades, the club continues to serve as a stop for second line parade participants as they make their way down North Claiborne Avenue.

The summer between her seventh and eighth grades, Irma's parents reconciled. Her father rented an apartment in the 4200 block of Melpomene Street next to a canal in a section of New Orleans known as Zion City. She said, "The big canal has since been filled in and the street is now called Martin Luther King Boulevard. Our apartment consisted of two rooms, a kitchen and a bath. With the increase in space, we thought we were moving up in the world. I still slept on my rollaway bed, but now I had my own private space in the living room."

During this time, while attending the Home Mission Baptist Church, Irma and several other neighborhood girls formed a gospel quartet. She also began writing scripts for the Tom Thumb weddings that were staged at her school as informal fundraisers. The tradition of these theatrical and comical mock weddings between two young children was inspired by the actual wedding of Charles Sherwood Stratton, a famous entertainer with dwarfism who performed as Colonel Tom Thumb in P. T. Barnum's circus.

Entering junior high, Irma was enrolled in McDonough No. 41 school in the 1100 block of St. Ann Street in the Tremé neighborhood, across the street from the area that was leveled in the 1962 urban renewal project that created Armstrong Park. This park is also the historic site of Congo Square, an open-air market and gathering place where, in the nineteenth century, free and enslaved people of African descent sold goods, practiced traditional customs, played music, danced, and socialized. Congo Square is considered a sacred place in New Orleans music history and, by extension, for American music in general. It continues to play a vital role in the community for its historical significance and as an outdoor venue for concerts, festivals, and cultural events. It is often the starting spot for second line parades.

The rhythms played in Congo Square had a direct influence on New Orleans music going forward, especially the bamboula, which became the basis of the second line parade beat. A similar musical tradition was carried forth in the chants and percussion of the Black Masking Mardi Gras Indians. While the origins of the Indians are complex, reflecting both the actual influence of Native Americans in New Orleans, and the romanticized Indian of American popular culture, their tradition of creating elaborate Native American–inspired costumes or suits, forming "tribes," and staging battles with one another on Mardi Gras day has enriched the culture of New Orleans. Some Indians say their extravagant suits pay tribute to local Native Americans who harbored escaped enslaved people. It is also possible that they were influenced by the flamboyant headdresses of the Plains Indians who were part of Buffalo Bill Cody's Wild West show, which had a four-month residency in New Orleans in the mid-1880s.

The first commercial recording to incorporate a Mardi Gras Indian chant was the swinging "Chocko Mo Feendo Hey" / "Indian Red" by Danny Barker and his Creole Cats, recorded in 1947 and released on his own King Zulu label, soon followed by "Jock-A-Mo" by Sugar Boy and His Cane Cutters, released on Chicago's Checker label in 1953. James "Sugar Boy" Crawford recalled that label owner Leonard Chess changed his pronunciation of "Chockamo" to the written "Jock-A-Mo."[14] When Crawford later recollected the story of adding the Mardi Gras Indian chants "Iko Iko" and "Jock-a-mo fee-na nay" to his classic rhythm and blues song, he admitted did not know what the words meant,[15] although the references in the lyrics to spyboys and queens on Mardi Gras day indicate that the song is clearly about Indian rivalry. In 1965, The Dixie Cups' "Iko Iko," with lyrics nearly identical to Crawford's, reached #20 on the *Billboard* Hot 100. Crawford eventually received a cowriter credit and a share of royalties. It seems an unlikely hit, with its stripped-down production of vocals, percussion, and acoustic bass, and with lyrics that approximate what might have been heard on the street on Carnival day, but teens across America were singing along with "Jock-a-mo fee-na nay."

This enigmatic phrase, first reported in the *Daily Picayune* during the 1879 New Orleans Mardi Gras as "Chick-a-ma-feeno," is derived from a Native American phrase ("achukmafehna" meaning "very good" in Choctaw) that could be used as a greeting or as a superlative,[16] or perhaps whatever a modern-day Mardi Gras Indian might want it to mean. In earlier days, the "battles" between tribes could turn violent, while today the competition is more or less centered on which chief has the prettiest suit, even if the vocal sparring and competitive rhyming between two rival chiefs can seem bellicose. Danny Barker wrote, "It's a macho thing to be able to say, 'I'm an Indian' on Mardi Gras Day, because he'd be charged up. They ain't gonna hear no shit from anybody."[17] In any event, the boastful songs of the Indians were another part of the musical milieu surrounding Irma, and "Iko Iko" would eventually become part of the "Second Line Medley" that she still performs at every show.

During her first year in junior high, Irma had many avenues to explore her budding talent. She said, "I was in Mr. Ashton Murray's homeroom. He was my social studies and music teacher, as well as director of the school chorus. Henry Carbo [the younger brother of Chuck and Chick Carbo of The Spiders, the New Orleans vocal group that recorded for Imperial Records in the mid-1950s] was a classmate in Mr. Murray's music class. Henry and I were the lead vocalists in the chorus. One of the operettas we performed was *White Gypsy*. We also gave a performance of the show tunes from the Broadway play *Show Boat*. I was a soprano then, and Mr. Murray had me sing the song 'Sweetheart, Sweetheart, Sweetheart.' I sang a lot of duets with Henry, who was a tenor. Anytime the chorus represented the school, the two of us sang the leads.

"All of the McDonough 41 teachers were like family. When the school put on the operetta, my mother was on strike at Southern Bell Telephone. The strike lasted almost six weeks, so money was tight. Miss Pierre, my homeroom teacher, helped my mother to get my costume. She actually bought the material so I could perform in the play, properly attired. Back then, teachers were more than just teachers. They sometimes took on the role of parents away from home. They taught us self-respect. They didn't allow boys to come to school wearing pants that hung around their butts, as many students do today. Girls had to dress in a respectful way, too.

"Another teacher who had a great impact on my life was Miss Dorothy Mary Carter Provost, my home economics teacher. In her class I learned how to sew napkins, aprons, and skirts, which were our seventh and eighth grade class projects. At the time, I also learned how to embroider, so I adorned my apron with flowers and other designs. Miss Provost liked my apron so much that she kept it to show to students in other classes. I never did get my apron back, which is regrettable. I had put a lot of work into that apron. Somehow, it just disappeared.

"I learned how to sew on a Singer pedal sewing machine, and to make my own versions of whatever was in fashion at the time. I could look at the dresses in the downtown stores, but back then we were not allowed to try on a garment, or even to return it if it did not fit. I still get material from Art 4 Now and make myself a dress for Jazz Fest [New Orleans Jazz and Heritage Festival] every year. Whatever the fashion is that year, I get enough material to make a dress or a two-piece set or whatever I decide."

Irma especially appreciated the school's annual "switch day," when the girls were sent to shop classes (which taught basic home repair and carpentry skills), and the boys went to study home economics. "We girls were taught different tools like the screwdriver, hammer, regular and needle nose pliers, monkey wrench, and saw, and how to use each one properly. We didn't make anything, but this kind of knowledge is really handy in life. In home economics class, the boys were taught some of the things girls learned, for example, how to make biscuits, thread a needle, sew on buttons, hem trousers, and mend a tear when necessary. These are all just good common sense things to know how to do." Irma's confidence in her mechanical abilities would serve her well in future years, especially as she traveled and came to learn basic automobile mechanics.

Irma reminisced about a time when students respected and appreciated their teachers. She said, "For Teacher Appreciation Week or other special occasions, Miss Pierre taught us to make rose corsages and boutonnieres from velvet crepe paper for all the teachers. It was Miss Pierre who sent students to each teacher's class to pin on a corsage or boutonniere and present a card of appreciation. The principal received a bouquet of fourteen roses. Miss Pierre instilled in us the importance of giving. Before there was United Way, there was the Community Chest, to which students made financial contributions. We were also taught the importance of giving to ourselves through saving. Each student was encouraged to open a school savings account, and we could deposit as little as ten cents a week. At one point I must have had as much as twenty dollars in my account. I thought I had big bucks!" This early training in money management would prove beneficial for Irma in later years sustaining a career as a working performer, but not before other desires came to the fore.

Irma said, "Junior high school ushered in my curiosity about life. I had already become a young lady with my first menstrual period when I was not quite ten years old. I was still living with both my parents on Felicity Street. My mother had not yet argued with and left my father. Becoming a young lady brought noticeable changes to my body. I thought I was hot stuff as my body developed its curves, forever leaving behind my tomboyish physique.

My inquisitiveness about sex did not really begin in school. Of course, I had little crushes on different boys. One in particular at McDonough 41 was Charles Brickley, who years later wound up working at Delgado Community College as a psychology teacher, where I took his class. Back in junior high though Charles was flattered about my slight crush, tickled to death, as a matter of fact. My friends and I used to tease him quite a bit because he was such a cute little boy, and very sweet.

"Then came my first experience with love, well, puppy love. I was sweet on a boy whose last name was Frazier. His first name now escapes me. He worked in the baker's shop up the street on North Claiborne Avenue. He said he was sweet on me, too, and we would talk when I went to buy doughnuts. Frazier gave me my first kiss. We kissed a lot, so much so that my lips were sore. I was still very young, around twelve years old and only in the seventh grade. So kissing was all we did. Even with the new experience of puppy love entering my young life, I continued to be a studious little thing.

"My classmate Jolene Jeff and I became very close, almost like sisters, because she was the only girl among her brothers and I was an only child. We both tried out to be majorettes, but were turned down. Our rejection made us wonder if it was because we were a little too endowed for junior high school girls with our big pretty legs. Then, too, neither one of us had very long hair or what seemed to be the preferred light skin color. So, we figured we simply did not fit the unwritten but well-understood majorette squad qualifications. Nevertheless, we did play on the same basketball team. For at least one semester, we shared the same homeroom. Sometimes after school I went by her house, where I met her mom and dad. I had no idea that her dad was the same Mr. Jeff who ran the Rosenwald Center that was close to where I lived when my parents got back together."

In junior high school, Irma made a recording of the school song when she and Henry Carbo were sent by their principal to Cosimo Matassa's Studio on Rampart and Dumaine Streets. It was her first recording session. Irma recalled some of the words to the song as, "Among all children on the Earth, how happy we would be, that we are living in a school, a happy family." At the beginning of each school day, the students recited the pledge of allegiance and a morning prayer, and then sang along with Henry and Irma's recording of the school song. The recording continued to be played each day, many years after Irma left McDonough 41.

CHAPTER THREE

All Grown Up

(1947-1957)

Irma assumed the responsibilities of an adult at a very young age. Pregnant at fourteen, she left junior high school to have her first child, while she worked at various jobs that included dishwasher, laborer, and dancer. By the time she was seventeen, she had given birth to two more children. During these years, she also found her first opportunity to be the lead singer of Tommy Ridgley's popular ensemble, and to work professionally as a vocalist outside of New Orleans.

In the 1950s (and for decades to follow), pianist, vocalist, and bandleader Ridgley was one of the stalwarts of New Orleans music, beginning with his 1949 debut recording, "Shrewsbury Blues" (named for his neighborhood in Jefferson Parish, adjoining Orleans Parish), on which his keening blues vocal was accompanied by Dave Bartholomew and his orchestra, in the popular blues-based style of artists such as Roy Brown and Wynonie Harris. He recorded for Decca, Atlantic, and Herald in the 1950s, and subsequently for a string of local labels through the 1990s. His group, The Untouchables, became a go-to New Orleans back-up band—always professional and reliable—for touring artists such as Sam Cooke and Little Willie John, at the Dew Drop Inn and later at the Municipal Auditorium, as he adapted his style to keep up with evolving trends. He also recognized a promising talent when he finally heard Irma sing. However improbable it might seem, this young mother, still a child herself and living with her parents, would soon find her feet on the ground as a prescient singer and entertainer.

Throughout the 1950s, Ridgley was a fixture at The Hi-Hat Club on North Villere Street, where he led the house band. The club was an important local venue where artists such as Dave Bartholomew, Smiley Lewis, and Professor

Tommy Ridgley's Ric Records publicity photo. (Photograph courtesy of the New Orleans Jazz Museum, David Kunian, Curator)

Longhair shared the stage with Ridgley. In fact, Professor Longhair's debut 1949 sessions for Star Talent Records were recorded at an impromptu studio set up in the club, yielding the first recordings of his hits "Mardi Gras in New Orleans" and "She Ain't Got No Hair" (later called "Bald Head"). In the back of the venue there was a jazz club called The Velvet Street Lounge, where musicians such as tenor saxophonist Nat Perrilliat played in a "bird's nest," out of the sight of the patrons. The entire area around Orleans Avenue, Basin Street, and Claiborne Avenue was a hot entertainment strip,[1] where music clubs such as the Colt 38 and Prout's Club Alhambra persevered through the 1980s.

While Irma had yet to fully embrace a vision of herself as a professional singer, she found another interest. "Living in such close quarters with my parents naturally piqued my preteen curiosity about sex," she said. "I did not act upon my curiosity until the summer between my seventh and eighth grade year. My parents and I went to visit my cousins who had moved from Laurel Street across the river to Algiers, near the Naval Base. To me it was a bit like being in the woods even though it was still considered New Orleans. Aunt Juanita and my cousins gave a lot of parties on the weekends, so I asked my parents to let me spend weekends with them. I lost my virginity on one of those weekends. They say you never forget your first, and that is so very true. His name was Eugene Jones. I thought he was my boyfriend, which in my young mind made sex with him okay. Adults didn't teach kids very much sex education back then. Many of us learned about it on our own through trial and error."

She continued, "My parents didn't talk to me a lot about life, meaning, experiences, and learning how to deal with growing up. And it was funny because my dad used to always tell me, don't play with boys. And here I am, the biggest, the baddest tomboy on the block, I could make China ball guns better than the average boy, I could shoot cap pistols and all that stuff. So what are you telling me? Don't play with boys. But later on in life, that was his way of telling me to not experience that which would make you pregnant. But by that time, it was too late."[2]

"The events of the summer between my eighth and ninth grades changed my life. I got pregnant. I had been sexually active from the time I was thirteen years old. Now at fourteen, I stayed home alone while my parents worked. The father of my baby was a handsome young man in his early twenties, who used to sit along the Melpomene Street canal during the day when my parents weren't home. His name was Percy Johnson, but we called him Turk. I will always remember how good-looking a young man he was, tall, thin, with a beautiful voice. He organized a little singing group; in fact, they recorded a song at one point. His group also sang with some other guys who lived in the Calliope Project. I started talking to Turk as he sat by the canal. He was handsome and talented, and I was inquisitive and promiscuous. The pregnancy was inevitable, I suppose."

That fall, when Irma began her ninth-grade school year at Carter G. Woodson Junior High School in the Central City neighborhood, she felt ill, but did not realize she was pregnant. She said, "I didn't really know what was wrong with me. I felt sick as a dog and slept a lot. I slept in school, returned home, and slept some more. My father became suspicious first. To be truthful, he already knew; he just wanted his suspicion confirmed. So he told my mother to take me to the doctor. And, of course, tests proved that I was pregnant. I was not allowed to stay in school because girls couldn't do that in those days as they can now. I attended ninth grade classes for less than a month. If I wasn't throwing up, I was sleeping. Continuing to go to school was impossible, even if I had been permitted." It was an unfortunate situation for Irma since she loved her teachers, and she had a thirst for learning.

The experience of being pregnant while in junior high school instilled in Irma a sense of resolve. She told writer Jeff Hannusch, "I was an outcast. I was told I was a disgrace and had to leave school. But I became determined to make something out of my life."[3]

In 1955, with his suspicions confirmed, Irma's father decided that she should get married. The problem was that Irma was not entirely sure who the biological father was since she had been sexually active with Percy Johnson and Eugene Jones at the same time. Percy Johnson was twenty years old at the time and Irma was only fourteen. Considering the age difference and the possible ramifications for Johnson as an adult having intercourse with a minor, Irma said, "I told my father that I thought Eugene (Genie, as I called him) Jones was the father, so he took the two of us down somewhere in St. Bernard Parish where we got married, and [then] played house for a few weeks. We lived in a small apartment, consisting of one room and a kitchen in the back of the rooming house where my parents used to rent from a Mr. Buck on the 4200 block of Melpomene Street. My dad helped us get a bedroom set and Eugene was supposed to be working to help pay for it. Predictably, my father wound up paying for it. Now that I look back, I recall that the first three of my children were born while I lived with my parents, a good arrangement, since I needed the help."

The marriage to Eugene Jones lasted less than a year, and while those were lean months for Irma financially, she felt fortunate to make a lifelong friend in her next-door neighbor. Irma said, "Josie Armstrong (everybody called her Kitty), my best girlfriend (then and now), moved next door. In fact, she moved in before Jean Marie was born. Unfortunately, within months, her husband was drafted into the Army, leaving her alone with three children, Larry, Sadie, and Bo (who was just starting to crawl). Then Kitty discovered she was pregnant with her fourth child, whom she later named Lucille. Kitty and I were pregnant at the same time, her fourth and my first. Since her husband was in the army, Kitty had to see the doctor at Camp Leroy Johnson. Kitty was originally from Bude, Mississippi, near Jackson, so she didn't know her way around the city too well. Therefore, I had to show her how to get to and from the base. You can imagine the two of us, very pregnant at the time, trying to board the bus?

"Also, remember that this was during the fifties, pre–civil rights movement, so it was not unusual for white bus drivers to choose not to stop the bus to pick up two pregnant Black women. Many times, it took the two of us much longer to return home because buses would pass us by for no other reason than drivers did not want to stop for us. Those many hours together gave us a lot of time to get to know one another. We became very close. Her fourth child, Lucille, was born in February, [and my] Jean Marie in May. We swapped baby and maternity outfits. I consider Lucille my daughter and she considers Jean Marie hers. I often say that I unofficially christened Lucille, and feel that she is my godchild. She was such a cute little baby. In fact, she grew up to look very much like me."

By the time Jean Marie was born on May 1, 1956, Eugene and Irma had separated and were no longer living together. Irma said, "I discovered that when he was supposed to be going to work, he was jumping the fence with Connie, my so-called best girlfriend who, would you believe, lived right next door. Many mornings, she would sit with us on the back porch of our apartment, drinking coffee and chit-chatting, all the while doing my husband behind my back.

"I am not now nor have I ever been a stupid woman. So when I eventually found out about them, I promptly put his few belongings in a brown paper bag, sat outside our front door with the bag next to me, and waited. When he showed up, I informed him that I wasn't going to let him in because he didn't live there anymore.

"Life is full of challenges, and life doesn't reserve its challenges for only the wise and worthy, I can tell you. Even though I had very little education and absolutely no formal training in anything, I still had to find a job doing something. I needed the money. If memory serves me, my very first job was as a dishwasher at the Beacon Restaurant on Napoleon at South Claiborne Avenue. I used to work nights because my parents could babysit Jean Marie only at night."

While the night shift solved the issue of finding babysitters, it presented a different problem for Irma. She said, "I didn't get off from work until two o'clock in the morning. I didn't have a car, so my only means of getting home was the Napoleon bus, which ran slow during early morning hours. My father grew increasingly worried about my safety, so he told me I had to find a job with hours from eleven to seven or one that would allow me to return home during daylight hours. This was easier said than done. It was some time before I found another job, so I stayed home for a while, caring for Jean Marie. Even though my dad wanted me to work, he did not push the issue. He saw that I was really trying to find work. I even tried to reconcile with my husband to relieve my dad of the extra financial burden. We rented a furnished one-room apartment with a stove and a refrigerator in what we call in New Orleans 'front of town' on Liberty Street. The reconciliation didn't last long, only long enough for me to get pregnant again. He was supposed to be going offshore to work, but I found out he was lying to me. He really didn't want to work. So I had to return to my parents and he went back to doing whatever he wanted to do without me and Jean Marie."

After returning home, Irma worked for a time at a nearby sweet shop, where she earned five dollars per week helping the owner in the store, as well as doing ironing and cleaning chores. However, being pregnant with a second child, Irma said she soon became too big to do the work.

Jean Marie was a year and three months old when James Edwin was born on August 24, 1957, in New Orleans. Irma had gone into labor that morning while washing Jean Marie's diapers on a washboard. Irma said, "No one was home with me but my Uncle Joe, my Aunt Alice's husband, who lived in a room in the back of the house. He kept saying, 'Irma, you better go to the doctor.' But, I just wasn't going because when I checked in the hospital for Jean Marie, I was there too long, I thought. In those days, doctors didn't believe in giving any kind of anesthesia or drugs for labor pain. Jean Marie was my first child that I delivered as a natural birth. The long hours of labor before she was born left me anxious about my next birth. I was just plain scared. I clearly remembered the hours of pain and the hospital staff's refusal to give me any water, even though I was extremely thirsty." She later commented, "I wasn't even given anesthesia for any of my children's births, except one stillborn. Only the white women got anesthetics for childbirth. This was the segregated South in the 50s."[4]

"So my decision was to remain home as long as I could. But, as I leaned over that wash board, the pains were coming harder and more frequently. I admitted to Uncle Joe that I should go as he warned me, 'You're going to have that baby right here at home!' The thought of that convinced me to leave.

"Uncle Joe got the landlord upstairs to drive me to the hospital. However, as fate would have it, baby James decided not to wait. He entered this world in my landlord's brand new 1957 Pontiac, just as we were turning off the Broad Street overpass onto Poydras Street, heading for Charity Hospital. It's a good thing that plastic covered the seats because James was born in the car. I didn't have to spend a lot of time at the hospital. In fact, I stayed only overnight, which suited me just fine. The medical staff kept me only long enough to make sure the baby was fine, and I didn't have any tears or temperature from infection. When I returned home, I took down the clothes I had hung up the day before, and life went on as usual. It's amazing to me now, when I think of it, how much a young girl could do such a thing. But I was fifteen. The body of a fifteen-year-old mother has remarkable and truly enviable capability.

"When Kitty discovered James had been born, she was just a little miffed about it. She was supposed to give birth before me, so she wouldn't speak to me for about a week. She marveled at the fact that I had had my baby in a car, stayed a few hours at Charity [Hospital], and then came home and took down the clothes. After she had Lucille, we really bonded as best friends, doing everything and going everywhere together."

Irma faced the reality that motherhood came with the responsibility of supporting her children, which meant taking a series of menial jobs—the only kind that were available to a young high school dropout. She said, "There were very few opportunities for a young, Black female. I didn't have any big ambitions. As a Black female, I couldn't buy a house or eat in many restaurants."[5] However, her father now insisted that she get a job, since he was now providing for Irma and her two children. She said, "I went to work as a dishwasher in a little diner called Kopper Kitchen on the corner of Carrollton and Tulane Avenue, owned by one of the Chehardy brothers, perhaps Lawrence. I worked the eleven to seven shift, remembering my dad's concern that I get home during daylight hours. Another good thing about that job was that I had to catch only two buses, the Washington Avenue bus to Carrollton, and then take the Tulane Avenue bus to the diner."

However, Irma's employment at the Kopper Kitchen was short-lived—approximately six months. She said, "As I worked, I had the habit of singing to keep myself company and to help the time go by faster. I had to do something to stay awake; the eleven to seven shift was unusually slow most of the time with very few dishes to wash, except on the weekends. My boss warned me a couple of times about my singing. Then one night he said, 'Look, I done told you about singing that n***** music. Do your job, but you don't have to sing that n***** music while you working.' Of course, I would shut up and stop singing for a while. Then one slow night a couple of weeks later, when once again I was trying to stay awake, I started to sing. I really didn't know that the boss was in the diner, so he fired me. That marked my first time being fired because of singing on the job.

"Unemployment led to my next job: dancing. One evening, cousins Joanne and Deedee came over and asked me if I wanted to make about fifteen dollars. 'Doing what?' I asked. 'Dancing,' they answered in unison. 'Dancing where?' 'At the Hi-Hat Club.'" She would soon find herself on stage, dancing in a modestly risqué manner to the music of Tommy Ridgley.

"My cousins came to pick me up, but there was a small problem. What would we wear? First there was the discussion of wearing something I used to play basketball in, or maybe something I wore to dance classes at

Rosenwald gym, where we learned tap and modern dance. Then there was a close examination of a pair of blue satin bloomers that went under the blue skirt of a costume I wore as a Y-Teen [similar to Girl Scouts, but in the YWCA] member in junior high school. The blue bloomers won out for my Hi-Hat Club debut. For my top we settled on a ruffled white eyelet cotton halter that bared my shoulders and stomach. I was sixteen, and even though I had had two babies, I was still quite shapely."

"The three of us danced our butts off to live music, played by Tommy Ridgley and his band. They played songs like 'Night Train' that had a good dance beat. The dance my cousins and I did was similar to the dancing popular in today's videos, stomach rolling, behind shaking, bumping, and grinding. We did it for only a couple of nights, though, on two consecutive weekends. The club owner didn't bother to check our ages, and we were all underage. That kind of nightlife was not very attractive to me. At first it seemed to be okay, but as much as I loved singing before an audience, that's how much I didn't like being on stage as a dancer. It wasn't long before the men in the club felt they could say anything to us as dancers—that they could make passes at them.

"I really don't know where I mustered the nerve, but I decided to ask Tommy Ridgley if he would let me sing. I should have expected his reply, I guess. 'Oh, you can't sing. You dance. You don't know nothing about no singing.' He laughed it off and I didn't bother him about it anymore. After the two nights on two consecutive weekends, and a total of sixty dollars, I called it quits. I did not care at all for the lifestyle or the way men got so familiar with the performers on stage. So the next time Ridgley asked me to dance, I refused. That ended my dancing career, but it did mark the actual beginning of my entertainment career."

With her dancing job over, Irma next went to work at Pete's Packing Company along the Mississippi River as a laborer, putting together bundles of soup greens. Her Uncle Joe, who was a longshoreman, told her that if she could get up early in the morning and leave with him, he could get her a job on the riverfront. Irma asked her dad if that would be a problem. He answered, "If you can get somebody to keep your babies for you because you know your mother and I have to work." Irma said, "The next person I consulted was Kitty who agreed to keep my babies for me. At the packing company, I worked from five in the morning to noon. So, Kitty did not have to keep my kids all day. Then there were days Uncle Joe helped out. If he didn't work on a certain day, he would return home and look after them a little bit.

"I made good money at the packing company. The pay was based on the number of pieces packed, and at the time I was packing soup bunches for which I was paid fifty cents a crate. A bunch consisted of a half head of cabbage, two carrots, three or four celery stalks, some parsley, some onions, and a potato, all wrapped together in a three-pound bag. A machine that looked very much like a Scotch tape dispenser twisted and sealed the bag at the top with a small piece of tape. Then I packed the bags by twelve in a square packing crate. I got better and better at this and was bringing home between one hundred fifty and two hundred dollars a week. For a sixteen-year-old, that was quite a nice little taste of change.

"Although a young mother, I was still quite shapely and promiscuous. In truth, I really wasn't so much promiscuous as I was full of myself. I have yet to know what the attraction was, but the packing company boss took a liking to me. Although short in stature, he was a handsome man, prematurely balding with a very deep cowlick that gave him a large forehead. Mr. Handsome wore a cap most of the time because he was self-conscious about his premature baldness. Since I was young, naïve, somewhat egotistical, and on some levels just plain dumb, I started dating him. I didn't have sense enough to find out if he was married. Consequently, not knowing anything about protection or paying too much attention to the connection between sex and pregnancy, I got pregnant again. I was just so ignorant about childbirth and stuff.

"During my third pregnancy, I was an LSU [Louisiana State University Medical Center] patient at Charity Hospital clinic, and I actually asked the doctor, 'How does a woman get pregnant?' He looked at me and laughed. I told him that I didn't think it was funny. 'This is my third child and I am only seventeen years old. I want to know.' He took the time to tell me, realizing I was serious. Using some charts and graphs, he showed me how women become pregnant and taught me about what they called the rhythm method, which indicated the days of the month women were fertile. He tried to explain the method to me as best he could with my limited understanding of it. Then he explained the importance of using condoms and other contraceptives. Condoms and the rhythm method were the only forms of contraceptives available to poor Black people back then. This knowledge was a real eye-opener, and I did not get pregnant again until three years later.

"Pregnancy naturally mandated my having to quit my job at the plant. To make matters worse, when I told the father that I was pregnant with his child, he denied the whole relationship. After the baby's birth, I returned to the riverfront to show him his baby. She looked so much like him that he could have spat her out, the only difference was that he was light-skinned and she was dark. After his repeated denial, I gave up on him. I tucked in my tail feathers, and took my baby and myself back home, resigned to raising her on my own along with my other two children. Her birth was eleven months and three weeks after that of my second child."

Tina (christened Ernestine) was born on August 3, 1958, in New Orleans. To help support her growing family, Irma took a part-time job as a waitress at the Pimlico Club located at 2525 South Broad Street, a modest venue that held between 150 and 200 patrons who were seated at tables. She earned four dollars plus tips each night. The Pimlico was a respectable place that offered quality entertainment, where a couple could dress up for a Saturday night out and forget the woes of the work week. They might order a "set-up," which consisted of a bucket of ice, a pint of liquor, a bottle of Coke, and two glasses. At some point, a photographer who was making the rounds of the nightclubs might stop by to commemorate their evening, for a fee, with a Polaroid souvenir photograph.

Saxophonist Roger Lewis, who was one of the original members of Deacon John and the Ivories, met Irma for the first time when he was performing at the Pimlico in 1957. "We were famous for taking people's gigs," he remembered. "We knew everybody's repertoire. We were a cover band, and we stole Eddie Bo's gig [at the Pimlico] by playing James Brown's 'Think.'"[6] Almost everyone in the band was also under-age, so Roger would sometimes act as a "spy boy," watching out for Musicians' Union representatives. He would become a key musician in Irma's career. "Deacon" John Moore would become a New Orleans institution, playing the popular rhythm and blues music of the day for fraternity parties, teen dances, Mardi Gras balls, and seemingly every Uptown social function. He also provided a tight and reliable backup band for artists at the Dew Drop Inn and other venues. He was still performing in 2025.

As fate would have it, Tommy Ridgley and the Untouchables were also performing regularly at the Pimlico Club at the time. Their reunion with Irma proved fortuitous because it launched her professional career, but not before she was fired for the second time for singing on the job.

Just as she had at the Kopper Kitchen, Irma sang while she worked, so much so that patrons began calling her "the singing waitress," even if her vocalizing as she waited tables did not go over well with the club owner. Then, she decided to make a bold move. She recalls, "I asked Tommy Ridgley if I could sing a song with him. This time, he allowed me to sing the popular Drifters song called 'There Goes My Baby.' This angered my boss who

Saxophonist Roger Lewis, pictured here at age seventeen, was a frequent member of Irma's early bands. He performs today with the Dirty Dozen Brass Band and other ensembles. (Photograph courtesy of Roger Lewis)

politely told me that he had not hired me to sing, and if I did it again, I was going to lose my job. Well, I guess you know what happened. One night when there wasn't a big crowd at the club, and I didn't have many tables in my working station, I decided to get up and sing a few songs to entertain the crowd. They were really enjoying themselves, and so was I."

Tommy Ridgley said, "I had met her once before, and she told me she could sing, but I never did get a chance to hear her. But anyway, she came up this night, she said, 'Well, if you say so, I'll go up on the bandstand,' and she sure did outdo Miss LaVell [who was singing with his band at the time]."[7] What is clear is that seventeen-year-old Irma commandeered the stage, as her desire to be an entertainer overrode any hesitation she might have had about jeopardizing her paying job. Her confidence in herself, however brash, and her irrepressible desire to sing outweighed every other impulse, and it worked, because she had just upstaged the established singer Lillia "Miss LaVell" White.

In that moment she had made an intuitive decision, both reckless and courageous, that would set the course of the rest of her life. She loved being in front of an audience who loved her in return—her playfulness and candor, and the unabashed joy she transmitted to them when she sang. It was a tipping point, even if the realities of motherhood and paying the bills demanded her first attention.

She also had a new job, albeit one that she could not imagine could ever support her family. Irma said, "The boss walked in and told me in no uncertain terms that I was fired—no surprise. Tommy Ridgley hired me on the

The 100 Men Hall in Bay St. Louis, Mississippi, in 2025. The venue continues to present live music, including a yearly festival dedicated to pianist James Booker. (Photograph by Scott Billington)

spot, and I started singing with his band regularly, but, understandably, not at the Pimlico Club. As a member of Ridgley's group, I began traveling to other places outside of New Orleans. I will never forget the first gig Tommy booked for me in Bay St. Louis, Mississippi, at the 100 Men Hall. For a costume, the only dress I had was a nice little Sunday dress. I had to do my own hair because I couldn't afford a hairdresser. Nevertheless, I fixed myself up decent enough to go on the job. Tommy picked me up that rainy night. Since it had rained all day, club attendance was small, so we didn't make a lot of money. Tommy was working for a percentage of the door. At the end of the night, we wound up making about two dollars each, which we used to share the expense of putting gas in the car to get back to New Orleans. This memorable experience marked my first earnings as a professional singer."

"As more proof of my naïveté, I didn't even know that I could actually make a living singing, so I felt that I really had to start looking for a real job. At the same time, my dad started complaining again about my still living with him and my mom with my three kids. I realized that I needed to find a place for myself. I found a job as a short-order cook at a restaurant on LaSalle Street. It's a nightclub now. There was a really nice guy named Ernest Lee Prader who used to come to the restaurant to buy lunch. I sized him up, thinking that here is a young man, apparently interested in me, who looks like he could make a few dollars, and be a way for my kids and me to get our own place away from my daddy. I decided to move fast, telling Ernest that if he got a place, I would move in with him. He seemed to like the idea of getting an instant wife and three children.

"The five of us moved into a small rooming house apartment on Thalia Street. We had one room, a kitchen, and a bath. Eventually, I had to accept the reality that I was using Ernest as just a way to get out of my dad's place. There was no true love there, an attraction, but not love. Who knows? At that age one can sometimes have a hard time telling the difference between love and something not love.

"While still living with Ernest Lee Prader and working on weekends at the Pimlico Club, I met my second husband, Andrew Thomas, whose name I still carry. Prior to that, my name was Irma Lee Jones from my marriage to Eugene Jones. Andrew was a very thin man about five seven or nine; he wasn't much taller than me. However, unlike me, he was light complexioned with somewhat wavy hair. Go figure, my liking a fair-skinned man. Once again, it was kind of an attraction. I can't say I was in love with him. Maybe I was, but who really knows? I certainly didn't. Because of this new interest, I left Ernest Lee in the house on Thalia Street, took my kids, and moved in with Andrew and his mother in her apartment, which was located on the opposite side of the Melpomene Street canal from where I used to live. It just goes to show that one never knows where life will take us."

Irma and her children lived with Andrew and his mother for a brief time. The two-bedroom apartment was small, but it was larger than Irma's parents' apartment, and Irma was happy for the change. After leaving his mother's apartment, Andrew, Irma, and the children moved downtown to the Seventh Ward, and then again uptown to Sixth Street. In 1962, Andrew adopted Irma's three children, and all of their surnames were changed to Thomas.

CHAPTER FOUR

Don't Mess with My Man

(1958–1960)

In November 1959, Irma made her first commercial recording, "Don't Mess with My Man," for the small Ron Records label in New Orleans. The company was founded by Joe Ruffino, who had gotten his start working as a salesman for Joe Banashak's A-1 Record Distributors on Baronne Street, selling records from local labels such as Ace, and independent national labels such as Atlantic, Imperial, and Specialty, to record shops and one-stops (subdistributors that carried numerous labels, providing a convenient "one stop" service where small shops could buy all the hits). After getting a feel for the record business, he decided to start his own labels.

Ron Records and its affiliated label Ric, named for Ruffino's two sons, were in business for only five years between 1958 and 1962, the year Ruffino died. Yet, they were important labels, not only because they released the first recordings by future New Orleans music icons Irma Thomas and Johnny Adams, but also because they represented a looser and more modern New Orleans rhythm and blues style, with artists such as Eddie Bo, and the updated sound of Tommy Ridgley. Irma's debut record became one of Ruffino's biggest hits, reaching #22 on the *Billboard* R&B chart in 1960 (Ruffino's other hit was Joe Jones's "You Talk Too Much").

In 1959, still living with Andrew and his mother, Irma continued to perform with Ridgley, which helped build her credibility as an artist. He was recording for Ric/Ron Records at the time, but when he asked Irma to go to an audition for the label, she didn't believe he was serious, and she did not go. A record deal was not something she could have envisioned. Yet, he persisted, showing up at her home to personally escort her to the studio.

The record label for Irma's first single, "Don't Mess with My Man." (Courtesy of the Concord Music Group)

At the audition, in Ruffino's second floor office on Carondelet Street, Irma met Dorothy LaBostrie, an important New Orleans rhythm and blues songwriter with a catalog of thirty or so published songs, of which an inordinate number were hits. Perhaps LaBostrie's most legendary contribution to American popular music was to clean up the lyrics to Little Richard's lascivious "Tutti Frutti" at Cosimo Matassa's studio in 1955. Originally, the song began "Tutti frutti, good booty," and became increasingly graphic from there. She penned Johnny Adams's first hit, "I Won't Cry," and cowrote McKinley "Li'l" Millett's first Specialty Records single, "Rich Woman," which was later covered by Canned Heat and the Fabulous Thunderbirds. It finally won the Best Pop Collaboration with Vocals Grammy® Award for Robert Plant and Alison Krauss in 2006. LaBostrie brought the song "Don't Mess with My Man" to Irma and taught it to her that first day at Ron Records, singing it *a cappella*. Irma remembered learning the song on a Monday, recording it on a Wednesday, and having it on the market two to three weeks later. Irma said, "With this record, I celebrated my first hit and first recording contract. I was thrilled when Kitty told me that she had heard my song on the radio."

With its slightly risqué lyrics, "Don't Mess with My Man" was an ideal song for the seventeen-year-old Irma, whose confidence and charisma were on full display. The song, recorded at the studio in the Ron Records office, does not have a typical New Orleans groove. Rather, it is a swinging, medium-tempo blues shuffle, with riffing horns, a bass line that would become a blues staple, and a raw-edged tenor sax solo by Robert Parker, whose instrumental "All Night Long" was a current local hit for Ron Records. He would later score a national hit with "Barefootin'." Other musicians include a young Mac Rebennack, who would later adopt the persona of Dr. John, on guitar, and Eddie Bo on piano. The sessions happened in a blur for Irma, who was too immersed in the moment to remember the other musicians who played with her. The song remains in her live concert set to this day, and the recording was inducted into the Blues Hall of Fame in 2025. The reverse side of the record, "Set Me Free," is a standard blues ballad with trebly electric guitar fills, showing a side of Irma that was not quite as brash, but that was well-suited to her voice.

"It's a funny thing about my first hit, 'Don't Mess with My Man,'" said Irma. "As soon as it hit the radio, it took off. Some years later, I was told that it was quite a big record on the *Billboard* R&B charts; it didn't do too badly on the pop charts either. Locally, it was taken off the radio because it was considered too suggestive. Boy, were they ever wrong! Compared to the stuff played on today's radio, 'Don't Mess with My Man' was whistle clean, almost pure.

"Of course, I didn't have any kind of management at the time, but it didn't take a genius to figure out that singing for fifty dollars a night was much more lucrative than waitressing for four dollars a night plus tips. One would think that my first gig as a recording artist would be with Tommy Ridgley's band, but it wasn't. Instead, it was with bass player Lloyd Lambert and his band at the Blue Eagle on Felicity Street. The Blue Eagle was a big hall, where customers gambled or played Keno, a board game in which a player picks a group of numbers and hopes they will match the winning numbers. The club also booked dances. Mr. Dave Brown, called Mayor of Rampart Street, owned the nightclub. He booked me for my first performance at The Blue Eagle."

Following her engagement at the Blue Eagle, Irma was booked for a series of one-night shows. She met and rehearsed with bandleader Al White and his band, and went on a two-week tour with the group. Irma said, "Fortunately, I could leave my children with Andrew's mother. The group consisted of five musicians, Andrew, Al White, and me, traveling in a Mercury station wagon that Al drove. We rode from New Orleans to Miami, stopping for gigs along the way. I remember playing some armories in Fort Lauderdale and Abe's 506 Club in Pensacola. My earnings were a big improvement. Fifty dollars a night for two weeks was not a bad take.

"My time on the road also had some interesting moments. By the time we got to Miami to play The Palms, the old Mercury engine had just about had it. So, Al had to get it fixed, which meant everybody in the group had to chip in for engine replacement. Additionally, we had to help pay for our hotel rooms, which were always small and cheap. Since I was not familiar with better class hotels, the ones we stayed in were like paradise to me. You have to remember that this was during segregation, a time when few hotels were available to Black people, so our accommodations were limited. Still, I guess they were okay, based on the standards of the fifties and sixties."

When Andrew and Irma returned to New Orleans, they had enough money to move out of Andrew's mother's place and rent their own apartment in one half of a shotgun double house on Sixth Street. Irma said, "We had a living room, bedroom, kitchen, and bath. Because of the three kids, I made the living room a bedroom and the second room was the kids'. We could not afford a stove or a refrigerator. In each room there was a fireplace between the rooms on both sides of the shotgun. On our side was a grate that extended out and curved around the fireplace somewhat like a protruding stomach, where wood and coal were placed to build a fire. This became my stove. I cooked beans and rice, setting a large pot atop the grate, and leaning it against the back wall of the fireplace. This had to do until we finally could afford a stove and later a refrigerator.

"For all practical purposes, our shotgun apartment wasn't so bad. It had a backyard and an alleyway, where the children could play. The rent was an affordable twelve dollars a week, which wasn't easy to pay, but Andrew and I managed. All Black folks know that one thing is sure: we definitely have skills when it comes to stretching a dollar as far as it will go. I cooked red beans on Mondays, butter beans on Tuesdays, pinto beans on Wednesdays, white beans on Thursdays, and tuna casserole on Fridays. On special days when I could afford them I would smother pork chops, or buy greens from the vegetable man, who came by with his pickup truck every week, singing "veg-tee-ble, veg-tee-ble, veg-tee-ble man is here."

During these years, there was a corner grocery store in nearly every neighborhood, where patrons could buy milk, eggs, and meats. Refrigeration was still in its early days; therefore, most families, including Irma's, kept perishables in an ice box. Every other day, she would buy a twenty-five-pound block of ice from the ice man, who announced his presence as he sang "Get your cold ice here." Singing merchants, known as street criers, provided a melodious soundscape throughout New Orleans neighborhoods as they advertised their goods and services through song. Merchants like the icemen carried

The Dew Drop Inn in 1953. (Ralston Crawford Collection of Jazz Photography, Hogan Archive of New Orleans Music and New Orleans Jazz, Tulane University Special Collections—used by permission)

their goods on hand-drawn or horse-drawn carts, others, like the Praline Lady, carried their goods in baskets. An example of these songs can be heard on the album *Street Cries and Creole Songs of New Orleans* by Adelaide Van Wey (Smithsonian Folkways Records). This tradition continued until the last prominent street crier, Arthur James Robinson, who called himself Mr. Okra, died in February 2018. He drove through neighborhoods in a pick-up truck filled with crates of vegetables, as he sang over a loudspeaker.

It was a welcome step forward when Irma and Andrew could afford to buy their own refrigerator. Irma said, "As luck would have it, I landed a weekly job at the Dew Drop Inn, owned by Mr. Frank Painia. I was making $12.00 a night, so one night covered the week's rent. Fortunately for me, he had heard about my record, 'Don't Mess with My Man,' so he signed me to do some gigs. I had changed my name to Irma Thomas by then even though Andrew and I were not married, but living together, common law."

The Dew Drop Café & Hotel, familiarly called the Dew Drop Inn, was an important and vital landmark in the history of New Orleans rhythm and blues, and for New Orleans culture in general, because Painia also booked jazz musicians and entertainers of all kinds. Located at 2836 Lasalle Street, the Dew Drop included a nightclub (sometimes called The Groove Room), hotel, twenty-four-hour restaurant, barber shop, and booking agency. Painia was also a civil rights activist, and while the club catered to the city's Black population, he welcomed everyone. It was an upscale place for a night out, where patrons dressed in their best clothes.

At least once, Painia went to jail when his customers were arrested.[1] Painia's grandson, Kenneth Jackson, recalled, "There were several instances where the police came here and found whites in here and just hauled everybody off in here and had everybody in the place arrested. They charged them with 'racial mixing.' So that went on for a while and there was an episode with a white actor, Zachary Scott, was arrested along with the rest of the people that were a part of that raid, and my grandfather had had enough so he sued the city, the mayor, the police chief, and ended up winning the lawsuit."[2] Irma further commented, "Even through segregation, Black and white musicians in New Orleans would get together privately and play."

It is perhaps a timely coincidence or an intentional statement that Elvis Presley's 1958 film, *King Creole*, which is centered on life on Bourbon Street, depicted Elvis's white character Danny being goaded to perform on stage with an all-Black jazz band, which could have hypothetically resulted in the character's arrest, at a time when the barriers of segregation had just begun to break down.

The list of musicians who played at the Dew Drop, from the mid-1940s until it closed in the early 1970s, included just about every popular entertainer in Black music, as well as many who were less well known or nearly forgotten. In its early years, the venue hosted jazz artists such as the Duke Ellington Orchestra and Ella Fitzgerald. By the late 1950s and early 1960s, the Dew Drop was presenting local stars such as Bernadine Washington ("exotic song thrush"), pianist/organist Allen Toussaint (who was first advertised in the *Louisiana Weekly* as "Alvin Toussiant [*sic*]," backing Lee Dorsey), Bubbles Mambo ("comic singer"), saxophonist Lee Allen, keyboardist James Booker ("Lil Booker at the organ and Earl King"), and rising R&B artist Ernest "Ernie K-Doe" Kador; stars of earlier years such as blues singers Roy Brown, Big Jay McNeely, Amos Milburn, and Charles Brown; and current national acts such as Joe Tex, Arthur Prysock, Ted Taylor, Little Johnny Taylor, Etta James, Solomon Burke, the Ike and Tina Turner Review, and B.B. King.

Since Painia was able to absorb the cost of accommodations for touring artists during the time of segregation, a group as large as the Ellington Orchestra could find a welcoming respite from the road, even as they had to cram themselves onto the small stage to perform. Along with a few other New Orleans hotels such as the Patterson, the Astoria, and the Golden Leaf, the Dew Drop was listed in *The Negro Motorist Green Book*.

However, the Dew Drop was more than a nightclub and hotel because it was the central gathering point for musicians in New Orleans—a home base for the local music scene. Musicians would often meet at the restaurant at lunchtime (Painia's brother ran the kitchen), and pass the early afternoon hours musing about their respective shows the night before, or about the latest gossip, musical and otherwise. The musician, songwriter, and guitarist Earl King wrote, illustrated, and published a mimeographed newsletter about the scene around the Dew Drop, which he sold for ten cents a copy. Allen Toussaint remembered, "Wherever musicians in town during those days were performing, they would all meet at the Dew Drop, and go and make their performance, and they would come back to the Dew Drop, which was the headquarters."[3]

The Groove Room was not a large venue, with a capacity of two hundred or two hundred and fifty patrons, who sat at tables with white tablecloths on the main floor or on a balcony which had a view of the stage. In addition to each night's main act, a typical show might include an opening musical artist, a shake dancer (who performed the derriere-focused dance style was the direct forebear of the ongoing bounce craze), and perhaps a comedian or a ventriloquist. Kenneth Jackson recalled an entertainer called Iron Jaw, who could lift a person sitting in a wooden chair with his teeth. In 1959, Miss Chi Chi, the "Exotic Cuban Bombshell," appeared as an opening act for Miss LaVell. Lillia LaVell White, the same singer whom Irma had upstaged at the Pimlico, recorded a series of singles for the Houston-based rhythm and blues label Duke Records between 1958 and 1964. Born in Amite, Louisiana, in 1929, she was a regular performer at the Dew Drop, listed in a typical advertisement in the January 10, 1959, issue of *Louisiana Weekly*: "Frank Painia presents double feature, 2 exotic dancers plus Miss Lavell & Bill Senigal's[*sic*] Ork."[4]

Shows were emceed by female impersonators or drag queens such as Bobby Marchan (who was also the lead singer for Huey Smith and the Clowns) and the glamorous Patsy Valdeler (born Irving Ales), the latter of whom Irma knew as Patsy Valdez, while others recall his last name as Vidalia. In a March 21, 1959, *Louisiana Weekly* advertisement, Patsy Valdeler is mentioned as the host of the "Big [St.] Joseph's Night Gay Ball" at the Dew Drop, at a time when the word "gay" was perhaps just coming into its current usage.[5] He also hosted a Gay Ball each Halloween.

Saxophonist Roger Lewis, who would soon be a part of Irma's touring band, also remembers Joe "Mr. Google Eyes" or "Mr. G" (after Billy Eckstine's nickname, "Mr. B") August as a sometime emcee. In the 1940s and 1950s, August had released records on labels as diverse as RCA, Columbia, Savoy,

On a typical night at the Dew Drop Inn, Deacon John and the Ivories back up singers Bobby "Blue" Bland and Joe Hinton. This is one of the few photographs depicting R&B musicians performing at the Dew Drop, with the band on the small stage and the singers on the floor. L-R top row: Deacon John Moore, guitar; Henry Joseph, baritone saxophone; Al Miller, drums; Roger Lewis, tenor saxophone; Lionel Vinson, alto saxophone; Oray Durban (correct spelling unknown), bass. Front row: Bobby Bland and Joe Hinton. (Photograph courtesy of Roger Lewis, photographer unknown)

and Duke/Peacock.[6] Lewis recalled, "He was a class act and he was an amazing singer. He could have played in Vegas."[7] At the Dew Drop in the 1960s, Irma met Esquerita, whose wild piano playing, flamboyant attire, make-up, and high pompadour hairstyle had been an inspiration for Little Richard. Many artists in the rock world, such as David Bowie and Prince, would later don the same mantle of sexual ambiguity.

"If you played the Dew Drop, you had made it in New Orleans," Irma said. "And I guess I made it because I played the Dew Drop quite often. I was the opening act for a while for someone else who was the headliner. Patsy Valdez was the 'host with the most' [also nicknamed The Toast] and he used to do this song called 'Hip Shakin' Mama.' He taught me all the verses, but I refused to sing all the verses because it was quite risqué. I actually recorded it without the risqué verses. It was what you call a double entendre type of song. You had to kind of read between the lines and figure out what they were talking about. But yes, the Dew Drop was the community gathering spot. Every local musician who didn't have a day job would be at the Dew

Drop during the course of the week on any given day."[8] In 2024, after years of neglect, the Dew Drop Inn reopened as a music venue and boutique hotel, with a room dedicated to Irma.

She recalled, "It was just a good place to hang among your buddies. I was one of the youngsters of that era who was able to go to the Dew Drop and perform there and find out if I had 'it,' whatever 'it' was that I was trying to seek, to find out if I had the ability to stand up in front of *the* audience—the hard-nosed audience—and perform and say, 'OK, I made it, they accepted me.'"[9]

Simultaneously, while singing at the Dew Drop Inn, Irma continued performing concerts with Al White, road gigs with Bill Sinegal, and shows with Robert Parker. She also began to work locally at the Saturday night teen dances held at Germania Hall on Bienville Street, and at the F&M Patio ("Frump and Manny's," after the proprietors' cleaning supply company, which occupied the same space) at Lyons and Front Streets; and at clubs such as the Saboo and the Baby Grand. The F&M Patio Bar on Tchoupitoulas Street was still open in 2025, under different ownership.

Irma and Andrew were both working steadily now. Irma said, "Andrew was a roofer by trade and he worked with his father when he wasn't with me on the road. Rare were the times when he did not travel with me. Due to my naïvete in the music business, I still was not charging the $300 or $400 a night that I should have been making. Instead, I started charging only a little bit more per night, thinking I was making quite a bit of money. A little bit of money could go a long way back in the late fifties and early sixties. But had I charged what I should have been charging, I would have been living like a lot of stars of that era. Having a manager would have made a big difference in my earnings.

"I also managed to book a one-week gig at the Regal Theater in Chicago. The pay was three hundred dollars, but we had to provide our own living arrangements. Andrew had relatives who lived in Chicago, so we didn't have the extra expense of a hotel. Playing on the same bill at the Regal Theater were Shirley and Lee, the headliners, whom I had idolized as a youngster, Gladys Knight and the Pips, Redd Foxx—also a headliner—and Al Benson as emcee."

The lavish Regal Theater, built in 1928, was a popular music venue, nightclub, and theater located at 4719 South Parkway (47th and Grand Boulevard) in the South Side of Chicago. With a seating capacity of approximately 3,000, the theater featured shows called revues that typically ran for seven days. Irma said, "I will never forget that early 1960 Chicago performance. We did five shows a day, the early part of the day, starting at noon, after the showing of two movies. Each performer sang two songs. My selections were 'Don't Mess with My Man,' and the flip side, 'Set Me Free,' the only two songs I had recorded at the time.

Performers who did more than two songs were headliners like Shirley and Lee, who sang 'I'm Gone,' 'Come Back to Me,' and 'Come On Baby, Let the Good Times Roll,' this last one doing quite well in sales at the time.

"I shared a dressing room with Shirley, Gladys, and Ruby of Ruby and the Romantics. Ruby's current hit was 'Our Day Will Come.' Normally, the stars had their own dressing room, but this time all of us shared the room. Evidently, we were kind of down on the totem pole, not yet having reached star status. It was fun being with them, though. Shirley still remembers it. I haven't seen Ruby for years, so I don't know if she also remembers. However, I have seen and spoken to Gladys Knight about sharing the Regal Theater dressing room. To her, it was a memory, long lost."

Irma began working again with Lloyd Lambert's band at the Sugar Bowl in Thibodaux, Louisiana, which most patrons and musicians called Hosy's Hill's place, after owner Hosea Hill. Like the Dew Drop, it was a major stop on the so-called chitlin' circuit—the informal network of Black theaters and nightclubs—and Hill would often coordinate bookings with Painia.[10] Irma remembered that during that time, Lambert's guitar player was often Clarence "Gatemouth" Brown, who would later become a major figure in the roots and blues music revival of the 1980s.

These years were a heyday in New Orleans for all the various genres that would come to be acknowledged as the bedrock of much American music, which thrived in a world that seemed invisible to mainstream media, while truly in plain sight. Almost every month, the Municipal Auditorium or the Coliseum Arena hosted a major touring show with artists such as Sam Cooke, Ruth Brown, Dee Clark, and the Drifters. WYLD's Rev. Herman Brown promoted gospel shows at the Booker T. Washington Auditorium, featuring the likes of Sister Rosetta Tharpe, the Swan Silvertones, and the Staple Singers. Lincoln Beach, an amusement park on Lake Pontchartrain, featured concerts each weekend by Art Neville and The Hawkettes, Roy Brown, or Tommy Ridgley. The Blue Eagle, which was sometimes booked by Frank Painia, rivaled the Dew Drop in presenting national touring artists such as the package show of Bobby "Blue" Bland and Little Junior Parker, and B. B. King and his Sensational Orchestra featuring Johnny Bond. The International Longshoremen's Association (ILA) Hall on Claiborne Avenue hosted weekly big band jazz concerts, with horn players such as Alvin "Red" Tyler or Warren Bell fronting a seventeen-piece band. The venue also hosted speeches by major figures such as Dr. Martin Luther King Jr. Throughout the 1970s and 1980s, it continued to be a regular chitlin' circuit stop for artists such as Clarence Carter and Tyrone Davis.

The dance halls, taverns, fraternity houses, and nightclubs that booked live music, not only in New Orleans but across Louisiana, may have constituted the single largest form of weekend entertainment for people from all walks of life, who gathered to socialize with friends and to dance to community-specific styles of music such as swamp pop, Cajun, rhythm and blues, and French Creole music (also known as "lala," which morphed into zydeco). (The word "Creole" means many different things in Louisiana, but all referring to a mixing of cultures and ancestry. In Southwest Louisiana, it refers to speakers of the Kouri-Vini dialect, itself a vestige of Haitian immigration, whereas in New Orleans, it usually means a person of mixed French, Spanish, and African descent in myriad combinations, or simply one of their US-born offspring.)

Since there was so much work for musicians, it was an era that fostered creativity in songwriters, singers, instrumentalists, and entrepreneurs alike. The plethora of music made for and by the community in daily life is the reason that most Louisianans who grew up during those years are very good dancers. Irma commented, "There were a lot more live music clubs back in the late fifties, early sixties. There were a lot of neighborhood music clubs where bands could go, singers could go and find out if that's what they really wanted to do. If they were good enough, [they] would be accepted."[11]

Given the fertile climate for music at the time, it is surprising that Joe Ruffino chose to cut just one more record with Irma, especially considering that she had just given him a major hit. Her second Ron single, "A Good Man" (on which she shares the writing credit), is a blues with stop-time verses in the mold of 'Don't Mess with My Man,' backed with "I May Be Wrong," a neatly arranged medium-tempo ballad with piano triplets. However, the record did not sell well, and Irma was released from her contract. She never received royalties for her Ron releases until Rounder Records bought Ric and Ron Records from Joe Ruffino's family in the 1980s and began paying her from the date of acquisition.

Making ends meet remained a challenge, but Irma used a skill she had learned in the country to put food on the table. She said, "While living on Sixth Street, when Andrew wasn't roofing, we used to subsidize the family income by going fishing. We loved to fish. I don't know why I don't fish as much as I used to. We would borrow a car and drive down to Bayou Gauche, towing a rented boat. The owner of the car was our friend, Morris Bland, who also liked to fish. Since we used a pole to fish, we didn't have to have a license, and we caught whatever fish would bite. I always caught a lot of fish, believing my pregnant belly was somehow the big draw for fish. Fish made many delicious dinners when we didn't have enough money for groceries. I would clean and cook them, making sure to pick out all the bones for the kids. Fried fish and mashed potatoes allowed us to eat really well. We had a good time, and times were not as rough as they sound. You have to be inventive when it comes to stretching a dollar. That was one thing I learned from my parents. Fishing was one of the ways we made money go as far as possible until times got better."

Still, her career was gaining momentum as she continued to find paying work. She said, "When I got started, I didn't have a choice. I was a teenage mother with three kids and an eighth-grade education, so my motivation was simple. I had to feed my family. I had to get out there and make something of myself. There was no welfare or anything like that back then. I had to struggle. My choices were to either take a menial labor job or to do something with the talent that God gave me."[12]

In a 2000 interview with John Sinclair, Irma summed up the positive aspects of her formative years: "I came up in a good time, I think, for music. It was a growing time. I didn't have a lot of female vocalists to style myself after, but I took from those I did learn from, which was Mahalia [Jackson], she was the gospel side of me, and Pearl Bailey was my showmanship side."[13]

Mahalia Jackson, the Queen of Gospel, was born in 1911 and reared in the Black Pearl neighborhood of New Orleans. The Mount Moriah Missionary Baptist Church, where she first gained her footing as a singer, still stands at 147 Millaudon Street. Her breakout hit in 1948 was "Move on Up a Little Higher," composed by W. Herbert Brewster. She toured widely in the United States and in Europe, and made many television appearances, including *The Ed Sullivan Show*. She sang at the 1963 Civil Rights march on Washington, just before the Reverend Martin Luther King Jr.'s "I Have a Dream" speech, and she sang five years later at his funeral.[14] The power of her singing left an indelible impression on Irma, who would later perform a regular Tribute to Mahalia Jackson set at the New Orleans Jazz and Heritage Festival.

While Pearl Bailey obtained a degree in theology from Georgetown University at age sixty-seven, much as Irma would resume her academic studies later in her career, she is remembered as a versatile actress, dancer, and singer. Born in Newport News, Virginia, in 1918, she began her career as a big band vocalist with Cootie Williams, Count Basie, and Cab Calloway. In 1946, she appeared in her first musical, *St. Louis Woman*. Her film debut the following year was *Variety Girl*. In 1967, she played the role of matchmaker Dolly Gallagher Levi in an all-Black production of the musical *Hello Dolly*, and hosted her own television show in 1971. She was awarded the Presidential Medal of Freedom by Ronald Reagan in 1988.[15] In all her endeavors, she exuded class, pride, and dignity, qualities that young Irma Thomas endeavored to emulate.

Irma could not have chosen two stronger role models, as she would soon define a style of her own and an attitude that would endear her to fans for decades to come.

DISCOGRAPHY

Singles

Don't Mess with My Man (D. LaBostrie)/Set Me Free (D. LaBostrie) Ron Records 328, 1959 (No. 22 R&B).

A Good Man (Thomas-Johnson)/I May Be Wrong (Allen-Johnson) Ron Records 330, 1959.

(Recording credits that appear at the end of each subsequent chapter are taken from the actual record labels. Therefore, some spellings and attributions will vary slightly from record to record.)

CHAPTER FIVE

Irma and Allen

(1961–1963)

In 1961, after she was dropped by Ron Records, Irma heard that the newly formed Minit label was conducting auditions, and she answered the call. The fledgling label was cofounded by Joe Banashak (coincidentally, the entrepreneur who had given Joe Ruffino his start in the record business) and disc jockey/promoter Larry McKinley, each of whom put up $650 as seed money. The partners also arranged for a national distribution deal with Los Angeles–based Imperial Records. Banashak, a Maryland native who had become a jazz fan while he was in the military, eventually gravitated to New Orleans after working for several other music-related businesses.[1] McKinley was the program director of WMRY radio, which may have had the first all-Black on-air staff in New Orleans,[2] and also the manager of budding artist Ernest "Ernie K-Doe" Kador. According to Banashak, McKinley was also "probably the hottest disc jockey in the city."[3]

McKinley's radio connections ensured that Minit Records would obtain local airplay, an unabashed conflict of interest, especially as the practice of payola—paying for airplay—was being actively investigated by the FCC following a 1960 Congressional hearing. Yet, the relationships between the local record labels and the disc jockeys, whatever clandestine favors might have been granted, helped build one of the most fruitful and exciting local music scenes in the country—a self-contained ecosystem of artists, musicians, record companies, radio stations, disc jockeys, record stores, and booking infrastructure, all enabled because local radio stations played local music. Irma commented, "There were some under-the-table arrangements made, but it worked."

There were numerous record shops, especially along the thriving commercial districts of North Claiborne Avenue, North Rampart Street, and Dryades Street. Operating a small label was a hustle, both in terms of the work required and the necessity of seeking any advantage that would get records played on the radio. Many highly regarded records that never would have attracted the investment of a major label were made by the New Orleans indies, including those released by Minit, as the label's roster came to include Ernie K-Doe, Jessie Hill, Benny Spellman, Aaron Neville, and Irma.

McKinley and Banashak's smartest move may have been to hire composer, pianist, producer, and arranger Allen Toussaint to oversee all aspects of the label's creative ventures, although their first choice had been Harold Battiste Jr., who was otherwise employed. The young Toussaint went on to produce hits for Minit that included K-Doe's "Mother In Law" and Hill's "Ooh Poo Pah Doo," both of which were awarded gold records to signify sales in excess of 500,000 copies. Ben Sandmel wrote, "The convergence of talent and acumen in the association of Toussaint, Banashak, and McKinley constituted a collective milestone, for Ernie K-Doe, Toussaint, the label's other artists, and, by extension, American popular music."[4]

Irma's husband Andrew had introduced her to Toussaint, his high school friend who was living at the time on Audubon Court. Born in New Orleans on January 14, 1938, Toussaint was leading a teenage rhythm and blues band called The Flamingos when he was only fifteen years old. While his arrangement with Minit would constitute his first job as a record producer, he had already acquired a reputation as a versatile pianist, touring with artists such as Shirley and Lee. He had also released his first album under his own name, albeit with an Americanized spelling: *The Wild Sounds of New Orleans* by Al Tousan, on the RCA label. The album did not attract much attention at the time, but it would later yield the hit song "Java" for New Orleans trumpeter Al Hirt.

Although Banashak and McKinley knew of Irma, they did not immediately sign her. John Swenson wrote, "In 1960, [both] Allen Toussaint and Irma Thomas showed up to audition at WYLD radio studio in New Orleans for Joe Banashak and Larry McKinley of Minit Records. The fledgling label was holding an open call for singers, session musicians, and songwriters and the respondents included Art and Aaron Neville, Jessie Hill, Joe Tex, Larry Williams, and Benny Spellman. Toussaint showed up to accompany singer Allen Orange, but the twenty-two-year old pianist walked out with creative control over the label's entire roster. Toussaint was about to make music history with Irma and the rest of the New Orleans R&B legends at that session."[5]

Irma remembers that her audition that day was not successful, and that it was Toussaint who ultimately brought her into the fold, some months later. She recounted, "I was turned down. I reminded [Allen Toussaint] of that many times. Well, I found out later that at that time, they were not looking for female artists, and Allen did not have control over whether or not I was accepted or rejected because he was just there as the auditioning musician. He explained that to me some years later because I used to blame him for that. He said, 'I have to explain to you, I was not in charge of that. I was just a musician.' And of course we became friends later."[6]

A surprise was on the way as well because Irma and Andrew would soon welcome into the world her fourth child, Andrea, who was born on September 20, 1961. Irma said, "In late 1960, early 1961, right in the middle of my transition from Ron Records to Minit, I discovered I was pregnant with my fourth child. I probably got pregnant during a road gig, maybe in Dothan, Alabama. The weather was very cold, which prevented us from getting out and about."[7]

As luck would have it, Irma and Andrew's home on Sixth Street was within walking distance of the Dew Drop, where she was still performing two or three nights each week, sometimes backed by Allen Toussaint on Hammond B3 organ (possibly with Check Badie on bass and Charles "Hungry" Williams on drums), or by James Booker on Hammond B3 organ. "Once I began to show, I had to consider concealing my pregnancy as long as I could. Back then, panty hose didn't exist. Since I worked in high heels, I had to wear stockings, held up by either garters or a garter belt. The garter belt worked perfectly in that it held up my stockings and gave me support for my belly as well. Having learned to sew in school, I knew how to make my own performance costumes. I also knew how to make some fancy brocade maternity tops that I wore with straight black skirts. I looked kind of cute for someone pregnant. Thankfully, pregnancy did not prevent me from performing for any of my gigs, such as for WTIX radio and other local stations."[8]

At the same time, she began a fruitful relationship with booking agent Percy Stovall. "Stovall booked many shows on the road, and he was very concerned about my traveling as an expectant mother. I assured him that I would be fine, so he booked me for a short trip to Pensacola, Florida, and back. Sometimes, we played five or six nights, then returned to New Orleans, but never longer or farther than Florida."

Roger Lewis recalled how Stovall took care of his musicians: "[He] would take money out and put it on the side, and he would give you your money when you got back to New Orleans."[9] This small act of prudence prevented his artists from spending all of their money while on the road, and ensured that they would come home from touring with money in their pockets. Irma added, "He always stressed being on time and being dependable. He said that's more important than talent most of the time and he was right."[10] They worked within a day's drive at venues such as the 100 Men Hall in Bay St. Louis, Mississippi, and Louisiana venues such as the Linnor Hall in Westwego, the Municipal Auditorium in Morgan City, and Haney's Big House in Ferriday. Stovall often worked the door himself, collecting the admission charge directly from patrons. The venues would make money by selling alcohol. He was able to pay Irma $125 per night. "To me, that was a lot of money," she said.

In later years, she was philosophical about the amount of money she made in the early years of her career. "I really think if I had started making large amounts of money back then, I would not have had any clue as to how to handle it properly. I probably would have been like a lot of other ones spending it and being stupid. I wasn't that kind of a spender. I've always been cautious with my money. But that amount of money would have made a big difference because a lot of the entertainers from that era who made that kind of money wound up either broke or dead." Her experience of having worked jobs at the very bottom of the labor pay scale was proving to be an asset, in addition to her grade school training in saving money.

Earl King told Jeff Hannusch, "Stovall was a rural bandit. He knew about every club, auditorium, and armory that held dances between Texas and Virginia. He had his own little circuits. When the tobacco workers got paid off, he'd book a solid month in those warehouses in the Carolinas. When they finished picking cotton, we'd be up in every little town in the Mississippi Delta. Same over in South Louisiana after sugar cane harvest. He was strictly for business. Nobody ever took advantage of Stovall. If you messed up once on him, that was it. I remember he'd come in a club at night before a gig and see some of the musicians having a drink. Well, he'd say, 'Uh-uh, boys. Ain't gonna be none of that tonight.'"[11] Stovall also booked shows such as the teen dances held at the Bay-Waveland Yacht Club in Bay Saint Louis, Mississippi, which was often packed well beyond its capacity of three hundred.

Stovall's band was called The Royals, which included, at various times, tenor saxophonists George Forshay and Frederick Kemp (and, for a brief time, Robert Parker), baritone saxophonist Roger Lewis, guitarist Leo Williams, bassist Walter Bourgeois, a drummer called "Big Nick," singer Joe Mizell (who would often open shows), and background vocalist Raymond Parker. Roger said, "Percy Stovall was the booking agent that used to book what we called the Chitlin' Circuit, from Texas to Florida, and we used to play all these little clubs. Irma was his featured artist."[12] The entourage would often include singer and coheadliner Johnny Adams, who had also gotten his start at Ron Records. Stovall also worked frequently with Solomon Burke, for whom Irma would be the opening act.

Roger recounted that Stovall had an International Harvester station wagon, like an early SUV, for traveling to shows. Irma remembers traveling in a windowless van, with six or seven musicians seated on cushions on the floor, along with luggage and instruments. "When Solomon Burke was with us, he did not ride with us because he had his own transportation," Irma said. Stovall sometimes traveled with the band as well. Dressing room accommodations were often limited, but Irma always managed to find a way to dress for the job, even if it meant using the ladies' room.

Concurrently, Irma was about to make the records with Allen Toussaint that would define her early career. In preparation for the recording sessions, Irma rehearsed with Toussaint and his musicians at his parents' house on Earhart Boulevard, in the section of New Orleans called Gert Town. Irma and Allen developed a deep friendship and a sense of comfort in one another's presence. She said, "We could talk about anything and everything. We would talk about how he used to call me one of the guys because they would be having a conversation about cars or something, and I could join right in, and I knew what I was talking about. And so I don't think he looked at me so much as the girl in the room, but as the person in the room, because I could join in no matter what conversation they were having, and I fit right in. There was never a time when they had to say, 'I'm sorry, Irma,' because they cussed, because that wasn't anything that they did among themselves. And if they did it, they didn't do it when I was around . . . We didn't have to walk on eggshells to be around each other."[13]

Years later, at a 2016 Jazz and Heritage Festival Stage interview that celebrated Allen Toussaint's life and legacy, Irma told Ben Sandmel, "We used to meet in his parents' living room. There were always five or six people, at least—K-Doe, Lee Dorsey when he wasn't working on someone's car [Dorsey worked in an auto body shop]. It was just like another home to us, and his parents were very hospitable. His mother was sweet and his father was as kind-hearted as he could be. Every now and then he would peek in to see how we were doing. I think his parents understood the genius of their son. For five or six hours each day, we would be in there singing."[14] It was a family atmosphere where nothing was forced, and where everything was on the table. This group of young musicians and singers were drawn to Allen's living room because it was a place for them to find their voices, while Allen experimented with his composing and arranging ideas. As a result, they were also well prepared when it came time to go to the recording studio.

Irma's Minit records were recorded at Cosimo Matassa's new studio on Governor Nicholls Street in the French Quarter, with musicians Chuck Badie on bass; Roy Montrell, Placide Adams, or Justin Adams on guitar; Nat Perrilliat on tenor saxophone; and Allen Toussaint on Hammond B3 organ or piano. The background vocalists almost always included Willie Harper and sometimes Allen himself, or Benny Spellman if a bass voice was needed. There were also usually two female vocalists, whose names Irma could not recall. The sessions were recorded live in the studio, including background vocals and strings, which were borrowed from the Louisiana Philharmonic Orchestra. "It was a pretty big studio," said Irma. "If anyone played a wrong note or missed a cue, the track would have to be recorded from scratch." It is clear that the rehearsals paid off because Allen's meticulous arrangements are beautifully realized. The one- or two-track recording technology of the day meant that the intricate sound balances had to be captured on the fly; therefore, Cosimo had to move musicians and microphones around in the studio until it sounded natural.

When asked about how he achieved such good-sounding records, Matassa was modest. "I go into the studio and listen to the sound of the instrument. I put a microphone on it, and I record it. Then, I go into the control room and listen. If it doesn't sound right, I go back in the studio and move the microphone until it does. Or maybe I try another mic."[15] His instincts were right because the records were beautifully recorded and balanced, and they sounded magnificent on the radio.

Irma's debut 1961 Minit single is a modest production, with Allen playing Hammond B3 organ with a small combo of guitar, bass, drums, and saxophone. "Girl Needs Boy," with its thirty-two-measure form and 4/4 swing tempo, sounds more like a 1940s standard than New Orleans rhythm and blues, but Irma sings it with aplomb, perhaps a reflection of her affinity for Pearl Bailey. It is the reverse side of the single, "Cry On," on which we get a glimpse of where Irma and Allen were headed, as well as the power of Irma's understated, emotional delivery. This ballad is an early defining moment for her. It was later covered, along with "I Did My Part," by singer Tracy Nelson on the 1968 debut album by the San Francisco rock band Mother Earth.

Their subsequent single followed the same pattern. Deborah Chessler's ballad "It's Too Soon to Know" had previously been recorded by The Orioles and Ella Fitzgerald. For Irma, Allen gave it a more contemporary, if slightly bland, pop treatment, with lushly arranged strings and background vocals. His own composition, "That's All I Ask" (attributed, as were most of his early compositions, to the pseudonym Naomi Neville, which was his mother's maiden name, due to a lopsided and unfair publishing agreement he had made under his own name when he signed with RCA) might have had a New Orleans rhythm and blues groove if it were not for the light touch of the rhythm section and the string-forward arrangement. As a body of work, Irma's two debut Minit singles were not an entirely auspicious start.

Then, on their first 1962 release, Allen and Irma began to hit their stride. Allen's "Gone" is a 6/8 ballad with a male doo-wop vocal group in support, but it is Ernie K-Doe's composition "I Done Got Over It" that stands out, with its syncopated background vocals, parade beat–derived rhythm, and a horn section with a slurred "tailgate" trombone. The song remains in Irma's set today, as part of her "second line medley."

The tailgate style was first popularized by the jazz trombonist Kid Ory. In his hands, the trombone no longer played the bass line, as it had in marching bands, but was free to play *glissandi* and counter melodies.[16] It is a signature New Orleans sound. The term "tailgate trombone" derives from the early jazz era when bands advertised their upcoming performances by playing on the back of wagons or trucks that rolled through the streets. The trombonist sat on the tailgate so that the slide would not hit the other musicians. In true New Orleans fashion of blending genres, here it was, the tailgate style showing up on a rhythm and blues record.

"It's Raining," also released in 1962, remains one of Irma's signature songs, and one of Allen's most enduring compositions. It is a standard blues ballad in structure, but the backing vocals and Irma's wistful delivery make it seem new. Allen recalled: "I remember when I was writing 'It's Raining,' she was sitting right there, and it began raining outside. I just wrote that song, then handed it over to her and sung a little bit of it, just to show her the melody, and it fit like a gown. Like an evening gown made and tailored for her."[17] Irma recalled, "He came out of the bathroom and said, 'I've got a song for you.' And he sat down at the piano and taught it to me then, but he wrote it that day. That's why we have such great respect for him because he could come up with them out of nowhere. It's like he was pulling them out of the air and they would fit the person he was writing it for."[18] She later commented, "You know, I call it the New Orleans national anthem because it's very fitting for this city. It does rain here a lot. And anybody who's having a melancholy moment can put on 'It's Raining' and go wherever their mind leads them."[19] The song was featured in Jim Jarmusch's 1986 film *Down by*

Law as costars Roberto Benigni and Nicoletta Braschi dance at the story's end, and has been covered by many other artists, including a 1981 version by Shakin' Stevens that reached #10 on the UK singles chart.

Irma added, "On the song 'It's Raining,' he didn't give me the second verse until we were actually in the studio and we were in the middle of recording. He stepped out from behind the piano and tiptoed over and put the second verse on the music stand. And I sang the second verse without even rehearsing. Back then you didn't make a noise in the studio because we didn't have all that technology we have today where you can tap it in or punch it in. You had to start all over again if you screwed it up. He had that kind of confidence in my ability and I was very comfortable with him. But it was nothing we thought about. It was just a thing that happened."[20]

The flip side of "It's Raining," "I Did My Part," is another outstanding performance and song, with a lilting street-derived beat and harmonized background vocals, with Allen's voice leading the way. New Orleans rhythm and blues historian John Broven wrote, "If any record represented a pinnacle of Toussaint's productions at this time it was Thomas's much-overlooked 'I Did My Part' . . . with an extended tenor sax cameo from Nat Perrilliat, forever inventive and with time to spare, not only in the break, but in the body of the song as well. It was no wonder that Perrilliat was a favorite Toussaint session man."[21]

On this record, there is a palpable sense of the bond between the vocalist and the producer/composer. Irma recalled, "He would teach us the song exactly the way he wanted the song to go, note for note how he wanted you to put in the little nuances. And, you know, sometimes you'd sneak in a few of your own, and he would have to leave them there because he didn't want to do the whole song all over again. But he was quite a person, an interesting person to work with in that his technique was very, very rigid in terms of what he wanted. And it was good. He knew."[22]

Allen often remarked that when he wrote, he heard Irma's voice in his head, and the songs he wrote specifically for her were so well suited for her that nothing ever seems forced. Irma had the ear to reach beyond the blues/gospel harmonic realm of many of her peers, perhaps a manifestation of her early enthusiasm for singers such as Nat "King" Cole; therefore, the melodies Allen wrote for her did not intimidate her. Allen later said, "Her love for singing translates when she's singing. She brings everything to the moment."[23] Allen was right because whatever imperfections anyone could hear in her singing, she was always present with the story embodied in the lyrics, and listeners were always moved.

Allen Toussaint and Irma Thomas at Jazz Fest in the 1990s. (Photograph by Daniel Untermyer, Ice Cube Slim Collection, courtesy of the New Orleans Jazz and Heritage Foundation)

Allen's daughter Alison Toussaint LeBeaux summed it up: "Irma really got my father, and I think a lot of that has to do with the fact that they started out so young together. . . . I think she just understood my dad and she understood his mind. And so throughout the times they worked together, if she was at the same function, when Irma came in he could actually breathe. He could relax. This is someone who knew him, who knew him from the very beginning, all the way through his career."[24] Irma commented, "There was just no hardship involved whenever I was working with him. He would have me sing a lot of his demos for people that he was writing songs for. I was a quick learner. When he wanted something done, he knew he could depend on me to sing it the way he wanted it sung."[25]

Around the time "It's Raining" was released, drummer Johnny Vidacovich heard Irma at the Saturday night teen dances at Germania Hall on Bienville Street, where she was backed by Tommy Ridgley, or one of the young house bands such as The Counts or The Jokers. Admission was twenty-five cents, with Cokes and chips available for purchase by the twelve- to eighteen-year-old audience. The tiny stage was in a corner in the back of the hall, originally built as a Scottish Rite Freemasons lodge, with windows that opened onto a patio. The young Vidacovich would station himself in the patio, prop his elbows on the open window ledge, and watch the drummers from his ideal vantage point.[26] Irma credited these Germania Hall "sock hops" with her popularity among teenagers.[27] Producer Ben Chace, who would work with Irma over sixty years later, commented, "You've got this entire generation of men in New Orleans who fell in love with Irma when they were teenagers. You never forget that kind of stuff. They either fell in love with her or they fell in love with the sound of her music. There's this whole generation of people. It's such a strong bond."[28]

Allen and Irma's streak of empathetic creativity continued. "Two Winters Long," "Somebody Told You," and "Hittin' on Nothing" were tailor-made for Irma's confident and sometimes sassy delivery. Each song is built on a variation of pure New Orleans groove, as Allen seemed to be fusing the city's birthright sounds—second line brass band parade beats, jazz, gospel, and the emerging fusion style that would be called funk—with his own compositional sense, creating new songs and arrangements that were both accomplished and quirky. It was an infectious and instantly recognizable new sound.

"Ruler of My Heart," the A-side of Irma's final 1963 Minit single, is another one of her defining moments, with an understated but powerful vocal that could be said to cement her future reign as the Soul Queen of New Orleans. Allen's delicate, filigreed piano motif leads to the dramatic bridge, giving the arrangement a tension that never quite resolves, even as Irma hums the melody while the song fades. There is not a wasted note.

The song's power was soon acknowledged by Otis Redding, whom Irma remembers as a kind and gentle man. After he heard Irma perform the song when she opened a show for him near New Orleans, he told her that he liked it and that he wanted to record it. Yet, when his record was released, the title had been changed to "Pain in My Heart," with the songwriters credited as Redding and his manager Phil Walden. It reached #11 on the *Billboard* rhythm and blues chart in November 1963, and #61 on the pop chart in February 1964. A lawsuit ensued, and subsequent pressings of the Volt single listed Naomi Neville as the composer. Irma later commented, "I love singing it. I mean, it's a great song."[29]

None of the Minit records were national hits, but they did very well regionally on both rhythm and blues and pop stations, and most New Orleans residents who grew up in the sixties remember them fondly. Irma recalled, "There was a time when I had records one, two and three with 'Cry On,' 'I Did My Part,' and 'Ruler of My Heart.' The label proved very lucky for me. We were going for a broad audience there. I broke the 'white radio station list' immediately with 'Cry On.' It broke the barrier, 'cause they didn't know if I was white or black."[30]

Her popularity prompted the local Coca-Cola Bottling Company to sign her to a promotional contract. The February 2, 1963, edition of the *Louisiana Weekly* reported:

> Irma Thomas, native of New Orleans, who has been hailed as one of this country's top recording artists, has signed an exclusive advertising contract with The Louisiana Coca-Cola Bottling Company. Miss Thomas, who has been singing professionally since 1958, will be heard on local radio stations. Special arrangements of the Coca-Cola musical jingle have been made featuring Irma Thomas.
>
> Officials of the Coca-Cola Bottling Company stated, "We are very happy Miss Thomas will be singing for Coca-Cola because we feel she is a very popular recording artist. In addition to her radio work, we expect she will do personal appearances for Coca-Cola to fit in with her heavy schedule."
>
> Irma Thomas' latest recording, "Two Winters Long," is a favorite with both teen-agers and adults and will probably hit the one-million mark in the near future. When it does, it will be her first "gold disc."
>
> Miss Thomas has made personal appearances throughout the United States, but at the present time, her heavy schedule keeps her in the New Orleans area. She is popular with the leading local night clubs and sings for many college fraternity and sorority dances.

Irma does not remember that she actually recorded a jingle, but she made many personal appearances for Coke at nursing homes, schools, and other venues. She also made a number of newspaper ads for the Helman-Speer Wig Company at 1228 Dryades Street. Part of her compensation was that she could buy her wigs at half price. The store had a sign in the window saying "Irma Thomas Buys Her Wigs Here."

Two more singles were released during the transition between Minit and Imperial Records, to which her recording contract would be soon assigned,

Irma Thomas was featured in a number of Coca-Cola ads in *Louisiana Weekly* in 1963. (Courtesy of Coca-Cola Bottling Company United)

including the string-laden, Allen Toussaint–produced “For Goodness Sake” / “Whenever (Look Up)” on Bandy, and “Foolish Girl” / “When I Met You” on the local Bumpa Records label. Warren Hildebrand, the owner of Mardi Gras Records, said that Bumpa was affiliated with his father Henry Hildebrand’s Watch label. Both songs were reissued on the 2022 compilation *NOLA Soul: Watch Records (Rare Tracks)*.[31] Watch was another important indie operation in New Orleans in the 1960s and 1970s, having released the Professor Longhair hit “Big Chief,” and Stop Inc.’s “Second Line,” both of which are still played on New Orleans radio stations every carnival season, along with several Johnny Adams songs, including his version of the country standard “Release Me.” Henry Hildebrand also ran All South Distributors, which was one of the largest record distributors in the South.

During this same period, Toussaint also used Irma as a backup singer, especially on split, three-hour sessions during which Irma would record two songs and another artist would record two more using the same band. Irma said, “Benny [Spellman] would be the baritone voice on the backup singers if Allen needed that sound, and I would be the alto section for the females. He wanted my female alto voice, but he didn’t realize how much it carried. They had to back me up against the wall to keep my voice in balance on Benny Spellman’s recording of ‘Lipstick Traces.’ It was a pretty big studio, and I was all the way against the wall farthest from the microphone, and you can still hear my voice over all those other parts. He kept saying, 'Back up a little bit more.'"

Irma told Jeff Hannusch, "We had a little family then. Just about everyone on Minit had a hit at one time or another—K-Doe, Benny Spellman, Aaron Neville. I sang background on their records and they did the same for me. It wasn't work then, it was fun."[32] Irma remembered that this musical coalition dominated the local airwaves as well. She said, "It was a very unique time for all of us. There wasn't an hour that went by that you didn't hear Ernie K-Doe, Benny Spellman, Fats Domino or Oliver Morgan. In those days New Orleans had radio stations that catered to New Orleans singers."[33] During this time, she garnered not only local radio airtime, but also a lengthy engagement at the Safari Lounge on Chef Menteur Highway, where she appeared with Danny White and the Cavaliers.

Irma said that working with Allen Toussaint could be ". . . interesting to say the least. He is a perfectionist. And because [of that] I got a lot of my technique in terms of how I learned to sing songs, how I learned songs from Allen. I give him credit for giving me some foundation on being a quick study. As I've gotten older that quick study part is still there, but remembering it is the part that's leaving me.

"But he was easy to work with in that he took time and he taught you specifically how he wanted the song to go in his head. He would bring it out of you. He'd keep rehearsing it till you got it exactly the way he wanted it. And of course, once you learn something, at least with me, once you learn something a certain way, no matter when you sing it or how you sing it, years later, it's always going to turn out the same way. But that's the way he worked with us."[34]

Allen and Irma were making history, and people are still listening to the records they made for Minit over sixty years later, particularly "It's Raining," which became a signature New Orleans song. In the hustle of the independent record business in the 1950s and 1960s, most 45 RPM singles were viewed by record companies and artists as ephemeral items, more like newspapers than as durable art. There was always the next hit to create, as soon as the current one was forgotten. It would be a few years before the long-playing album evolved into more than a collection of tracks put together to capitalize on a hit, at least outside the jazz and classical worlds. Yet, even though Irma would have bigger hits, and even though other producers, notably Scott Billington (the coauthor of this book) and the songwriter/producer Dan Penn, would work with her over a longer period of time, the twenty tracks she made with Allen Toussaint are those that many people remember first, especially in New Orleans. The synergy of that moment, both for Irma and Allen, and for New Orleans rhythm and blues in general, still resonates.

It was also during this time that Irma developed a passion for bowling, a sport that was a big part of recreational life in New Orleans during the 1950s and 1960s, perhaps due to the popularity of televised bowling tournaments during that era. Alleys such as the Garden Bowl, Aubry's, Bowlarama, Major Lanes, Paradise Lanes, Sugar Bowl Lanes, and Delta Bowl drew patrons who formed competitive leagues. According to Mike Scott's article on the topic for *The Times-Picayune*, "The game was such a part of the fabric of local life that bowling alley impresario Dominic Fazzio—who with his family operated a number of New Orleans bowling alleys, usually with the Fazzio brand attached—even earned a mention in John Kennedy Toole's quintessentially New Orleans novel *A Confederacy of Dunces*."[35]

After playing a show at the Sands on Jefferson Highway in Metairie with Tommy Ridgley and the Untouchables, Irma and the band drove across town to the Delta Lanes. "I bowled all night, averaging like 98 or 100," Irma told Angus Lind, adding, ". . . it didn't cost much and we had a lotta fun." Irma kept up this hobby for years, and was cited in the Kegler's Kix column in the *Louisiana Weekly* for a series score of 530—the highest in her league. The guitarist Walter Washington is also mentioned for rolling a single game of 190.[36] "Is the bowling serious?" Irma responded to Lind, "You better believe it. If you're going to do something, why not all the way?"[37] The anonymous writer of the bowling column in the June 16, 1962, issue of *Louisiana Weekly* noted that "Irma Thomas, Lee Dorsey, Tommy Ridgley, Chris Kenner, Larry McKinley and Buddy Lewis were all seen at the Delta Lanes," and that "Yours truly always seem [sic] to get lucky against K-Doe."[38] Mildred Dix, one of Irma's league mates, said, "Bowling was our social outing. We would all go as couples and meet up at the bowling alley."[39]

Bigger things were yet in store for Irma when Minit (as well as the Imperial label) was acquired by Liberty Records in 1963. Of all the Minit Records artists, Irma and Ernie K-Doe were the only two whose contracts were included in the deal. Concurrently, and perhaps part of the reason why Minit's hit streak slowed, Allen was drafted into the United States Army in January 1963, and his creative partnership with Banashak went on hiatus. Writer John Broven also noted, "Meanwhile, Larry McKinley had been forced to sell his stock in Minit in the wake of the payola disc-jockey scandal that erupted at the turn of the 1960s. Joe Banashak, however, never dropped a beat as a record man and was now looking for hits on Instant Records."[40] In the 1970s, Banashak's Bandy label would repackage ten of Irma's Minit sides as the album *Irma Thomas Sings*.

DISCOGRAPHY

Girl Needs Boy (Naomi Neville)/Cry On (Naomi Neville) Minit Records 625, 1961.

It's Too Soon to Know (Deborah Chessler)/That's All I Ask (Naomi Neville) Minit Records 633, 1961.

Gone (Naomi Neville)/I Done Got Over It (E. Kador) Minit Records 642, 1962.

It's Raining (Naomi Neville)/I Did My Part (Naomi Neville) Minit Records 653, 1962.

Two Winters Long (Naomi Neville)/Somebody Told You (Naomi Neville) Minit Records 660, 1962.

Ruler of My Heart (Naomi Neville)/Hittin' on Nothing (Naomi Neville) Minit Records 666, 1963.

For Goodness Sake (Naomi Neville)/Whenever (Look Up) (Naomi Neville) Bandy Records 368, 1963.

Foolish Girl (Ken Kerr)/When I Met You (Ed Freeman-David Levine) Bumpa Records 711, 1963.

The Minit sessions were produced by Allen Toussaint. Musicians include Allen Toussaint, piano and Hammond B-3 organ; Chuck Badie, bass; Roy Montrell, Placide Adams or Justin Adams, guitar; Willie Harper, Ernie K-Doe, Allen Toussaint, and Benny Spellman, backing vocals.

CHAPTER SIX

The First California Sessions

(1964)

The mid-1960s were a potent and transitional time in American popular music. Rhythm and blues was quickly evolving into the new sound called soul music, with its overt incorporation of gospel vocal styles, and a sophisticated songwriting approach that aimed for pop accessibility while retaining a gospel or blues tonality. At the same time, British bands such as the Beatles and the Rolling Stones were achieving their initial popularity with a back-to-the-roots sound that paid homage to American pioneers such as Little Richard, Carl Perkins, and Chuck Berry. Both of these phenomena would figure into the next phase of Irma's career.

Liberty Records, which retained the Imperial brand as a flagship label, clearly had big hopes for Irma, their new artist. The company's first move was to bring her to California to record with producer Eddie Ray and arranger Hidle Brown "H. B." Barnum. Eddie Ray is a pioneering record executive who eventually became the first Black vice president of A&R at Capitol Records. He produced or signed artists as diverse as Ricky Nelson, Fats Domino, Ernie K-Doe, Johnny Rivers, and Pink Floyd. He later served as a commissioner of the US Copyright Royalty Tribunal. H. B. Barnum is a first-call arranger who worked with Gladys Knight & The Pips, Aretha Franklin, Count Basie, The Jackson 5, Frank Sinatra, and countless others, contributing to some 100 gold albums.

Irma could not have been placed in better hands. The records she made with them are among her most successful, both commercially and artistically. She also had the benefit of Ray's songwriting reach, as he brought her material from writers such as Jackie DeShannon, Randy Newman, and Jerry Ragovoy. Yet, it was Irma's composition "Wish Someone Would Care" that was her breakthrough national record. Eddie Ray wrote:

Portrait postcard of Irma Thomas. (Photograph by Magnolia Studio, 1962, courtesy of the Louisiana State Museum and the New Orleans Jazz Museum, David Kunian, curator)

[Liberty Records president Al] Bennett suggested that I bring Thomas to Hollywood to produce her with top studio musicians and expand her record sales potential, which at that point had been limited to the Southern region. I brought Thomas to Hollywood for two weeks to give us a chance to know each other and to review hundreds of songs from popular West Coast songwriters. From them, I was planning to select ten for her to record on an album.

Thomas was in her early twenties, and this was her first trip to California. She was definitely not a conversationalist, quite introverted, and probably homesick for her two [*sic*] young children back home in New Orleans. On numerous occasions during her visit, I asked her if she was a songwriter or had any original songs that we should consider for the recording session. Her answer was always, "No, sir." After I finally decided upon the ten songs, with no objections from Irma, I hired arranger H. B. Barnum to write the arrangements and set a recording date.

The night before the recording session, we had a little pre-recording party at Barnum's home in the Hollywood Hills. During the party I noticed Ms. Thomas

> sitting alone at the piano, softly playing and singing. I went over and heard this one sentence of the song, 'Sitting home alone, thinking about my past, wondering how I made it, wondering how long it's going to last.' Noticing my presence, she stopped.
>
> "Please keep singing, Irma," I encouraged.
>
> Reluctantly she began again, this time with feeling and emotion I had never heard expressed by her before.
>
> "Whose song is this, Irma?" I inquired with interest.
>
> "Oh, this is just a little something I wrote," she quietly replied.[1]

Ray gave an expanded account of the moment in an interview with John Broven:

> I'd been asking her, "Did you have anything?" I went through maybe a hundred different publishers, you know, doing that type of looking for that song or something different. And she said, "Well, it's just a little something I wrote," and I said, "Well, I've been asking you . . . ," then I stopped. I called H. [Barnum] over. I said [to Irma], "Sing this phrase."
>
> And H. said, "I guess the party's over."
>
> I said, "Yep."
>
> "I guess I'm going to have to go to work."
>
> I said, "Yeah."
>
> "I guess you want [it for] tomorrow morning's session."
>
> And I said, "You're damn right."[2]

Irma has never played piano herself, but otherwise concurs with this account. Since her debut Imperial recording session at United Western Recorders in Hollywood was set for the next day (December 5, 1963), they ended the party, and Barnum went to work writing the arrangement for the song. However, there is more to the story, because the song did not make its actual debut at the pre-session social gathering. Rather, Irma had written the song with a collaborator in New Orleans.

It came together during a visit with her friend Connie LaRocca at the office of the restaurant Connie and her husband owned, Jim's Fried Chicken, on the corner of South Carrollton and Earhart Boulevard. "It was there for years," Irma recalled. "They made the best fried chicken and had the biggest chicken legs. My mother worked for them for a hot minute after she lost her job at the Southern Bell Telephone Company." In fact, Vader Todd had naïvely cosigned a loan for a friend, which her friend had not repaid, resulting in Todd's wages at Southern Bell being garnished.

"We were at her office and this young man, Sax Kari, was playing the piano. And I said, 'That music sounds good.' So I just started singing the words that were in my head." Their mutual ad libs evolved on the spot into the composition "Wish Someone Would Care."

"When I went to California to record, I sang the song *a cappella* [for Eddie Ray]. It wasn't until years later when I ran into Sax Kari, and he said, 'You didn't give me credit for the music.'

"I said, 'Credit for the music on what?'

"And he said, 'I Wish Someone Would Care.'"

"I said, 'Nobody told me I was supposed to do that.'

"When you're naïve about things you don't know, I mean, it wasn't like I was trying to steal anything from him. I even told the people in California that a piano player was playing this when I started singing it. They didn't ask me what his name was, and I didn't volunteer because I didn't know I was supposed to. So after that, he was like, okay, you didn't know and he just let it go."

Chicago-born Isaac Columbus "Sax Kari" Toombs Jr. was a versatile and successful bandleader, producer, and entrepreneur (he produced the hit "So Fine" by the Falcons) who had spent time in Oklahoma City, Indianapolis, and Detroit before landing in New Orleans in the early 1960s, where he managed Esquerita and produced records by Chris Kenner and others. He remained active in the music business almost until his death at the age of eighty-nine in 2009.

Lyrically, the song is a reflection on Irma's marriage, which was not giving her the emotional or business support she needed. Andrew was increasingly jealous of the attention she was receiving from her fans. "So I just started singing these words and I was singing about how I felt at that time. And I came up with the song, 'Wish Someone Would Care.' And I mean, I was just rattling it out because I was pissed at the time when I did it. And I always tell people I hope I'm never that angry again in life because I was really that upset with what was going on in my life at that time . . . but evidently there were a lot of folks, other folks, who weren't happy campers either because it became pretty big in the charts."[3] Irma remarked that the song came from her heart, which is probably why it sold so well. She truly wanted someone to stand beside her and care.

Each of the four songs they recorded at her first United Western session is a gem: "Wish Someone Would Care," "Break-A-Way," "While the City Sleeps," and "Another Woman's Man."[4] The songs are simply produced, with a tight rhythm section and background vocals by Darlene Love and the Blossoms, and with appropriate gospel-tinged chords on "Wish Someone

Would Care," and "Another Man's Woman." The drummer on "Break-A-Way" sounds like a New Orleans musician, who logically would have been first-call Los Angeles session player and New Orleans native Earl Palmer, but some accounts say it was Ed "Sharkey" Hall, who was recording with Sam Cooke during this same period. In any event, Palmer would be a commanding presence on many of Irma's other Imperial tracks. On this session, Ernie Freeman played piano, and Carol Kaye played bass. Irma remembers that songwriter Jackie DeShannon was present, and that possibly she played guitar. As a recording artist, DeShannon was a regular presence on the charts in the 1960s and 1970s, with songs such as "What the World Needs Now Is Love" (written by Burt Bacharach and Hal David) and the self-penned "Put a Little Love in Your Heart." Her musical world was similar to Irma's, crossing boundaries between pop, country, and rhythm and blues. "Break-A-Way" would have a new life when it was used in the soundtrack of the 2008 film *The Secret Life of Bees*.

Irma's recollection of the musicians who accompanied her on these sessions is vague, although she remembers Kaye because of the novelty, at the time, of a woman playing bass. As always, she was there to sing, and it was all a whirlwind for her. Kaye's recollections are similarly hazy. Noting that she was working hundreds of dates each year during that time, Kaye could only recall, "I did receive good re-use fees for her big hits. I think she was a good singer, nice to work with."[5] Yet, as luck would have it, Irma had stepped into one of the greatest hit-making environments of the day, more recently made famous in the 2008 film *The Wrecking Crew*, the latter-day nickname for the revolving cast of studio musicians (which included bassist Kaye, who has expressed her disdain for the term) who played on hundreds of hit records at United Western and other studios.

Los Angeles was becoming a home for talented New Orleans musicians who found greater opportunity on the West Coast. Along with Palmer, ex-Specialty Records A&R executive Harold Battiste Jr. now lived there, where, in addition to serving as Sonny and Cher's musical director, he and fellow New Orleanian Mac Rebennack conceived of the character of Dr. John, The Night Tripper, borrowing the name of the legendary nineteenth-century New Orleans healer Dr. John Creaux. They initially approached New Orleans pianist Ronnie Barron to front the Dr. John act, but it was eventually Mac himself who donned the mantle of the conjuring hoodoo man, playing the role with great panache. Battiste produced and arranged Dr. John's psychedelic debut album, *Gris Gris*, which also featured New Orleans vocalists and recent Los Angeles residents Shirley Goodman (of Shirley and Lee) and

Tami Lynn. He would move back home, after thirty years, where he joined the faculty of the Jazz Studies program at the University of New Orleans. Earl Palmer would become one of the most recorded musicians of all time, with a discography that includes records by Jan and Dean, Frank Sinatra, and Count Basie, and the theme to *Mission: Impossible* television series. Plas Johnson, a saxophonist from Donaldsonville, Louisiana, was also a much-employed player in the Hollywood recording studio scene.

Recording engineer/entrepreneur Bill Putnam established the United Recording Corporation on Sunset Boulevard in Hollywood after he moved to the West Coast, following the success of his Universal Recording Corporation in Chicago. Later, he purchased the adjoining Western Studio and renamed the complex United Western Recorders. The studios were marvels of contemporary technology. Putnam was an innovator whose UREI (United Recording Electronics Industries) and Universal mixing consoles and related audio processing gear set a standard for high-end recording. Artists who recorded there ranged from the Beach Boys (the tracks to *Pet Sounds*) to Frank Sinatra to Radiohead. The studio was huge in comparison to Cosimo's, with enough room for a full orchestra, and its new multitrack recording machines enabled the overdubbing of additional sounds after the initial tracks were recorded. Still, "one-take Irma" (as Allen Toussaint called her) didn't have to perform a song more than a couple of times before Ray was satisfied that they had a final take.

"Wish Someone Would Care" became Irma's biggest hit record. Alison Fensterstock wrote, "It's a song that comes straight from a heart so broken that the singer can't even imagine finding all the pieces, let alone how they might fit back together; a song about a yearning that's deeper than romance or physical want, an anguished, purely existential desire for the relief of being seen. At the time she recorded the song, Thomas was twenty-two, the mother of little kids in the middle of her second divorce. She was angry and tired, and she wished someone would care. The slow-burning, meditative ballad was as devastating as a hurricane, and it scooted up to No. 2 on the [*Cash Box*] R&B chart and No. 17 on the [*Billboard*] Hot 100 [in March 1964]—still her highest-charting hit to date."[6]

The *Billboard* Hot 100 chart on May 2, 1964, reflected the attractive eclecticism of Top 40 radio of the era. The Beatles "Can't Buy Me Love" was #1 (there were five other Beatles songs in the Top 40) and fellow New Orleanian Louis Armstrong's "Hello Dolly" was #2. Other artists in the Top 40 were the folk group The Serendipity Singers, rhythm and blues crooner Bobby "Blue" Bland, and surf music icons Jan and Dean. By the end of the 1960s, radio formats would begin splintering into niches as FM programming gained popularity, with the result that Top 40 radio no longer offered this kind of diversity.

In the wake of the success of "Wish Someone Would Care," Irma began touring sporadically, often booked by the Shaw Agency in New York. While she was on the road, Andrew's mother took care of the children at her home on Peniston Street. Irma performed three times at New York's Apollo Theatre, opening for main acts Dionne Warwick, The Miracles, and Garnett Mimms (whose band walked off during one performance after he reprimanded a musician in mid-set). She appeared in four shows each day, backed by the house band for one or two songs. Irma said, "I've always enjoyed being in front of an audience. I can't remember whenever I was afraid of being in front of an audience, in terms of having stage fright. Now, I've had a fear, not of being on stage, but of what the audience was thinking. I was nervous in 1964 when I played the Apollo Theater for the first time and I was told that if they didn't like me, they would throw rotten food at me. My knees were a bit shaky when I walked out there. I didn't have any doubts that I could sing, but I had doubts whether a New York audience would accept me. And so, when I made it through the first song and I didn't have anything thrown at me so, okay, I thought, and I was alright after that."[7]

Even with the full schedule, there was still time for fun. During one stay in New York, she bowled her all-time high score of 288. Bowling was a way for her to unwind at home and on the road.

At a weeklong engagement at Baltimore's Royal Theatre, opening for James Brown, she improvised a monologue as an interlude in "Wish Someone Would Care." Brown was running late, and she needed to stall for time by extending her performance. She would later record the monologue as a set piece with producer Jerry "Swamp Dogg" Williams in Los Angeles.

Still, the gigs with the Shaw Agency were one-offs, and she continued to work mostly locally along the Gulf Coast. She remembers that Eddie Ray had taken her to meet the owners of a West Coast booking agency with which Liberty was hoping she would sign. Irma said, "He just brought me over there and showed me around, and I talked with various people and what have you. But once again, I wasn't aware of what that was, what that meeting was all about. I just thought he was introducing me to some people he thought I needed to know. I didn't find out until sometime later that they were actually a big time agency, but they never told me that." Perhaps a manager or even Ray himself could have helped her navigate the steps it would have taken for her to have become a full-time international touring artist, but she did not grasp the opportunity presented or make a connection that stuck. Another mitigating factor was that she had four children to care for in New Orleans. "I didn't know what the hell I was doing. I came back home and I had local jobs around here that I was able to make a living with. So it didn't bother me."

She added, philosophically, "I actually don't have any regrets. I really don't because, like I say, hindsight is 20–20. A lot of the artists who signed with those major agencies wound up being either drug addicts or drunkards. So why would you want to mess up your life doing things that you have little control over? I mean, I wasn't a drinker or a smoker to begin with, but when I look back at the folks who actually signed with all these different agencies and they were always on the road and going all the time, they didn't wind up in such a great position. So, you know, I may have made more money then, but I don't know what kind of brain situation I would have been in terms of my thinking about my career and my family. And my family at that time was more important to me. I was working to try to support my family. It wasn't about being a superstar." Throughout her career, Irma would remain wary of putting her career in the hands of others, or putting herself in situations over which she had no control. For her, it was a matter of priorities. Singing was her job, not her career, and as long as she was supporting her family, she was disinclined to chase anything that seemed speculative.

The team of Eddie Ray, H. B. Barnum, and Irma Thomas returned to Hollywood in April and May 1964 to record eight more songs that would be included on her debut album, *Wish Someone Would Care*, as well as her next single release, "Anyone Who Knows What Love Is (Will Understand)." A few of the songs that were chosen as album tracks are interpretations of classic blues ballads such as Percy Mayfield's "Please Send Me Someone to Love" and Little Willie John's "I Need Your Love So Bad," both of which may have brought back memories to Irma of her father's record collection. They are sung with understated confidence, with a skilled guitarist, who may be the Coasters' guitarist Adolph Jacobs,[8] punctuating Irma's vocal performance with stinging fills. The album also includes another Irma Thomas original, "Straight From the Heart," a timeless-sounding 6/8 ballad, written about the heartbreak that seemed to be endemic in her romantic relationships.

However, it was the single of "Anyone Who Knows What Love Is (Will Understand)" backed by "Time Is on My Side" that was the masterpiece of her Los Angeles sessions. "Anyone Who Knows What Love Is (Will Understand)" is a pop song written by the team of Judith Arbuckle, Randy Newman, Jeannie Seely, and Pat Sheeran. The idea for the song came to then twenty-three-year-old (and future country music star) Seely when she was working as a secretary at Liberty Records on Sunset Boulevard. She told *Billboard*, "I got the idea for the song from a pantyhose ad in a magazine. It read: 'Anyone who knows what comfort is . . .'" In her head, Seely could hear the chords she wanted in the song, but couldn't find them herself on the company piano. When she ran into nineteen-year-old songwriter Randy Newman in the hall (Newman was working at the time as a staff writer for Metric Music, the music publishing company associated with Liberty Records), she asked if he would help. As he told *Billboard*, it was one of only three songwriting collaborations in his career.[9] Of course, Newman went on to become a renowned artist and songwriter with a famously acerbic wit, and a much-hired film score composer. Irma would also record his songs "While the City Sleeps" and "Baby Don't Look Down" for Imperial. He felt a connection with Irma since he had spent much of his youth in New Orleans, and he would later record with her when she sang his iconic song "I Think It's Going to Rain Today" with her on her Rounder Records *Simply Grand* album.

Irma sings "Anyone Who Knows What Love Is (Will Understand)" beautifully, with just the right mixture of vulnerability and been-through-it-all worldliness. H. B. Barnum's dramatic backing vocal arrangement, performed by Darlene Love and the Blossoms, seems heavily inspired by the Flamingos' 1959 hit version of "I Only Have Eyes for You." It received the full United Western Recorders treatment, utilizing the live echo chambers that were the studio's trademark (in fact, several of Phil Spector's later "Wall of Sound" productions, which were characterized by their layers of reverb-drenched instruments, were made in the same room). Irma's vocal, with much less reverb, is an intimate sonic contrast. While her singing style has its roots in gospel music and blues, she was proving herself capable of taking on just about any melody and singing it as it was written. She embellished a song only gently, and only when the storyteller in her decided it was needed. The track is a masterpiece of 1960s pop, with a band that anecdotally included pianist Leon Russell, bassist Carol Kaye, and drummer Earl Palmer. Yet, Irma's disarming vocal is likely the primary reason that "Anyone Who Knows What Love Is" is the song in her catalog that has been most licensed for film and television use.

The song rose to #52 on the *Billboard* pop chart, and attracted enough attention that she appeared on the nationally televised *American Bandstand* show in Philadelphia on August 29, 1964, lip-synching to the record, after which she was interviewed by host Dick Clark. It is a sweet interchange in which she cites her admiration for Nancy Wilson and Etta James, coming across as demure and still a touch shy. She told Clark that she started singing

Irma's children bundled up to visit Santa Claus during Christmas season 1964. L-R: Tina, niece Gina (Andrew's brother's daughter), James, Andrea, and Jean Marie Thomas. (Photograph courtesy of Tina Thomas)

in church at the age of five. The progressive-minded Clark replied, "I think a lot of people get their start singing in the choir in the church or in temple or wherever their place of religion is." She told Clark, "I have a feeling for songs where if they have something like a story going on, I put myself in the same situation and it always comes out pretty nice." Irma made her own sparkle-topped dress for the appearance. She signed autographs after the show.

"That was huge!" Irma told the *LAist*. "First of all, to even be invited to be on the show was a major coup. I would put it to the equivalency of being nominated for a Grammy®. I mean, those things just didn't happen. At that time, the record company I was with must have had good rapport with Dick Clark because that's how I got on there."[10]

On the show, Irma's smile included an uncharacteristic gold tooth, the result of a rowdy gig at a fraternity on Broadway Street in New Orleans. Irma said, ". . . they really got carried away. Everybody was jumpin' on top of everybody else, and this one fellow was really drunk and he fell into the microphone stand and knocked my front teeth out! I stopped using a mic stand after that."[11] She said, "The only thing I could afford to get over the weekend was an open face crown. So in a lot of my earlier photos, I have a gold tooth, which I hated. I couldn't wait to get that out of my mouth. And after I got rid of it, I looked like I was ten years younger." She remembered that she did not smile as broadly as usual in her publicity photographs from that era.

"Anyone Who Knows What Love Is" experienced a revival when it appeared six times in Charlie Brooker's Netflix television anthology series *Black Mirror*. According to executive producer Annabel Jones, the song was used numerous times throughout the series because it was a way of "nesting all the episodes together in an artistic universe of sorts." Brooker saw the song as one of "earnest beauty" which had "the sound of a timeless haunting classic."[12] Brooker felt such an affinity for the song that he told the BBC News' *Desert Island Discs* that he would choose it as one of eight recordings he would take with him to a desert island, along with the Beatles "Tomorrow Never Knows."[13]

The song was used in a variety of scenes over a thirteen-year period. It was first aired in season one, episode two ("Fifteen Million Merits") on December 11, 2011, when actress Jessica Brown Findlay sang along with Irma's recording. On December 16, 2014, actress Janet Montgomery sang it in a karaoke scene (season two, episode four, "White Christmas"); on October 21, 2016, actress Madeline Brewer sang it while holding a person at gunpoint (season three, episode five, "Men Against Fire"); on December 29, 2017, Irma's recording of the song is recalled by a man involved in traffic accident (season four, episode three, "Crocodile"); on June 5, 2019, actress and singer Miley Cyrus fictitiously composes the song (season five, episode three, "Rachel, Jack and Ashley Too"); and on June 15, 2023, Irma's recording of the song plays in the background when actress Annie Murphy walks into a bar to meet her ex-boyfriend (season six, episode one, "Joan Is Awful").

Irma said, "I got a nice sized check. We got a nice surprise with that one . . . I still get residuals [from the album that included the song] because a lot of movies use songs from it."[14] *Billboard* commented, "The story of 'Anyone Who Knows What Love Is' is not over. It has been heard on other TV shows, including *Big Little Lies, Orphan Black, NFL GameDay Morning* and a promo for HBO's *Here and Now* as well as trailers for the films *Moonlight* and *Jurassic World: Fallen Kingdom*."[15] It also appeared in the Hulu series *Casual* and in the Netflix series *Dead to Me*. In 2018, the song peaked at #2 on *Billboard*'s Top TV Tunes chart, forty-four years after its release. In 2025, the song had been streamed over sixty-five million times on Spotify, and was featured again in the Amy Schumer film *Kinda Pregnant*.

While Irma did not initially earn royalties for her early recordings, she eventually began receiving her share of income for these and other uses, both as an artist and as a songwriter, due in large part to the work of the Rhythm and Blues Foundation. Founded in 1988 at the initiative of singer Ruth Brown and her attorney, Howell Begle, with seed money from Atlantic Records founder Ahmet Ertegun, the Rhythm and Blues Foundation brokered a deal with most of the major record companies. For legacy R&B artists such as Ruth Brown herself and Irma Thomas, any unrecouped expenses would be forgiven, and a flat artist royalty of 10 percent of sales would be paid going forward. The Foundation also assisted in the task of locating artists who had not kept up their record company contacts. Irma said, "Right after [Hurricane] Katrina, I started getting my royalties a lot better. Some of the companies who [were] holding royalties for me said they couldn't find me. I said, 'I don't know why you couldn't find me. Anybody in New Orleans could have told you where I was.'"[16]

It remains standard practice today for record companies to recoup the cost of the recording sessions and advances, and sometimes promotional expenses, from the income they receive, before artist royalties are paid. The result is that the artist does not receive payment beyond advances or session fees until sales or licensing income generate enough income to pay back all the money the record company has spent. Further, the royalty rates on many recording agreements from the 1960s were far lower than 10 percent. Many artists did not pay much attention to their contracts at the time they signed them because their immediate concern was airplay on the radio, which resulted in more and better performance opportunities. Additionally, few people in the business at the time—executives, songwriters, and musicians alike—could have anticipated there would be a windfall of income from their records forty or fifty years later. Sometimes, the recoupable amount could even grow, when new expenses were generated when repackaging older tracks into new compact disc reissues.

Thus, it was not until Rounder Records acquired the Ric and Ron labels in the 1980s that Irma also began receiving royalties for "Don't Mess with My Man." Irma also receives a pension. She said, "I'm a lifetime member of the American Federation of Musicians, so I get my pension checks from them. Sometimes, you can pay a light bill with it. At least I get something."[17]

The B-side of the 45 RPM record "Anyone Who Knows What Love Is (Will Understand)" was "Time Is on My Side," a track with a similarly enduring legacy that would eventually become one of Irma's most beloved songs. However, in spite of her unerring vocal and a backing track that made it a breathtaking record, her initial relationship with the song was one of frustration and disappointment.

The song was originally recorded by trombonist Kai Winding on a 1963 Verve Records session that was produced by pop-jazz impresario Creed Taylor, and written and arranged by Jerry Ragovoy (using the songwriting pseudonym of Norman Meade). The Winding recording features background vocals by the trio of Dionne Warwick, Dee Dee Warwick, and Cissy Houston, but the only words they sing are "time is on my side" and "you'll come running back," with the trombone playing the melody. For Irma's recording, lyricist Jimmy Norman was brought in to write verses for the song. H. B. Barnum provided a spectacularly arranged track, with Earl Palmer on drums, and a tough blues guitar solo over which Irma delivers a monologue. Darlene Love and the Blossoms sound like a full choir as backing vocalists.

Jerry Ragovoy was a New York–based songwriter, arranger, and producer who was responsible for a number of highly regarded rhythm and blues records that were later covered by pop and rock artists, including Erma Franklin's "Piece of My Heart" (covered by Big Brother and the Holding Company, with Janis Joplin), Garnett Mimms's "Cry Baby" (Janis Joplin), and Lorraine Ellison's "Stay With Me" (Bette Midler, Steve Marriott, and others). In 1969, he founded New York's Hit Factory, which became one of the top recording studios in the city. In the 1970s, he produced Dionne Warwick, The Paul Butterfield Blues Band, and Bonnie Raitt. When Irma signed with Rounder Records in the 1980s, he would again become a source of new songs for her.

In September 1964, only months after the release of Irma's version of "Time Is on My Side," the Rolling Stones released their own version of the song (in fact, they recorded it twice). During their early years, the Rolling Stones often indulged their obsession with American rhythm and blues, covering songs such as the Valentinos' "It's All Over Now" and Solomon Burke's "Cry to Me." Perhaps they were paying tribute to a sound they loved, but their version of "Time Is on My Side" sounds small in comparison to Irma's. Mick Jagger even copied Irma's spoken interlude. Yet, their version became their first Top Ten US hit in December 1964.

The success of the Stones' version of the song rather than Irma's was long a subject of distress among her fans, and a touchy topic for Irma herself because, by most appraisals, Irma's record is definitive. The most obvious reason that it was not a hit is that it was the B-side of "Anyone Who Knows What Love Is (Will Understand)," which by all standards was a successful record, and that Imperial did not promote "Time Is on My Side" as the hit side of the disc. Perhaps a perceptive disc jockey could have chosen to flip the record, but it didn't happen. Further, at the time, Irma was getting airplay on Top 40 pop radio stations, so it was not as though radio was ignoring her.

In any event, for years Irma refused to perform the song, not because she did not like it, but because she felt her listeners would think she was covering a Rolling Stones song, rather than the reverse. It was not until 1992, at the Jax Brewery in New Orleans, when Bonnie Raitt asked Irma to sing "Time Is on

My Side" as a duet, as part of an ABC Television New Year's Eve special, that the song was restored to her set. Producer Ken Ehrlich said, "Bonnie Raitt agreed to host on the basis that I could get Irma Thomas to sing with her. If I didn't get Irma Thomas, Bonnie wasn't coming."[18] Irma recalled, "I put it back in my repertoire because she came down to New Orleans and did a New Year's Eve show and invited me to be a part of that celebration. And that's the song we did together. And her statement was, 'Irma, look at us. Time has definitely been on our side. Put that song back in your repertoire.' And I did follow her instructions. So it's back to stay."[19]

Bonnie Raitt, the blues-influenced multiple Grammy®-winning guitarist and singer, had long championed her musical influences. Early in her career, she took the blues singer Sippie Wallace (the coauthor of one of Bonnie's signature songs, "Women be Wise") on the road with her. Later, blues pianist Charles Brown and vocalist Ruth Brown would open shows for her. With the ABC Television broadcast, she had become Irma's champion as well.

"Time Is on My Side" gradually achieved recognition as one of Irma Thomas's finest recorded moments. It was featured in the films *Ferris Bueller's Day Off* in 1986, *The Secret of My Success* in 1987, *She's Out of Control* in 1989, and *Opportunity Knocks* in 1990. The song was also featured in an episode of HBO's *Six Feet Under* in 2005. In 2021, her version of Ragovoy and Norman's song (and not the Rolling Stones cover) was inducted into the Grammy® Hall of Fame.

The saga finally came full circle on Thursday, May 2, 2024, at the New Orleans Jazz and Heritage Festival, when Irma was invited to perform the song with the Rolling Stones. *Variety* reported, "Jazz Fest always welcomes a crowd from far beyond New Orleans, but there were still plenty of locals in the crowd, and there was a palpable feeling of pride at watching one of their own [zydeco accordionist Dwayne 'Dopsie' Rubin] onstage with the international superstars." *Variety* noted:

> But that particular "one of us!" vibe would ratchet way up with the next guest, none other than the "Soul Queen of New Orleans," Irma Thomas. Thomas originally recorded "Time Is on My Side," a song the young Stones turned into one of their earliest hits. "We heard this great song in 1964," Jagger said, confirming the worst-kept secret in New Orleans, as Thomas was escorted onto the stage [by her husband Emile] and took her place alongside the band. It was one of those rare moments where Mick Jagger was not in control of his stage. Thomas is a Jazz Fest regular, with her shows at the Gospel Tent always a must-see and a highlight of any festival weekend. At 83, she is still a poised and commanding presence, and nothing about that changed because

she was now onstage with the Rolling Stones. Jagger mostly provided vocal support and harmony for Thomas' vocals. Their version of "Time Is on My Side" was pretty much a note-for-note cover of her version, but in a sadly common syndrome of the era, theirs was the hit. At least some karmic balance was achieved on Thursday.[20]

Eddie Ray, H. B. Barnum, and Irma could not have predicted the long-lasting reach of the two-sided single of "Anyone Who Knows What Love Is (Will Understand)" and "Time Is on My Side," neither for the impact it would have on Irma's legacy, nor for the durability of these two songs. In terms of overall impact and reach, it was the most significant record of her career.

DISCOGRAPHY

Singles

Wish Someone Would Care (Irma Thomas)/Break-A-Way (J. DeShannon, S. Sheeley). Imperial Records 66013, 1964. Producer: Eddie Ray. #17 pop.

Anyone Who Knows What Love Is (Will Understand) (Seely-Arbuckle-Sheeran-Newman)/Time Is on My Side (Norman Meade-Jimmy Norman). Imperial Records 66041, 1964. Arr. and Cond. by H. B. Barnum. Produced by Eddie Ray. #52 pop.

LP

Wish Someone Would Care, Imperial LP 9266, 1964.

Side A: 1. Wish Someone Would Care (Irma Thomas) 2. I Need Your Love So Bad (H. Dunham) 3. Without Love (There Is Nothing) (D. Small) 4. Please Send Me Someone to Love (Percy Mayfield) 5. Another Woman's Man (H. B. Barnum, J. Norman) 6. Sufferin' with the Blues (Pemberton)

Side B: Time Is on My Side (J. Norman, N. Meade) 2. While the City Sleeps (Randy Newman) 3. Straight From the Heart (Irma Thomas) 4. I've Been There (G. Usher, W. Martindale) 5. I Need You So (I. J. Hunter) 6. Break-A-Way (J. DeShannon, S. Sheeley)

Ernie Freeman or Leon Russell, piano; possibly Adolph Jacobs, guitar; Carol Kaye, bass; Ed "Sharkey" Hall or Earl Palmer, drums; Darlene Love and the Blossoms, backing vocals; others

Arranged by Conductor—H. B. Barnum

Engineer—Eddie Brackett

Producer—Eddie Ray

CHAPTER SEVEN

Times Have Changed

(1965–1969)

In mid-1964, Eddie Ray left Liberty Records to take a new job at Capitol Records where he was given responsibility for the company's new Tower Records division, and where he eventually became vice president of A&R. Irma felt somewhat abandoned by Ray's departure from Imperial. Ray said, "Irma, when I saw her several years later, I ran into her in New Orleans. And she said, 'You know, I'm mad at you. I'm mad at you. You left me all alone.' I left and went to Capitol. And then they brought in somebody who produced her from New York or somewhere, and nothing ever happened. She said, 'You shouldn't have done that. You shouldn't have left me over there.' And I said, 'Irma, I'm sorry, but I had to. This was a move I couldn't refuse.' It was a good move for me."[1]

At the same time, Liberty Records president Al Bennett, who also became the company's owner in 1965, was steadfast in his commitment to Irma, bringing her back to United Western Recorders in August 1964 with staff producer and arranger Nick De Caro, who again enlisted arranger H. B. Barnum on several songs.

Nick De Caro was a multitalented arranger, musician, and songwriter who moved to Los Angeles from Cleveland after his discharge from the army, at the suggestion of his friend and fellow future record producer Tommy LiPuma. His diverse credits include arrangements for James Taylor, Bonnie Raitt, and the O'Jays, and the arrangement of the string section on Gordon Lightfoot's "If You Could Read My Mind." He was also a career session keyboard player, performing artist, and bandleader who was especially popular in Japan.

(Photograph courtesy of the New Orleans Jazz Museum, David Kunian, Curator)

The records he made with Irma are ambitious, though perhaps not as focused and uncluttered as her work with Eddie Ray. For her sessions in August 1964, she recorded Van McCoy's ballad "Times Have Changed," with a solo soprano voice—possibly Darlene Love—dominating the intro. The record might now seem dated to contemporary ears, but it reached #98 on the pop charts. McCoy was a prolific writer with over 700 copyrighted compositions that included hits such as "Baby I'm Yours" by Barbara Lewis, "When You're Young and In Love" by Ruby and the Romantics, and "Walk Away from Love" by David Ruffin. Yet, he is most remembered for his 1975 disco hit "The Hustle," which reached #1 on the *Billboard* pop and R&B charts and won a Grammy® award. He never had a major hit with Irma, but he provided her with a number of memorable songs. Tragically, he died of a heart attack in 1979 at the age of thirty-nine.

The flip side of the single, "Moments to Remember," was perhaps more satisfying. Composed by Los Angeles songwriter Richard Berry (who wrote the frat party anthem "Louie Louie") and arranged by H. B. Barnum, the song borrows its chord changes and vibe from Martha and the Vandellas' 1963 hit "Heat Wave," with big background vocals, a tight horn section, and a chugging baritone sax. Irma is at her joyful best on this rollicking up-tempo song.

The follow-up single, Van McCoy's "He's My Guy," was recorded in December 1964 at United Western. It is a classic rhythm and blues ballad that fared well commercially, reaching #63 on the pop charts. As surprising as it might seem, this would be her last charting record with Imperial, perhaps a byproduct of the "British invasion" that was now dominating American radio. "Things got slow for most musicians during the 'British Invasion,'" Irma said followed by a sigh.[2] The reverse side of the single, "(I Want a) True, True Love," hints at the Motown sound that was in fact holding its own against the Brits, with its fusion of non-blues chord changes and bluesy vocals, supported by big orchestration. A contrast is Randy Newman's "Baby Don't Look Down," with a groove that suggests the downhome blues of Jimmy Reed. Several Nick De Caro productions from the same period remained unreleased at the time, including "Long After Tonight Is Over" (written by hit-making team of Burt Bacharach and Hal David) and "Think Again," both of which feature a string section. The George Goldner composition "Maybe" is a beautifully sung ballad.

Still, Imperial was not giving up. Only a month later, in January 1965, the label sent Irma to Mirasound Studio in New York City to record with Jerry Ragovoy. Van McCoy continued to supply excellent material with "Some Things You Never Get Used To," a pure pop song with a complicated melody that shifts between major and minor tonalities. It is a powerful and beautifully orchestrated track, arranged by Gary Sherman. The mix is not as drum-heavy as her West Coast recordings from the same era, but the record is so spacious and welcoming that it is puzzling to consider why it was not a hit. The record's B-side, "You Don't Miss a Good Thing (Until It's Gone)," is a gospel-influenced ballad cowritten by Irma and Jerry Ragovoy—another slice of plain-spoken truth from Irma in the mode of "Wish Someone Would Care." After her spoken interlude, Irma leans into the song with such force that she overloads the microphone, causing a few dramatic moments of analog tape distortion. As Allen Toussaint had observed when he asked Irma to sing her background vocals as far away from the microphone as possible, Irma's voice is a formidable and loud instrument. Her microphone technique is usually impeccable (she will turn her head if she sings an especially powerful note), but the passion and spontaneity of this vocal is hard to top in Irma's discography.

During the same week, Irma and Ragovoy recorded "I'm Gonna Cry Till My Tears Run Dry," written by Doc Pomus, Mort Shuman, and Scott Fagan, a prime example of the accomplished songcraft centered on New York's Brill Building in the 1960s. Irma recalled that Ragovoy was not happy with her timing on the first few takes, and that he wouldn't let it go. "He really pissed me off. I sung it mad because I was mad," she recalled. Pomus would again write for Irma in later years. The flip side, "Nobody Wants to Hear Nobody's Troubles," is another bluesy ballad that follows the pattern of her first collaboration with Ragovoy. One more Ragovoy-produced single ensued: McCoy's "It's Starting to Get to Me Now" and Roy Alfred's "The Hurt's All Gone."

Another song that was recorded at these sessions, "Live Again," was not released until 1992, on a greatest hits collection. Written by the hot hit-making team of Burt Bacharach and Hal David, it is an exemplary 1960s pop song with a twisty and typically catchy Bacharach melody. It is difficult to understand why it stayed on the shelf. The recording was complete and fully realized, with a horn section and other overdubs, and it stands with the best of Irma's work. Imperial/Liberty was providing Irma with top-notch songs, producers, arrangers, studios, and musicians, but still nothing clicked, perhaps because her music was too "adult" for the mid-1960s market, or perhaps because the label did not have a properly targeted promotion plan for her records. Whether commercially successful or not, the team of Irma Thomas and Jerry Ragovoy hit another artistic peak.

During this period, she toured only intermittently, again booked by the Shaw Agency, playing at theaters such as the Howard in Washington, The Royal in Baltimore, and the Apollo in New York. For transportation for her road trips, she bought a new blue "deuce and a quarter" Buick. She recalled, "Coming back from New York, I had a real bad accident and I wound up in Kings Mountain, Georgia in the hospital. I was traveling with my youngest daughter [Andrea] and she was in the back seat sleeping. Andrew was sleeping, too. The car flipped over several times and it stopped near a ravine, but it didn't go in the ravine. So I consider myself very blessed. I had an injury to my lower ribs. They didn't break, but they were bruised real bad. I spent two weeks in the hospital and the only way they would let me come home was to fly. And I had to fly on one of those puddle hoppers, which I can't stand, but that was the only way I could come home.

"I was doing the driving at the time that it happened and it was in the late afternoon. I had a cold drink cup, and instead of reaching down without looking down, I looked down and then I took my eye off the highway and I wound up on the shoulder. Instead of gradually getting back off the shoulder, I jerked the car back and of course it went into a tailspin. Seat belts would have probably saved me from the injury that I had." The hazards of the road did not escape the attention of her family. Her son James commented, "That just really got me worried. I was basically a worrywart about my mom going on the road all the time. I didn't know when she was going to come back. Things happened in the world. It scared me and I was worried about a lot of things."[3] Years later, Irma was involved in another on-the-job accident, coming home from a gig in Breaux Bridge, Louisiana. She was not seriously hurt, but the driver was hospitalized and her red and white Pontiac Grand Prix was badly damaged.

For her last sessions of 1965, Imperial made the logical move of recording Irma at home in New Orleans with producer and songwriter Allen Toussaint, who had returned from military service. Allen's ballad "Take a Look" was chosen for the single release from their sessions, backed by the mid-tempo "What Are You Trying to Do." It is notable that these recordings follow the direction of Irma's work with Nick De Caro and Jerry Ragovoy, with full orchestration that does not suggest a strong New Orleans connection, as Toussaint's later work with Lee Dorsey and others would. Perhaps the album track "Wait, Wait, Wait" is their most successful collaboration from this period—a slow churchy song that later became a fan favorite. These sessions would mark the final time that Irma and Allen would collaborate on new material in the studio, leaving the legacy that would forever define both of them, although Allen would again provide songs for Irma on her future Rounder Records albums. In 2022, "Take a Look" gained a new life when it was used in a television commercial for Philadelphia Cream Cheese.

By 1965, Irma's marriage had become strained to the breaking point, and she and Andrew separated (and eventually divorced). Then, at La Ray's Recreation Center on Dryades Street (now Oretha Castle Haley Boulevard), a sprawling entertainment complex that included banquet facilities and a 1,000-capacity nightclub called The Village Room, she met Victor Despenza, who managed the facility's thirty-two-lane bowling alley. As they got to know one another, he offered to help her with her business paperwork. Despenza's mother owned the Shadowland club at 1921 Washington Avenue, so he knew the nightclub business. Irma and Despenza began a professional partnership that ultimately developed into a personal relationship, and they rented a home together in Pontchartrain Park in the New Orleans neighborhood called Gentilly, near the lakefront of Lake Pontchartrain.

La Ray's Recreation Center ad from *Louisiana Weekly*, November 9, 1963.

Developed beginning in the mid-1950s, Pontchartrain Park was a community of 680 families, with a golf course, school, college, park, and picnic grounds. In June 1959, a new section at 4301 Mithra Street opened offering families a new way of life based on home ownership, but paying for it like rent, advertised "as low as $77.50 per month." The developers gave those on the GI Bill the opportunity to purchase a home with no down payment.[4] The GI Bill of Rights is an act adopted in 1944 by the United States Congress to provide federal government benefits for the readjustment into civilian life of returning World War II veterans with funds for college education, unemployment insurance, and housing.

Irma's children remembered Pontchartrain Park as a fun and safe place to live, where everybody knew everybody, where the neighbors watched out for each other, and where youngsters could play football in the street. The family spent time together at the beach on days off from school and work. James said, "We never got into any trouble because Mom said that she better not get a phone call from the neighbors while she was on the road. So she never did."[5] Middle child Tina said, "She made sure we had everything. We used to want the clothes that other people had, but when mom started making clothes, we felt like we were special because nobody had what we had. She might make the same outfit, but it was a different pattern, you know. It would

Irma at the famous Marquee club, London, March 11, 1966. (Photograph by Steve Richards, courtesy of Bill Millar)

be like, maybe the sleeves were different or the top a different color, but it was the same. So, everybody wanted to know where we got our clothes."

Their grandfather was also a presence in their lives, especially when they visited the bar he had opened, called Percy's Place, at the corner of Magnolia and Felicity Streets, where they would drink soda and eat potato chips. However, at that time in her life, Irma was never one to choose to hang out in a bar. "I guess I got that from my mother. My daddy would go out sometimes, but rarely would she go with him. I'm not a big bar person."

In March 1966, Irma embarked on a three-week tour of England, which had been arranged through Percy Stovall. It was an exciting prospect, but Stovall may not have had a complete picture of the commitment he was making on behalf of his artist. She traveled alone, flying from New Orleans to London and meeting the driver who would effectively become her tour manager. She recalled, "I didn't think they even knew who I was, but when I got off the plane, there was this huge banner saying "Welcome to England Irma Thomas.""[6] The reception had been arranged by soul music fan and authority Dave Godin, who owned the Soul City record shop in London.[7]

But that may have been the end of any star treatment. "We spent [nearly] a month over there traveling from city to city. As soon as you finished your show, you changed clothes, got in the car, and drove to the next city. I had brought three suitcases of clothes with me thinking I was going to be playing at one venue. [She had purchased a four-hundred-dollar wardrobe for the tour, and ended up wearing only two of the dresses.] At the little townhouse-type hotel where I was staying, I packed a few things to take on the road with me, thinking I'd be able to come back to get fresh clothes, and it didn't happen that way. There were different musicians in each town, but they knew the music that I was doing. They were prepared, but I wasn't prepared, because no one really filled me in on what you do when you go overseas and travel. If I had known the tour was going to be like that, I wouldn't have taken it. It was not at all glamorous."

In fact, the tour was a grueling ordeal. She began with rehearsals on March 10 at the Roebuck in London, where Stevie Wonder was also working through his repertoire with a British band. Then, she zigzagged across the country, as promoter Roy Tempest packed in as many shows as possible. For instance, on March 11, she played three shows in London: at the Marquee, the Club West Indies, and the Cue Club. On the March 12, she was off to Nottingham for a show at The Dungeon; then the next night she traveled farther north to Salford, for shows at two different clubs. On March 18, she performed on the *Ready Steady Go!* television program, which was taped at the Flamingo in London, and then proceeded to play a midnight show at Partido Club.[8] Tony Burke of *Blues and Rhythm* commented, "The touring would have been bad then—the UK didn't have the motorways, and facilities on the road would have been bad (no cafes etc.)."[9]

She was not alone among touring American artists in England, The weekly magazine *Record Mirror* featured advertisements for a regular cast of visiting US artists: The New All-Star Club in London featured artists such as Doris Troy and Clarence "Frogman" Henry, while The Flamingo and the All Nighter Club in London were promoting shows by Lee Dorsey, Ben E. King, and Stevie Wonder, along with British blues stars John Mayall and the Blues Breakers.

British music author Bill Millar and Irma Thomas in 1966. (Photograph by Steve Richards, courtesy of Bill Millar)

Bill Millar wrote about Irma's appearance at the Marquee in London on March 11:

> Irma Thomas came on early in a dazzling full-length sequined white gown. Looking extremely tall (high heeled shoes did it) and pencil slim. She sang, in order, "My Boy," "Time Is On My Side" (the best and most powerful number of the evening), "Monkey Time" (demonstrated with a dance), "Can't Help Myself," "Take A Look" and "Don't Mess With My Man," introduced as her earliest record and one that she absolutely hated. Nonetheless, a terrific swinging, rockin' number which made a splendid change. Followed on with "Rescue Me," "What Are You Trying To Do" and the last number, which I requested, "It's Raining." It had not been rehearsed so she sang it totally unaccompanied which I've never seen any singer do before (not an R&B singer, that is). It required tremendous guts and she was amply rewarded with enthusiastic applause. In some ways it was disappointing she didn't close with a longer number but she had another two dates to do the same night.[10]

Irma said, "The only memorable part of the tour in terms of whom I met was when Mick Jagger and Keith Richards came over and caught the set in Manchester. We chatted for a few minutes and they told me how much they liked 'Time Is on My Side.' That's the one and only time that I said anything to Mick Jagger. Keith has been working in and around the United States, and he's spoken to me a couple of times, but he didn't have any comments about the song."[11] The venue in Manchester was the Twisted Wheel, which also promoted an all-nighter on which she shared the bill with Wilson Pickett. It is likely that she also played at two other clubs in the area, the Princess and Domino, which were about five miles apart and owned by the same person as the Twisted Wheel.

"I came home sick. I really didn't get any bed rest until it was time for me to come back to the States. I wasn't eating very much. I slept through breakfast, and I had learned some lessons about not eating before going on a show, to give myself space to sing, so I was really killing myself—I lost about fifteen or twenty pounds. When I got back home, I don't think I had five hundred dollars after four weeks over there. The fans were great, but the tour was a mess. The learning curve can be a beast. I was learning by trial and error, and I learned a lot from that tour."

In fact, the tour was so strenuous that she lost her voice. Irma sought out New Orleans ear, nose, and throat specialist Dr. Samuel Zurik for treatment. She said, "My throat specialist told me I had a choice of doing one of two things. I could shut up for three months, or I could get an operation." She decided to give her voice a rest.[12] She communicated by writing on a pad that she carried everywhere. Vocalist Carol Fran substituted for Irma on the shows that Percy Stovall had already booked, but Irma insisted nonetheless on going on the road. She recalled telling Stovall, "Look, my voice is gone, but my body is still working. The people could actually see me, but I just couldn't sing. Because a lot of folks, you know, they don't see the entertainer, and they make the assumption 'there they go again, lying,' but I wasn't lying. That worked out beautifully." After that experience, she concentrated on singing from her diaphragm, to help prevent future vocal cord strain.

Irma and Victor soon made the decision to start their own booking agency, and Irma severed her long relationship with Percy Stovall. Victor began running her band as a formal business, withholding taxes from the musicians and paying for unemployment coverage. Irma and the band, which they called the Toronados (after the sleek Oldsmobile model), rehearsed at the house she and Victor shared on days when they were not working, and she cooked red beans for everyone. Roger Lewis recalled, "Vic Despenza, trombone player and school teacher, he was a real nice guy. The thing about that band, we rehearsed for almost a year. Vic paid everybody for rehearsals like going to work. [We had] two trumpets, George Forshay on tenor

Irma Thomas and the Toronados, L-R: Lionel (last name unknown), trumpet; Gabe (last name unknown), trumpet; Joe Gunn, drums; Irma Thomas; George Forshay, tenor saxophone; Russell Obay, sitting in on alto saxophone. Not pictured are guitarist Walter Washington, baritone saxophonist Roger Lewis, and bassist Dave Bonds. (Photograph by Jonas Bernholm, used by permission; musicians identified by Roger Lewis)

and baritone, Walter Washington on guitar, and Dave Bonds on bass. Man, that was a hell of a band." Irma also recalled the well-regarded saxophonist Humphrey Davis Jr. as a key player in the band. To open shows, Walter Washington and Dave Bonds performed a routine based on the popular duo Sam and Dave, covering hits such as "Hold On, I'm Coming." The band even had choreographed moves. The Toronados also served as a house band at Shadowland, where they backed artists other than Irma.

Irma's son James remembers the band's drummer, Joe Gunn, letting him sit in with the band during a rehearsal, performing the Aretha Franklin song "Respect." Still in grade school at the time, James recalled, "That was the very first time I ever played drums with a live band."[13] He was the only of Irma's children who would pursue music as a vocation.

Irma and the band soon tapped further into the lucrative Southern fraternity and sorority circuit, playing shows in college towns such as Tuscaloosa, Alabama; Oxford, Mississippi; and Jackson, Mississippi, and meeting artists such as Ike and Tina Turner and Doug Clark and the Hot Nuts along the way. In New Orleans, Irma played a yearly show at the uptown Valencia Club, which she called "The Rich Kids Club." She also recalled a particularly memorable gig in Mississippi: "At the Heidelberg Hotel in Jackson, we were hired by a sorority that paid us in advance. At the beginning of the evening,

Irma accepts a Certificate of Merit from the Mayoralty of New Orleans from an unidentified mayor's aide at the Hullabaloo Scene club, circa 1968. Following the success of the *Hullabaloo* television show, which was a teen dance program modeled on *American Bandstand*, a number of Hullabaloo Scene franchised clubs opened around the United States. The New Orleans area had two of them: one at 2047 Airline Highway in Metairie, and the other at 3305 Lafitte Street in New Orleans. (David Nelson photograph, courtesy of the Louisiana State Museum and the New Orleans Jazz Museum, David Kunian, Curator)

the girls poured all kinds of liquor into a number three galvanized tub, and that's what they drank. They would all be passed out by the end of the night."

She told Jeff Hannusch, ". . . those were the superstar days. I made a hundred and twenty dollars a night when I was on the road and twelve dollars a night when I played at the Dew Drop. I thought that was big money. I had a nice house in Pontchartrain Park and plenty of gigs. I couldn't have been happier."[14] She and Victor played golf together almost every day. She said, "I was able to be a mom and an artist, and enjoy my work."

Imperial gave it one more try with Irma in 1966, this time by arranging for her to be produced by James Brown. Hot off the success of his single "Papa's Got a Brand New Bag," one of the first hit records that would be identified with the new genre called funk (which was also brewing in New Orleans, especially with the Meters, who would become Allen Toussaint's house band for several years), it might have been reasonable to think that he would take Irma in that direction. Yet, Brown succumbed to his weakness for over-arranged sappiness, big string section and all, saddling Irma with a song that loosely borrows from his "It's a Man's Man's Man's World" and other songs, called "It's a Man's-Woman's World." The record seems out of step with the era, and, for the first time on record, we can hear Irma trying her best, but seeming uncharacteristically disengaged. She considers it the worst record she has ever made.[15]

The later Imperial sessions were undoubtedly costly, and the label believed enough in Irma's talent to keep trying, but the mismatch with James Brown seems to have been the breaking point, and she was dropped by the label. Rhythm and blues was veering toward the more visceral "Southern soul" sounds emerging from Memphis's Stax Records and from Muscle Shoals, Alabama's FAME Studios, and toward the stripped-down funk side of James Brown. It was a tougher, more immediate take on rhythm and blues that peeled away most pop music affectations, resulting in a tougher, bluesy sensibility. Concurrently, the rock world would be turned on its head by the psychedelic sounds of the Summer of Love in 1967.

The grown-up, orchestrated balladry toward which Imperial had steered Irma, no matter how beautifully it was executed, was no longer finding a home on the charts. In 1967 and 1968, her contemporaries were performing funky, up-tempo soul songs such as Etta James's "Tell Mama" and Aretha Franklin's "Respect," which also had the advantage of being perceived as a women's anthem. Yet, Irma's producers and record companies had continued to give her songs and a production approach that fit an older template. They were often good songs, and she accepted them, but they were out of step.

Then, in 1967, the most obvious next move for Irma happened when she signed with Chicago-based Chess Records. Chess was best known as the groundbreaking label that brought Chicago blues to its highest level of visibility, with unfailingly well-produced records by Muddy Waters, Sonny Boy Williamson, Little Walter, and Howlin' Wolf, and through the pioneering rock and roll records of Chuck Berry and Bo Diddley. Now, the label was finding success with an up-to-date rhythm and blues sound, with Little Milton ("We're Gonna Make It"), Fontella Bass ("Rescue Me"), and Etta James. While most of their records were made in Chicago, the label would send Etta James to the FAME Studios in Muscle Shoals in 1968, resulting in her #23 *Billboard* pop hit "Tell Mama." Irma remembered her excitement: "Of course, I was a bit excited. Who wouldn't be? Chess was a hot label at that time."[16]

Irma and fellow singer Laura Lee were the first Chess artists to record at FAME, where Aretha Franklin had just tracked her breakthrough song on Atlantic Records, "I Never Loved a Man (The Way I Love You)." Producer/

studio owner Rick Hall paired Irma with his house rhythm section of guitarist Jimmy Johnson, drummer Roger Hawkins, and bassists Tommy Cogbill or David Hood (who would later strike out on their own, establish their own studio, and acquire the nickname The Swampers), along with the Memphis Horns (Wayne Jackson, Andrew Love, and cohorts). Spooner Oldham played keyboards on the three songs he cowrote for the sessions with Dan Penn. It is a fresh sound, and the songs chosen by Rick Hall and Irma were appropriate for her. The records she made at FAME exemplify the Southern soul style at its very best, capped by Irma's focused and passionate vocals. It is worth noting that in a hit-making environment such as FAME, with its signature sound and in-house crew of writers and musicians, it is still the singer who must ultimately deliver the goods, and that's what Irma did on these sessions.

She arrived in Muscle Shoals with Victor Despenza for three days of sessions, and soon settled into the relaxed atmosphere. "The studio was not huge, and the musicians and I had a real camaraderie," she commented. "What I appreciated was that no one told me how to sing."

Chess released three singles in 1967 and 1968, following the established pattern of a ballad on each A-side and a funkier, up-tempo number on the B-side. The Paul Kelly–Clarence Reid song "A Woman Will Do Wrong" features Irma double-tracking her voice and harmonizing with herself for the first time, culminating in a searing vocal crescendo. Reid was a writer and producer who became associated with TK Records in Hialeah, Florida, where he worked with Betty Wright, KC and the Sunshine Band, and others, but he was perhaps best known for his "party" records (performed in the R- and X-rated comedy genre that included artists such as Redd Foxx, Rudy Ray Moore, and LaWanda Page) that he released using his alter ego pseudonym, Blowfly. Kelly is the prolific writer and composer who was responsible for Angela Bofill's hit, "Personally." He would later write several more songs for Irma, including the title track of her debut Rounder Records album in 1986, *The New Rules*. "Cheater Man," an up-tempo song written by Dan Penn and Spooner Oldham, features the Memphis Horns playing a fanfare riff that is every bit as catchy as the part they played on Sam and Dave's "Soul Man," which was recorded the same year at Stax.

Dan Penn is one of the greatest songwriters to have emerged from the Southern soul music era, as well as one of the key figures at FAME. He would cowrite hits as diverse as the Box Tops' "Cry Like a Baby," James Carr's "Dark End of the Street," and Aretha Franklin's "Do Right Man Do Right Woman" (which was the reverse side of the single of "I Never Loved a Man [The Way I Love You"]). He would become a principal character in Irma's career, as he provided songs for her over a period of twenty-five years, and sometimes assumed the role of producer, notably as the coproducer with Scott Billington of her Rounder Records album of his songs, *My Heart's in Memphis*.

Yet, it was not a newly composed song but a cover of Otis Redding's "Good to Me" that resonated with radio stations. The song had been released originally on Otis's 1966 *The Soul Album*, and it was an ideal song for Irma, reaching #48 on the *Billboard* rhythm and blues charts in February 1968. The script had been flipped. Irma was now having a hit with her cover of one of Otis's songs.

However, the great promise of her records on Chess never came to fruition. The label was exerting pressure on her to sign an exclusive agreement with Phil Walden Artists and Promotions, with whom it may have had an arrangement, or perhaps because it simply wanted her to have a booking agent who could put her in front of people. The Walden organization, which also managed or booked Otis Redding, Sam & Dave, Percy Sledge, Etta James, Al Green, Joe Tex, Clarence Carter, and others, was owned by the same Phil Walden who was behind Otis Redding's cover of Irma's "Ruler of My Heart" (as "Pain in My Heart"), on which writers' credits were initially assigned to Redding and Walden. It is probably no coincidence that Redding's songs were favored on the Chess sessions, which would have resulted in publishing income for Walden's client. Walden would later establish the Capricorn Records label and achieve great success with the Southern rock group the Allman Brothers Band. However, Irma would not agree to Walden's 25 percent booking and management fee (a percentage that remains more or less standard in 2025), and she was subsequently dropped by Chess.

She told Art Schuna, "At that time 25% of somebody was a lot of money and they weren't guaranteeing me anything, but they wanted me to give them 25% of me. And I said 'No, you haven't done anything other than the recording. You know, you're not guaranteeing how [many] bookings you're gonna provide me with.' And I was a mom at the time [with kids] and I wasn't gonna sign away 25% of my life to someone who wasn't guaranteeing me nothing."[17] She added, "It's too bad, because I really liked that Muscle Shoals sound."[18]

What would have happened had she signed with Walden? Irma needed someone like him if she was ever going to have a breakthrough as a national touring artist, beyond the one-off gigs that the Shaw Agency had provided for her. Walden was a relentless promoter of Southern music, with connections strong enough that Otis Redding was featured at the pivotal 1967 Monterey Pop Festival (which was influential in launching the careers of Janis Joplin, Jimi Hendrix, and The Who). There were no guarantees, even for Walden, whose first iteration of Capricorn Records went bankrupt, and who personally fought to overcome substance abuse problems. After his death in 2006, he was eulogized for his work in promoting Southern music by former president and fellow Georgian Jimmy Carter.

Most of the songs Irma recorded at FAME remained unissued until twelve of them were released in Japan on the P-Vine Special label in 1984, as *Down at Muscle Shoals*. Finally, in 1991, Andy McKaie of MCA Records released a slightly expanded version of the album in the United States as *Something Good: The Muscle Shoals Sessions*, as part of an ambitious program of definitive reissues of the Chess catalog. In the intervening years, Irma thought highly enough of two of the songs, Dan Penn and Spooner Oldham's "Good Things Don't Come Easy," and Carole King and Gerry Goffin's "Yours Until Tomorrow," to record versions of them for her 1986 debut on Rounder Records, *The New Rules*—a smart choice considering that no one had yet heard the Chess versions. Another Otis Redding song recorded for Chess was "I've Been Loving You Too Long," which became a tour-de-force performance piece for Irma. At Chess, she had experienced another artistic peak that had not achieved commensurate success in the marketplace.

DISCOGRAPHY

Singles

Times Have Changed (Van McCoy) Arranged by Nick De Caro. Produced by Nick De Caro/Moments to Remember (Richard Berry) Arranged by H. B. Barnum. Produced by Nick De Caro Imperial Records 66069, 1964. #98 pop.

He's My Guy (Van McCoy). Produced and arranged by Nick De Caro/(I Want a) True, True Love (J. D. Willingham-H. Berry) Arranged by H. B. Barnum. Producer: Nick De Caro Imperial Records 66080, 1964. #63 pop.

Some Things You Never Get Used To (Van McCoy). A Jerry Ragovoy Production. Arranged by Gary Sherman/You Don't Miss a Good Thing (Until It's Gone) (Thomas-Ragovoy). A Jerry Ragovoy Production. Arr. and Cond by Jerry Ragovoy. Imperial Records 66095, 1965.

I'm Gonna Cry Till My Tears Run Dry (Pomus-Shuman-Fagan)/Nobody Wants to Hear Nobody's Troubles (A. Steward). Arranged by Gary Sherman. A Jerry Ragovoy Production. Imperial Records 66106, 1965.

It's Starting to Get to Me Now (Van McCoy)/The Hurt's All Gone (Roy Alfred). Arranged by Gary Sherman. A Jerry Ragovoy Production. Imperial Records 66120, 1965.

Take a Look (Allen Toussaint) / What Are You Trying to Do (Allen Toussaint). Imperial Records 66137, 1965.

It's a Man's-Woman's World (part 1)/It's a Man's-Woman's World (part 2) (James Brown). Imperial Records 66178, 1966.

Somewhere Crying (Oliver Sain Jr.)/Cheater Man (Dan Penn-Spooner Oldham). Arranged by Rick Hall and Staff. Produced by Rick Hall. Chess Records 2010, 1967.

A Woman Will Do Wrong (Paul Kelly-Clarence Reid)/I Gave You Everything (Terry Woolford-Larry Hamby). Prod. by Rick Hall & Staff. Chess Records 2017, 1967.

Good to Me (Otis Redding-Julius Green)/We Got Something Good (Maurice Dollison). Arranged & Produced by Rick Hall and Staff. Chess Records 2036, 1968 #42 R&B.

Tracks

Live Again (Burt Bacharach, Hal David). Produced by Jerry Ragovoy; Think Again, produced and arranged by Nick De Caro; Long After Tonight Is All Over, produced by Nick De Caro, arranged by HB Barnum; Maybe; released on *Time Is on My Side: The Best of Irma Thomas, Volume 1*, EMI Records 97988, 1992.

LPs

Take a Look, Imperial LP 9302, 1966.

Side A: 1. Take a Look (Naomi Neville) 2. Teasing, But You're Pleasing (Naomi Neville) 3. I Haven't Got Time to Cry (Mel Carter, Zelda Samuels) 4. You Don't Miss a Good Thing (Until It's Gone) (Irma Thomas-Jerry Ragovoy) 5. Some Things You Never Get Used To (Van McCoy) 6. Anyone Who Knows What Love Is (Will Understand) (Seely-Arbuckle-Sheeran-Newman)

Side B: 1. It's Starting to Get to Me Now (Van McCoy) 2. Times Have Changed (Van McCoy) 3. He's My Guy (Van McCoy) 4. Baby, Don't Look Down (Randy Newman) 5. What Are You Trying to Do (Naomi Neville) 6. Wait, Wait, Wait (Naomi Neville)

Down At Muscle Shoals, P-Vine Special/Chess PLP 6013. Recorded June and July 1967 at FAME Studios, Muscle Shoals, Alabama, released in 1984.

Side A: 1. We Got Something Good (Maurice Dollison) 2. Good to Me (Otis Redding) 3. Here I Am, Take Me (Maurice Dollison) 4. Security (Otis Redding) 5. Let's Do It Over (Dan Penn-Spooner Oldham) 6. Somewhere Crying (Oliver Sain Jr.)

Side B: 1. A Woman Will Do Wrong (Paul Kelly-Clarence Reid) 2. Yours Until Tomorrow (Gerry Goffin-Carole King) 3. I Gave You Everything (Terry

Woolford-Larry Hamby) 4. I've Been Loving You Too Long (Jerry Butler-Otis Redding) 5. Don't Make Me Stop Now (Maurice Dollison) 6. Cheater Man (Dan Penn-Spooner Oldham)

Arranged and produced by Rick Hall and staff

Collective personnel: Jimmy Johnson or Albert Lowe, guitar; Roger Hawkins, drums; Tommy Cogbill or David Hood, bass; Carl Banks, keyboards; Wayne Jackson, trumpet; Andrew Love, Gene "Bowlegs" Miller, Charles Calmers and/or Aaron Varnell, tenor saxophone; Floyd Newman, baritone saxophone; Spooner Oldham, keyboards on "Cheater Man," "Good Things Don't Come Easy," and "Let's Do It Over"; other musicians

CD

Something Good: The Muscle Shoals Sessions, Chess 93004. Recorded June and July 1967 at FAME Studios, Muscle Shoals, Alabama, released in 1991.

1. Cheater Man (alternate mix) (Dan Penn-Spooner Oldham) 2. A Woman Will Do Wrong (Paul Kelly-Clarence Reid) 3. Good to Me (Otis Redding) 4. We Got Something Good (Maurice Dollison) 5. Let's Do It Over (Dan Penn-Spooner Oldham) 6. I Gave You Everything (Terry Woolford-Larry Hamby) 7. I've Been Loving You Too Long (Jerry Butler-Otis Redding) 8. Security (Otis Redding) 9. Somewhere Crying (Oliver Sain Jr.) 10. Don't Make Me Stop Now (Maurice Dollison) 11. Good Things Don't Come Easy (Dan Penn-Spooner Oldham) 12. Here I Am, Take Me (Maurice Dollison) 13. Yours Until Tomorrow (Gerry Goffin-Carole King) 14. We Got Something Good (Maurice Dollison)

Arranged and produced by Rick Hall and staff

Musicians as on *Down at Muscle Shoals*

CHAPTER EIGHT

Los Angeles and Oakland

(1970–1975)

In the late 1960s, Irma's career became increasingly challenging. She continued to work across the Gulf Coast, especially in Mississippi and Florida, but she was now carrying a smaller band. As rock became a dominant musical sound, with the burgeoning counterculture reflecting the anti-establishment principles of many younger people, there was less demand for traditional rhythm and blues. Even Motown would go psychedelic with songs such as the Temptations' "Ball of Confusion." The radio market had changed as well, with the wide-open formats of FM and college stations reflecting an anti-Top 40 aesthetic. While some small, independent labels continued to be the incubators of emerging musical talent, most of them were dependent upon affiliations with major labels for distribution and marketing. As a result, no label, large or small, was promoting Irma's records to local radio stations.

Further, in tandem with changing musical tastes, the rhythm and blues scene in New Orleans was not what it had been even five years earlier. Lincoln Beach had closed in 1965, and the Dew Drop Inn would soon shut its doors as a music venue. Many writers have commented on this unanticipated byproduct of the civil rights movement, as wider entertainment options became available to everyone. The documentarian Candacy Taylor, who developed a traveling *Green Book* exhibition in conjunction with the Smithsonian Institution, wrote, "In less than a decade after the passage of the Civil Rights Act, at least half of the *Green Book*'s Black-owned businesses were closed." The community activist Georgia Ayers said in 2015, "We got what we wanted, but we lost what we had,"[1] while the linguist and social historian John McWhorter wrote, "Once Black people had access to the vaster

(Photograph courtesy of the New Orleans Jazz Museum, David Kunian, Curator)

resources, wider variety and sometimes higher quality available in mainstream stores, they took their custom elsewhere."[2] While Irma's audience had always reflected a broad demographic, even the teen dances that had been a mainstay of her bookings were backing off, as they shifted away from rhythm and blues, and leaned toward rock.

Then, on August 17, 1969, Category 5 Hurricane Camille made landfall along the Gulf Coast near Waveland, Mississippi, causing widespread catastrophic damage and destroying many of the nightclubs where Irma earned her living. While her musicians were able to collect unemployment benefits (due to the business details that Despenza and she had so carefully arranged), she thought about applying for a day job to support her family, but did not believe she had the necessary skills. To compound her difficult situation, her relationship with Despenza had come apart, and she wanted out. She commented, "He went where he wanted to be, and I went where I wanted to be." The relative stability and prosperity she had achieved at Pontchartrain Park was suddenly in peril. It was a rough patch as she was again a single mother with four children to support, without dependable income to do so. She ultimately decided to make a clean start in Los Angeles, where several relatives had relocated, reasoning that it would be easier to find work there. After all, she had a national hit record only a few years earlier, and her previous experiences in Los Angeles had been positive.

A few months later, on January 1, 1970, Irma rented a U-Haul truck, packed it with whatever belongings would fit, and drove across the country with Tina and James (whom his sisters call Jimmy). Initially, they lived with Aunt Rose (the same relative who had once bandaged Irma's foot with turpentine and cobwebs), who now had come to Irma's rescue again.

Jean Marie and Andrea stayed in New Orleans so they could finish the school year. Then, Irma arranged for them to travel by Greyhound bus to Los Angeles. Perhaps she had recalled her own experience when she rode the bus from Greensburg to New Orleans by herself at the age of eight. However, there was a snag. Andrea recalled, "We were on the bus, and the bus stopped to do a pickup. We went to the bathroom. My big sister, sweet as she is, put her purse down and lost the bus tickets." Thankfully, the bus station employees managed to contact Irma, and the tickets were replaced. Irma had raised her children to be responsible and self-possessed. Nonetheless, as Andrea commented, "We got there, but that was scary."[3]

Balancing the tasks of motherhood and career was never easy, but Irma's children were always her first consideration. After several months at Aunt Rose's, friends told her about an apartment on 41st Street. She said, "Believe it or not, I could rent that place for $125 per month, and it was a three bedroom apartment, with kitchen and bath." Jean Marie, who was only fifteen years younger than her mother, added, "We lived on a block where everybody got along. When my mom would go out of town, our neighbor next door would help. We felt like we were all grown anyway." James said the family "never had want of anything at all." Jean Marie remembered that when she graduated from high school, she already had the knowledge and confidence to go out into the workplace, earn a paycheck, make a budget, and pay her bills—skills that many of her classmates had yet to develop. Tina came to admire her mother's travels. "Eventually, I became a traveler like her. I wanted to travel and go to different places because of her. So it taught us to be very independent. I don't care where she was, if she spoke, we listened."[4] Andrea learned how to be resourceful from her mother. She said, "When I graduated from the sixth grade, we had to have a white shirt and a blue skirt. I found a skirt, but my skirt was too long. I didn't really know how to sew at that time, but I took some safety pins, sewed my skirt, and made it work." Irma's children flourished and were happy in California. Jean Marie added, "Mom always chose some nice little areas."

Irma did her best to impart her hard-earned lessons about romance on her children. When James graduated from high school, she presented him with a box of condoms, saying, "Whatever you do, don't open it in front of everybody else." Jean Marie said, "I got married young. I had my first child at 18. I was almost like my mom, but two or three years older. I got married and went overseas with my husband because he had no choice but to go into the service so that we could have a family, so we could have a life." Andrea took the opposite route. She said, "I waited a little late to start my family. So I joke with her and I tell her, you see how well I listened to you? And she was saying, okay, Andrea, it's okay now. You can have children. You can have a baby."[5]

Soon, a new recording opportunity presented itself when Irma signed with Wally Roker's recently founded Los Angeles-based Canyon Records. Roker had first made a name for himself in the music business as a doo-wop singer with the Heartbeats, whose "A Thousand Miles Away" was a hit in 1956. He subsequently worked as an executive for a number of record labels. For Irma's debut Canyon single, Roker enlisted arranger Monk Higgins, who, while living in Chicago, had made notable contributions to records by Cash McCall, Junior Wells, Etta James, and Gene Harris. "Save a Little Bit for Me" has a loping up-to-date groove, while "That's How I Feel About You" is a ballad that foreshadows the popular quiet storm rhythm and blues radio format of the 1980s. Both songs feature Higgins's trademark large horn section, and prominent background vocals.

For Irma's second single, Roker brought in producer Jerry Williams Jr., whose colorful persona and self-deprecating sense of humor are exemplified by his alter ego, Swamp Dogg, especially on his 1971 *Rat On!* album, which features a photo-illustration of him riding a giant rat. David Kunian, the curator of the New Orleans Jazz Museum, remembered meeting Swamp Dogg, and characterized him as "a hilarious entertainer in the Redd Foxx/Richard Pryor vein."[6] But there was also a serious side to Williams, who had a long and storied career as an A&R executive, producer, and songwriter. He wrote hits for country, pop, and R&B artists such as Doris Duke, Johnny Paycheck, and Gene Pitney. He was still releasing new music in 2024.

Williams took an unorthodox approach for the production of his first single with Irma. Upon getting the assignment, he made an arrangement with his friend George McGregor to create two instrumental tracks to which he could write lyrics for Irma to sing. According to the liner notes of *Turn My World Around*, the Shanachie Records album on which they were rereleased in 1993, the tracks were recorded at Muscle Shoals Sound in Alabama, with the Memphis Horns and pianist Spooner Oldham in support. Legend has it that McGregor flew to Los Angeles with the tapes the day after he cut them, and that Williams immediately wrote lyrics (assisted by Troy Davis on "We Won't Be in Your Way Anymore"). The next day, he overdubbed Irma's vocals and delivered the final masters to Roker.[7] Whatever the process, "I'd Do It All Over You" and "We Won't Be in Your Way Anymore" are classic Southern soul tracks that Irma sings with assurance, even if the hook "I'd Do It All Over You" is atypically gimmicky for her. Interestingly, McGregor gets no songwriting credit on either track.

On subsequent recordings Williams would give her songs on cassette tape for her to learn that night in her hotel, for the next day's session at his Jamland Studio in Los Angeles. This approach was different from that of other producers with whom she had worked such as Allen Toussaint, who would often sit with her to go over the songs he wanted her to learn; even demonstrating how he wanted her to sing them. Irma was not entirely happy with the results. She said, "Jerry Williams wanted me to sing in keys that were not comfortable. And so I was screaming half the time." Williams kept asking Irma to give him more vocally, but Irma said, "I don't scream." Therefore, according to Irma, Williams raised the key of the songs to force her to push harder. Two of the songs, including "A Woman's Viewpoint" (an excerpt of the monologue that she had developed while stalling for time for James Brown), were released on a Roker Records single. However, none of the three Roker-affiliated singles achieved any level of success.

As her opportunities to make records continued without a pause, work as a performer in Los Angeles was not easy to find. She remarked that at that point, her singing "was not so much a career as a job," and she needed to work. Club owners either offered too little, or expected her to guarantee a minimum against the cover charge collected at the door—to pay to perform. Irma recalled, "And I said, like hell. So my Uncle Perry, my Aunt Rose's husband, told me, 'They have a store that's opening up, maybe you ought to go down and get you a sales clerk job.' I said, 'Well I don't have any experience.' He said, 'Yeah, you have experience. You've been selling yourself for years to the audience. You can do it.' So I applied for a job, and on my application they asked me questions like, where did you graduate from school? And of course, I had not graduated. But anyway, I put a school on it that no longer existed. But I got the job as a salesperson in lingerie. And so I started working the day job. And at the time minimum wage was a dollar-seventy-five an hour. But I would have rather worked for a dollar-seventy-five an hour and earn my living doing that as opposed to paying a club owner to work in his club because that wasn't the way I was told it was supposed to happen. So that's what I did. I started working in Montgomery Ward [on La Cienega Boulevard]."[8] She told Keith Spera, "Technically, I hadn't lied—I've always been selling me."[9]

After six months selling lingerie, an opening came up in the department that sold sewing machines and vacuum cleaners. It was a commission job that afforded her the opportunity to make more money. Irma said, "To demonstrate the sewing machines, I would cut out clothing for my girls at home and sew them on the job to demonstrate the sewing machines. So my boss would come by and say, 'What [are you doing]? And I said, 'I'm demonstrating the sewing machine.' And I would show him that the finished product is not bad. I sold a lot of sewing machines."[10]

Following the passage of the Equal Opportunity Between Men and Women in Employment Act of 1972, Irma applied for a position in the Montgomery Ward automotive department. Irma said, "As we traveled on the highways back in the early days of my career, we weren't able to pull in and get something fixed every time you wanted to. So when they would raise the hood up, I would be out there being nosy. So I learned all the parts of the engine and everything. I knew what I was doing." In addition, her manager had mentored her. He told her, "When you sell an engine to a person with an older car, make sure you make them aware that they need to get the carburetor rebuilt and they need to buy new spark plugs and wires because you can't put old stuff on new stuff and expect it to work properly." She sold five engines in her first week, and none of them were returned. After being promoted to assistant manager, she faced a customer who did not want to be waited on by a woman, but her male colleague told the customer, "She knows more than I do about what you want, so you need to talk to her."[11]

At the same time, through her acquaintance Shirley Goodman (of Shirley and Lee), who was also now living in Los Angeles, Irma was hired by Harold Battiste Jr. to sing on a session of the pop duo Sonny and Cher, for which she was paid eighteen dollars. "They had about ten of us. In fact, the guy I was dating at the time, Walter Golden, they used him, too. He couldn't sing a lick. I don't remember the name of the song, but we must have sung it fifteen or twenty times." In a remembrance of Battiste, she recounted, "He was very business-like, got right to the point, but he was a very nice man."[12]

Then, also on the recommendation of Goodman, she was signed by Atlantic Records producer and A&R executive Jerry Wexler to the label's Cotillion imprint. It seemed like a big break, complete with a $2,000 signing bonus. With its roots in the early rhythm and blues music of artists such as Ruth Brown and the Drifters in the 1950s, Atlantic was now a major label, and a part of the WEA (Warner-Elektra-Atlantic) powerhouse that was proving to be an adept and culturally connected rival of legacy major labels such as RCA, Decca, and Columbia, with hits by artists as diverse as Aretha Franklin and Led Zeppelin.

For her first Atlantic sessions, Irma returned to familiar territory. On November 12, 1971, she traveled to Malaco Studios in Jackson, Mississippi, to work with New Orleans arranger and producer Wardell Quezergue, who was hot off 1970 hits by King Floyd ("Groove Me") and Jean Knight ("Mr. Big Stuff"), recorded the previous year at the same studio, using Malaco's house musicians. Irma would grow to appreciate Quezergue's genius, although he was another in a line of producers at the time. She said, "I didn't really get to know Wardell till I moved back to New Orleans. Then I got to know who he really was." "Full Time Woman" is a big, orchestrated ballad, with strings, horns and a vocal chorus surrounding Irma's strong lead. The flip side of the single, "She's Taken My Part," uses the same kind of heavily syncopated groove heard on "Groove Me," a Quezergue trademark. It is difficult to imagine a more impressive label debut. In fact, Wexler described it in a 2007 interview as one of his all-time favorite recordings.[13] Yet, the record failed to attract any notice.

Next, in May 1972, Atlantic sent Irma to Detroit to work with Motown producer Joe Hinton, but the results were a mixed bag. On songs such as "Shadows of the Sun," "Waiting for Someone," "Our Love Don't Come That Easy," and "Try to Be Thankful," Irma sounds out of place and uncharacteristically restrained. Instead of the edgy Southern soul of the Chess recordings and her first Cotillion single, her muted vocals are lost in the lush arrangements and complex background vocal parts. Mississippi songwriter Bobby Gentry's song "Fancy" fares better, returning Irma to Southern soil, although the key chosen for the song pushes Irma to the very top of her range. She delivers a strong yet strained interpretation of the Jules Styne-Sammy Cahn standard "Time After Time." Again, the imaginative contemporary soul music arrangement would have been better for her in a lower key.

Still, Atlantic did not give up, as the label continued to send her on a tour of many of the current hit-making studios in the country. With Hinton and Atlantic arranger Arif Mardin, she traveled next to Criteria Studios in Miami, where engineer Tom Dowd famously recorded hits by a wide array of artists, from Aretha Franklin to Derek and the Dominos. "It's Eleven O'Clock (Do You Know Where Your Love Is)," with its novelty newscaster introduction and Latin percussion, and "Could It Be Differently" are both heavily orchestrated pop/rhythm and blues songs, presumably arranged by Mardin, that certainly could have been funkier. Her Miami session begs the question of how she would have fared at TK Records, only a few miles away in Hialeah, which was more in touch with a raw and vital Southern soul sensibility.

Finally, she journeyed to Sigma Sound Studios in Philadelphia, which was famously turning out TSOP (The Sound of Philadelphia) hits by the Three Degrees, the O'Jays, Harold Melvin and the Blue Notes, and the Spinners, produced either by Kenny Gamble and Leon Huff or the talented arranger/producer Thom Bell. Irma was assigned to the Young Professionals Team: LeBaron Taylor, Phil Hurtt, and Bunny Sigler, a veteran producer and songwriter who worked often with Gamble and Huff. The Philly sound, with its soaring strings and funky bottom, fits Irma surprisingly well, although the Hurtt/Sigler songs chosen for the session (especially "Adam and Eve") might not have been the best choices.

In the end, it all went wrong, and Atlantic never released a follow-up single to "Full Time Woman." According to Irma, Arif Mardin told Jerry Wexler that she didn't have *it* anymore, and she eventually received a letter telling her she was released from her contract. When all the Atlantic material was finally released in 2014, she told Keith Spera, "They kept trying to tell me, 'Sing like Diana Ross.' Well, I'm not Diana Ross. I'm Irma Thomas. Why would I want to sing like Diana Ross? That didn't make any sense to me. I wasn't a neophyte. I had been in the business for quite a few years. I was angry because they weren't letting me be who I was. They were trying to make me into somebody I wasn't. It's difficult for an artist to do your job if you've got somebody who ain't sure what they're doing, dictating how you do it." Thus, her high, almost wispy vocals on some of the Detroit tracks were the result of Hinton's direction. She added, "I was praying that those songs would never come out. I didn't think it was my best work. I had totally wiped that out of my mind—that's how bad I felt about those recording sessions."[14]

Years later at the 1992 Grammy® ceremony, where Irma had received a nomination for her live album, *Live! Simply the Best*, on Rounder Records, she met Jerry Wexler in person for the first time. She recounted to Spera, "I told him, 'For somebody who don't have *it* anymore, I ain't doing too bad, am I?' He smiled. He realized the mistake he had made, allowing someone else to tell him what to do with his artist." In retrospect, it seems like a lost opportunity for all.

While Irma was in Los Angeles, she began another journey when she passed her GED (the high school equivalency exam), establishing a base for continuing her education, which would be a lifelong pursuit. She commented, "In 1971 when I passed the GED, I was asked if I wanted to return to school. Thinking back, I wish I had made the decision then because attending college was much cheaper in those days. In fact, it was free. All I had to pay for were my books. But I had a family to feed and I couldn't afford to take off and go to school, so I chose not to pursue education just then. The California GED test was grueling, an eight-hour ordeal, beginning at eight o'clock in the morning. I did okay. My weakest area was math, as it is with a lot of people. I often wonder why math intimidates so many of us, but it does. Anyway, I promised the lady [who administered the GED test] that I would eventually go back to school. She understood my decision to put off extending my education, since my children were still young and needed me to take care of them."

Following two years of frustration in finding paying gigs in Los Angeles, Irma made the decision to relocate again, this time to Oakland, when work in Northern California proved easier to secure. The owner of the Club Western, who provided one of her few good-paying Los Angeles gigs, had made some initial connections for her, and she commuted back and forth for several months before bringing her family with her. She was also able to obtain a transfer from the Los Angeles Montgomery Ward to the company's Oakland branch. Her eldest daughter, Jean Marie, admittedly the rebellious one, was adamant about staying in Los Angeles, where she would stay with her Great Aunt Rose and graduate high school, get married, raise a family, and permanently settle.[15]

Even after two failed marriages, and having four children, Irma felt that she did not grow up until she moved to California. She viewed her years there as growing years, both spiritually and mentally. She said, "I faced a side of life that I had not faced in New Orleans, and it made me learn about people that my eyes had not been open to in New Orleans, especially in the music business. I moved to California in hopes that I could further and enhance my musical career, but in fact, it was just the opposite. It made me change the way I approach music from the stage." She went on to say that through watching other performers, she learned that audiences want to be acknowledged and respected, and that they should not be taken for granted. She saw the performance side of the business from a new perspective, and she decided to make a change in how she interacted with her audience. She said, "I enjoyed the change because it allowed me to be who I really was to begin with."[16]

Roger Lewis remembered his surprise at running into Irma in Oakland during a year when he took time off from playing in Fats Domino's band. Lewis said, "I moved to Las Vegas, and from there to San Jose, California. I hooked up with the brother of the young lady I was with at the time, who played twelve string guitar, bass drum, sock cymbal [high hat cymbal], harmonica around his neck, and we worked up as a duo. We were doing great until he decided he needed more money than me.

"That broke up, and I wound up doing a one man band act in a club. During that time, Irma had moved to Oakland. I was practicing one day, and I had the radio on, and it came over the radio that Irma Thomas was playing at this club down the highway not too far from where I was staying. So I said, 'OK, I'm going down there and check out my home girl, and I put my baritone in the back of the car. She was surprised to see me, and I was surprised to see her. She said, 'Where your horn at?'

"She was playing with a group at the time called the California Playboys. A hell of a band. A cat played B3 organ, with a tenor player, a guitar player, and drums. I sat in that night, I wasn't expecting to get any money, I was just sitting in, but I think she gave me $125, that was a lot of money."[17] Later, at the invitation of Sy Simon, who briefly managed Irma, Roger would return to New Orleans to again be part of her band.

Oakland was an exciting place for Irma's son James. He acquired his first set of professional drums there, and was subsequently asked by his friend Michael Bennett, who wrote the hit song "Because I Love You" with future Tower of Power singer Lenny Williams, to join their band. Irma gave him permission to do so, with the provision that his schoolwork could not suffer. During this period, he also auditioned for ex–Sly and the Family Stone bassist Larry Graham (who had formed the band Graham Central Station), but could not go on the road at age sixteen.[18]

In 1973, the remainder of Irma's recordings with Jerry Williams Jr. were finally released on LP as *In Between Tears* on Williams's Fungus label, a short-lived joint venture with the German audio tape manufacturer BASF (which flirted briefly with a record label division). The album cover is an attention-getting period piece: an illustration of Irma doing what appears to be a seated yoga pose inside a teardrop, with a crying face in the background. The album brings together sessions cut at studios around the country, with at least a couple of songs featuring Southern roots rock guitarist Duane Allman, who was also an in-demand rhythm and blues session player. To add another layer of creative evolution, Williams made a second version of the album that he called "Phase 2," on which he replaced most of the musicians from

Irma performs on *The Jay Payton Show*. Payton was an Oakland disc jockey and emcee who modeled his show on the nationally televised *Soul Train*. Musicians and dancers are unidentified. (Photograph courtesy of the New Orleans Jazz Museum, David Kunian, Curator)

the original sessions with new players. This second version was released as the 1993 Shanachie label album, *Turn My World Around*. In 2007, Williams released a compact disc with all the songs from both versions as *Swamp Dogg Presents Two Phases of Irma Thomas* on his SDEG label. Despite the pastiche of production approaches, it was a successful artistic pairing because the songs and the sound generally complimented Irma.

The album included the full version of Irma's monologue, which was now called "Coming From Behind" (and credited to Jerry Williams Jr.). It was also released as a two-sided single. The monologue has its awkward moments as it summarizes Irma's world-weary observations on the dynamics between men and women, as she declares "I'm in love, but I'm miserable," teetering between admonishing men in general for their unfaithful ways, while expecting at the same time that her own cheating man will come back. Irma was surprised that she was not credited with the authorship of the monologue on the album. Irma said, "When I saw him some years later, he said, 'You ignored me,' and I said, I ignored you on purpose because you stole my

Irma performing with the Dave Bartholomew Orchestra during a visit home to New Orleans, circa 1970. (Photograph by Jim Ellis, courtesy of the Louisiana State Museum and the New Orleans Jazz Museum, David Kunian, Curator)

song. You know you didn't write that. Why would you take credit for something you didn't do?"

At this point in her musical career, it might have seemed that she had reached an impasse, even though she was supporting her family with her job at Montgomery Ward and with local gigs. The promise of another hit record, even with the backing of major labels such as Chess and Atlantic, had not materialized—as if the soul music era had passed her by—and she was no longer touring nationally. Yet, her commitment to herself as a singer was undiminished, and her career would soon get a boost as she began traveling back to New Orleans.

In December 1974, Irma accepted a six-week engagement at the River Queen Lounge on the forty-first floor of the Marriott Hotel in New Orleans. Tommy Ridgley's band backed her up. *The Times-Picayune* took notice:

> The sweet young girl who sang for all those high school proms in the early 1960s is a little older now, but she still knows how to please her audience . . . Miss

> Thomas doesn't force herself on you, she just sings, smiles and lets you grow to like her. Irma Thomas is a personal singer. She mixes country, blues, soul, and some of those good old rock and roll tunes which made her popular locally in the early 60s. Her songs are about love, and love lost, and the overall mood is mellow. Her renditions of "Killing Me Softly" and "Help Me Make It Through the Night" are a case in point. But Miss Thomas is not all serious. She has a fun side, too. She just might ask you to help her along with one of her lighter numbers, and before you know it, you'll gladly respond. For a relaxing, enjoyable evening, it's Irma Thomas, back in New Orleans at the Marriott Hotel.[19]

It is noteworthy that two contemporary hit songs—not her own—are mentioned. Irma had been incorporating current rhythm and blues and Top 40 songs into her set for years, in addition to the songs she recorded. If a sweeping observation could be made about New Orleans music, it might be that musicians of all kinds see themselves as entertainers first, and therefore will do what is necessary to please their audiences. Irma was always listening for a hit song in which she and her fans could relate, and one that would keep her set up to date. This was a practice she continued for many years in her shows.

During one of her return trips to New Orleans, Irma bought an inexpensive sewing machine so she could make a dress for Tina's high school graduation back in Oakland. She also recalled mailing envelopes of cash to Tina so she could purchase groceries.

In the spring of 1975, Irma made her debut appearance at the New Orleans Jazz and Heritage Festival (familiarly called Jazz Fest). The Festival was founded in 1970 by promoter George Wein, who had more or less invented this kind of multistage outdoor event with his Newport Jazz Festival. The Jazz Fest website points to a critical moment during the debut festival, involving the gospel singer Mahalia Jackson: "While attending the Louisiana Heritage Fair in Congo Square (then known as Beauregard Square), she and Duke Ellington, who also appeared at the event, came upon the Eureka Brass Band leading a crowd of second line revelers through the Festival grounds. George Wein, producer of the Festival, handed Ms. Jackson the microphone, [and] she sang along with the band and joined the parade . . . and the spirit of Jazz Fest was born." Wein soon hired two young New Orleans music enthusiasts, Quint Davis and Allison Miner, to act as the festival's creative directors, and the event blossomed into a yearly celebration that provided an unprecedented showcase for Louisiana's indigenous music styles. The festival relocated to the much larger New Orleans Fairgrounds horse racing track, where it remains today. In 2004, Jazz Fest began partnering with the concert promoter AEG Live, which brought in more big-name baby boomer acts from around the world, but the core of the festival remained intact.[20] Both Quint Davis and George Wein would be significant champions of Irma's career throughout the years, bringing her to Europe on a number of occasions.

Irma would appear at every subsequent Jazz Fest. The event would mark a turning point not only for Irma and her career, but for the culture of New Orleans rhythm and blues and Louisiana "roots" music in general. Instead of being regarded as a temporal, commercial artifact, New Orleans rhythm and blues was presented at Jazz Fest as a cultural expression, and as music of lasting and universal value (something the Newport Folk Festival had accomplished for various styles of folk music a decade earlier). Further, appreciation for the artistry of a performer such as Irma Thomas or Allen Toussaint began to reach ears around the world that may have missed it in its popular incarnation, as Jazz Fest pilgrims made their way home. Many music fans were attracted to music with qualities that resonated with them as authentic: music that was created outside the pressures of the marketplace that had developed within the context of local social tradition. New Orleans rhythm and blues, with its distinctive rhythms and unmistakably celebratory character, fit the bill.

Missing her aging parents and finding that her old fans were eager to hear her again, Irma was now returning to New Orleans with increasing frequency. She said, "I kept in touch with my dad often. Even when I would come back from California, I would make it a point to go visit him and my mom. Then my mom wound up living [in Los Angeles] with my oldest daughter because she got sick and I didn't want to put her in a nursing home. So I sent my mom to live with my oldest daughter, Jean, because she was an LPN [licensed practical nurse], and that's where she was when she passed [in 2006]. But I used to call her at least once a week. We would chat on the phone for as long as she felt like talking because she didn't want to talk a long time."

1975 was a pivotal year for Irma, both personally and professionally. During her engagement at the Marriott, she met her third husband, Emile Jackson, while hanging out after hours with friends at Mason's Mardi Gras Lounge on South Claiborne Avenue. The Mardi Gras Lounge was part of a large entertainment complex, known as Mason's Las Vegas Strip, that included the lounge, a coffee shop, a hotel, and several other bars.[21] (A shabby remnant of the hotel, offering hourly rates, was still standing in 2025.) Irma had gone to the lounge to hear her musician friends, singer Germaine Bazzle, saxophonist Alvin "Red" Tyler, and bassist Chuck Badie.

All that remained of Mason's Las Vegas Strip in 2025 was Mason's Motel. (Photograph by Johnette Downing)

Emile recalled his first encounter with Irma. "She passed by me, but I didn't know who she was. She was just a woman. I was just looking at her, and she had a ravel hanging on her behind [a thread was hanging from her dress]. I told her, but she looked at me and walked on off." In fact, Irma had gone to the bar to verify that she did indeed have a ravel. "Then, after a few minutes she came on back. She tapped me on the shoulder and had me take it off. If I had known who she was, I wouldn't have done anything, [thinking that] she wouldn't want to talk to me no way." Then he bought her a drink at the bar. She introduced herself simply as "Irma."

The next day, both Irma and Emile were back at Mason's. Irma was sitting with a group of women on the balcony of the club. Emile tried to buy a round of drinks for her table, but she insisted on paying for it herself. Finally, after some back-and-forth banter, she let him buy the second round.[22]

Originally from Gonzales, Louisiana, Emile had spent several years working as a seaman on commercial ships that docked in the port of New Orleans. He had traveled the world, sometimes staying at sea for three or four months at a time, visiting Europe and ports as far away as Okinawa and Singapore. When he met Irma, he was working at the Rayne Memorial United Methodist Church at 3900 Saint Charles Avenue. Parishioners

Emile Jackson at the New Orleans Jazz and Heritage Festival, circa 1992 (Photograph by Daniel Untermyer, Ice Cube Slim Collection, courtesy of the New Orleans Jazz and Heritage Foundation)

remember his immaculately maintained Cadillac, which was always parked out front.[23] He soon started his own landscaping business after the cousin of one of the California Playboys, who had come to New Orleans to accompany Irma at the Marriott, needed help on a job. Emile saw that it was a good business, and he soon had a number of clients of his own.

At the time, while she was still based in California, Irma was signed to an exclusive agreement with New Orleans manager Sy Simon, but as she and Emile became closer, the couple said they became aware that some of Simon's accounting details did not add up. When Emile accompanied Irma to a gig at Smackwater Jack's in Baton Rouge, where she was backed by a band called The Dynamic Four, the club owner took Emile aside and confided in him about Simon's business practices. Irma said, "[Simon] was doing two contracts. He was doing a contract for me and then he was doing a contract for himself. And he was actually stealing. Here's a woman with four children buying her own home, working a day job, and playing on weekends, and you're going to steal from her? Terrible. Just terrible. So I got a lawyer, who was Fats Domino's lawyer, to write a letter and broke that contract off."

Irma and Emile began a long-distance romance, but the couple ultimately decided that they wanted more, especially after Emile asked Irma to make a decision: did she want to stay on the West Coast, or did she want to build a life with him in New Orleans? Irma said, "It's funny because when we met, I wasn't looking for a husband. I don't think he was looking for a wife either. I had a show to do out of town, and I hadn't rented a car or anything, and I needed transportation to go. And he says, 'I'll bring you.' But anyway, we got to know each other to the point that we were dating. On one particular show, he brought some pots and pans with him because we were going to be out there for a few days. I said, 'Why are you bringing all them pots and pans?' He said, 'I want you to cook me some red beans.' I said, 'What?' He said, 'Yeah.' So I cooked him some red beans. And after I cooked red beans, he proposed."[24] When asked what would have happened if the red beans were not to his liking, Emile laughed and jokingly said, "Well, I knew who she was at that point."[25] Finally, in 1976, she gave her notice at Montgomery Ward and moved with her youngest children back to New Orleans, this time for good.

DISCOGRAPHY

Singles

Save a Little Bit for Me (Mamie Galore-Dee Ervin-Monk Higgins)/That's How I Feel About You (Vee Pea-Dee Ervin-R. Brooks). Producer: Wally Roker and Staff. Arranger: Monk Higgins. Canyon Records 21, 1970.

I'd Do It All Over You (Jerry Williams Jr.)/We Won't Be in Your Way Anymore (Jerry Williams Jr.-Troy Davis). Producer: Jerry Williams Jr. Arranger: Jerry Williams Jr. Canyon Records 31, 1971.

These Four Walls (Len Farr)/Woman's Viewpoint (Irma Thomas) Arr. and Prod. by Jerry Williams Jr. Roker 502, 1971.

Full Time Woman (Alice Stuart)/She's Taking My Part (Adams-Hamilton-Savoy). Produced and arranged by Wardell Quezergue. Cotillion Records 41444, 1972.

She'll Never Be Your Wife (J. Williams Jr.)/You're the Dog (J. Williams Jr.-G. Bonds-C. Whitehead). Produced and arranged by Jerry Williams Jr. Fungus Records 15119, 1973.

In Between Tears (part 1)/In Between Tears (part 2) (Jerry Williams Jr.-T. Davis). Produced and arranged by Jerry Williams Jr. Fungus Records 15141, 1973.

Coming From Behind - Part 1 [A Monologue Rap] (Jerry Williams Jr.)/Coming from Behind - Part 2/Wish Someone Would Care (Irma Thomas). Produced and arranged by Jerry Williams Jr. Fungus Records 15353, 1974.

LP

In Between Tears, Fungus Records FB 25150.

Recorded at Capricorn Sound Studios, Macon, Georgia; Muscle Shoals Sound, Muscle Shoals, Alabama; Sigma Sound Studios, Philadelphia; and Jamland Studios, Los Angeles, 1973. Produced by Jerry Williams, Jr.

Side A: 1. In Between Tears (J. Williams Jr., T. Davis) 2. She'll Never Be Your Wife (J. Williams Jr.) 3. These Four Walls (L. Farr) 4. What's So Wrong With You Loving Me (C. Whitehead, J. Williams Jr.) 5. You're The Dog (I Do The Barking Myself) (C. Whitehead, G. Bonds, J. Williams Jr.)

Side B: 1. Medley: Coming From Behind (Monologue) (J. Williams Jr./Wish Someone Would Care (I. Thomas) 2. Turn My World Around (C. Whitehead, J. Williams Jr.)

"I'd Do It All Over You" and "We Won't Be in Your Way Anymore," the two Jerry Williams Jr.–produced tracks on Canyon, were added to the 1993 Phase 2 rerelease of this album as *Turn My World Around*, Shanachie 9201.

Collective musicians on the Fungus sessions include Duane Allman, Jimmy Johnson, Alan Schwartz, guitar; Robert Popwell, bass; Jerry Williams Jr., Spooner Oldham, George McGregor, Rodney Thomas, piano; Paul Hornsby, organ; Wayne Jackson, Joe Davis, trumpet; Andrew Love, Charles Chalmers, tenor saxophone; Floyd Newman, baritone saxophone; Joseph DeAngelis, French horn; Eleanor Rigby, Sabrina Wilson, Sandra Rhodes, Charles Chalmers, Donna Rhodes, background vocals; strings arr. by Richard Rome

CD

Full Time Woman: The Lost Cotillion Album, Real Gone Records RGM-0224, recorded at Malaco Studios, Jackson, Mississippi; Pac-Three Recording Studio, Detroit, Michigan; Criteria Studios, Miami, Florida; Sigma Sound Studios, Philadelphia, Pennsylvania; Recorded 1971–1972, released 2014.

1. Full Time Woman (Alice Stuart) 2. All I Wanna Do Is Save You (writer unknown) 3. She's Taken My Part (Adams-Hamilton-Savoy) 4. Shadow of the Sun (Merriam-Milton) 5. Waiting for Someone (Trenita Womack) 6. Fancy (Bobbie Gentry) 7. Time After Time (Jules Styne-Sammy Cahn) 8. Our Love Don't Come That Easy (Mitchell-Shelby) 9. Turn Around and Love You (Weiss) 10. Tell Me Again (Crutchfield) 11. Try to Be Thankful (writer unknown) 12. It's Eleven O'Clock (Do You Know Where Your Love Is) (writer unknown) 13. Could It Be Differently (writer unknown) 14. A Song with No Name (aka Song For Jim) (Hurtt-Sigler) 15. Adam and Eve (Hurtt-Sigler)

CHAPTER NINE

Back Home in New Orleans

(1976–1984)

In 1976, Irma Thomas and Emile Jackson were engaged to be married, and began living together. Emile was initially skeptical of marrying someone with kids, but most of their respective children were now old enough to be living on their own. Their youngest children, Andrea, Wayne, and Rogerlynn, moved in with the couple. Just as the marriage license they had obtained was about to expire, they were married in 1977 in their living room by Judge Frank A. Marullo Jr.

Irma remembers, "I decided to marry my ten percent. I offered him the job of being my manager. I've gone through some pretty bad management in my career and he had absolutely no idea about show business when I offered him the job. But he had great business sense and that's very important to me. And I told him, 'What you don't know, we'll find out from somebody else, but you will learn the business. It's better. It's easier than you think.' And the rest is history."[1] Previously married, Emile has three children: daughters Darell and Rogerlynn and son Wayne. As of January 2025, Irma and Emile collectively had seven children, twelve grandchildren, fourteen great-grandchildren, and one great-great-grandchild.

After so many years as a single working mom, Irma said, "I had to learn how to be a wife because I had been so busy doing everything for myself." She also appreciated how the business aspect of their relationship worked out: "I can't say enough for Emile. He takes care of the band, the bookings, and the money. All I have to worry about is being Irma and putting on a good show."[2] She attributes the key to their success as a working couple to communication. She put it simply, "Conversation. Agree to disagree."

(Photograph courtesy of the New Orleans Jazz Museum, David Kunian, Curator)

Over the years, their blended families came together. Emile had been very young when his daughter Darell was born, but as soon as Darell's mother, Cleo Stokes, discovered she was pregnant, she left New Orleans for California. Her conservative family did not approve of the pregnancy, nor of Emile, and even Emile's own parents told Darell that their son was too young and inexperienced for marriage. As a result, she did not tell anyone where she was going. Emile finally spent one day with Darell when she flew to New Orleans at the age of fourteen, but then they fell out of touch again. Once Irma and Emile were together, he told her, "I have a daughter somewhere in California and I really want to find her," so Irma decided to do some detective work to track her down. After calling information in Los Angeles and obtaining two phone numbers for people named Stokes, she succeeded on her second try (and, as it turned out, both Stokes families were living in the same building). At the same time, Darell was looking for her dad, calling every Emile Jackson in the White Pages in the New Orleans vicinity. After she was reunited with her father, she and Irma became close friends, and they joke that Irma is Darell's "bonus mom." Darell's yearly visits to New Orleans provided the occasion for Irma to bring the entire family together at her home, for Thanksgiving and other holidays.

Irma also reached out to Ms. Stokes, and the two women got along very well. When Ms. Stokes finally returned to New Orleans, Darell said, "Irma played tour guide and drove us all around and showed my mother all of the old places that my mom remembered that may have been still standing. She took us to my Mom's old neighborhood."

Of her father, Darell recounted, "He likes the street and so do I. You know, it's funny. I didn't grow up with him, but we have very similar ways. He's out and about, going to get his hair cut or his nails done. I am the same person. We might go sit at Ruth's Chris [Steakhouse] bar, something like that, places he liked to go. And we would just talk." They are both social and like hanging out with people, especially in a nightclub. Darell said, "I started working in hotels way back when they first met me. I love the social element of life. The hotel industry is perfect for me because I love hospitality." Today, she works as a corporate meetings and events director.

In contrast, she said, "Irma is a homebody. She likes to be at home watching shows, cooking, and talking on the telephone. That's Irma. She might want to be in there arranging her clothes in her closet." Emile likes being out on the town, but, Darell said, "at the end of the night, he's coming home."[3]

Many years later, when Irma and producer Scott Billington were sitting in a café in New York City, where they were recording tracks with pianists John Medeski and Norah Jones, Scott decided to ask Irma the possibly too-personal question of what made her and Emile tick as a couple. He had known Irma for over twenty years, and was curious. Unabashed, she told him, "First, Emile is a gentleman. Second, when we got together, we made a pact. We did not want to grow old and be broke, so we decided to save our money, to invest it well, and to ensure that we would be comfortable as we aged. That was our goal."

Paradoxically, now that she was home, she began getting requests to perform in California. Emile was selective about the jobs he accepted, always refusing to agree to a price that was less than he felt she was worth. Even if that meant that he turned down many jobs, and that Irma did not tour as extensively as she might have, he established once and for all that Irma Thomas was a premium act. It was a strategy that worked, especially as Irma began performing for local conventions and headlining regional festivals.

Irma said, "I was blessed to find a good husband to be my backbone. I'm living fine, as far as I'm concerned."[4] Darell remarked that in the music business you have to be able to say no, and Emile does that for Irma.

Her return to New Orleans was proving to be a good career move, but perhaps it was inevitable. She explained, "It's called the New Orleans vaccination. Once you're vaccinated by the City of New Orleans you cannot leave. You can go away and spend some time away, but you'll always come back home. You manage to find your way back here some kind of way."[5] If Irma had been from Houston or Atlanta or almost any other American city, the revival of her career might not have happened, at least in the same way. Music has a place of elevated stature in New Orleans, and its citizens cherish their local entertainers. It is a self-contained world. Musicians such as Louis Armstrong, Mahalia Jackson, Harry Connick Jr., or Wynton Marsalis had to leave in order to cultivate larger audiences, but their hometown roots sustained them, and they were regarded as local heroes. Irma's years in California had not resulted in national stardom, but she was now on a path to stability and success that perhaps only New Orleans could provide.

Irma's 1976 Jazz Fest show, on which she was backed by Tommy Ridgley's band, was recorded and released by Island Records, a major international label founded in Jamaica by Chris Blackwell in 1959, which had a roster of artists such as Bob Marley, U2, Grace Jones, and Cat Stevens. Irma breezed through a set of her older hits for an adoring audience who clearly knew every word, before performing covers of her friend Shirley Goodman's (as Shirley and Company) "Shame, Shame, Shame" and LaBelle's "Lady Marmalade." Roger Lewis, who was sitting in with the band that day, reported that the band was tight, even though the musicians did not know they were being recorded. Irma sounded energized in her delivery.

At Jazz Fest in 1977, Irma was featured not only on her set at the Fairgrounds, but also at a nighttime concert on riverboat the *President*, along with Allen Toussaint and zydeco accordion player Clifton Chenier. Built in 1924, and having a reported capacity of 3,100 passengers, the *President* was a three-decked, sidewheel river excursion boat on the Mississippi River in New Orleans that included a music club for onboard entertainment. From World War II until the mid-1980s, the boat hosted weekend dances and concert cruises, and subsequently became a floating music venue that seldom left the dock. It was a stop for national touring artists such as Tina Turner, the Mamas and Papas, and Gil Scott-Heron, as well as a regular gig for locals such as the Neville Brothers and Irma. Writer Doug McCash reported, "Irma Thomas used to take off her shoes after a couple of songs—she was right at home."[6]

Other Jazz Fest concerts on the *President* that year featured Sonny Rollins, Charles Mingus, and Henry Butler in a triple bill; and Ella Fitzgerald with the Tommy Flanagan Trio and Roy Eldridge, with opener Al Belleto. It was clearly a venue for the festival's biggest stars. By early 1988, the *President* had moved upriver to St. Louis, and Jazz Fest had forsaken the evening shows (concerts were also staged at the Municipal Auditorium), focusing only on the main event at the Fairgrounds.

During this time, Irma discovered that she had a brother, Robert Goldman, who was working as a porter at the New Orleans airport. She remembered, "He knew me, but I didn't know him. And I used to wonder why this guy always wanted to do our luggage when Emile and I would be coming in from trips at the airport. As it turned out, he was my brother. When I looked at him, I said, yeah, you're definitely my brother. It was from my dad's side. But I didn't meet him until I was in my thirties, at my father's bar. So, you know, I kept close to my parents, but I didn't know that at all. He was eight years older than me. When I lived in the country, in Hammond, Louisiana, when my daddy would come to visit me with my great aunt and uncle, he would go up the highway and leave money for him [my brother] with his mother. We called him Sonny."

Irma's recording career led to her being recognized as a New Orleans music icon, and a more durable presence than an artist who had had a few hits a decade earlier. She was soon approached by producer John Fred (Gourrier) to make a new recording for the Ville Platte, Louisiana–based Maison de Soul label. Fred was a Baton Rouge musician who had a #1 hit in 1967 with "Lucy in Disguise (With Glasses)" as John Fred & His Playboy Band. While the resulting album, *Soul Queen of New Orleans*, was heavy on songs she had recorded for Minit and Imperial, including yet another version of "Wish Someone Would Care," several were given attractive updated arrangements, although the synthesized strings were a novelty that would soon wear thin. Fred also found several well-considered new songs for Irma, including Dan Penn's "Friendly" and Kim Morrison's "Don't Blame Him." She also covered Kris Kristofferson's "Help Me Make It Through the Night." Irma laughed as she said, "It was one of those sessions that you do all in one day. I came in one morning and he had pre-recorded a lot of the musical parts of it. I got there about 10:00 a.m. that morning and I came out of the studio at 5:00 p.m. and I had an album cut."[7]

Maison de Soul is the blues, zydeco, and R&B label created by South Louisiana entrepreneur Floyd Soileau, following his success with Cajun and country records on labels such as Flat Town (nicknamed for his hometown of

Ville Platte, Louisiana). While it was a local operation with limited national distribution, Maison de Soul's regional reach was impressive, with good presence in Louisiana record shops, and with racks of records in restaurants, truck stops, and any place that might appeal to a tourist. Soileau would eventually have a major international hit with Rockin' Sidney's "My Toot Toot" and the various cover versions that followed. Though Irma's record was not an especially important milestone in her career, it kept her name in front of her core Louisiana audience.

A year later, another door opened when Baton Rouge businessman, songwriter, and author Cyril E. Vetter became interested in Irma. Vetter's artistic projects, which have included books on photographer Fonville Winans and architect A. Hays Town; the audiobook/novel *Dirtdobber Blues*; and the album/video *Deacon John's Jump Blues*, have enriched Louisiana culture for many decades. His motive was simple: "To give her that opportunity to have the kind of global superstardom which I always felt she deserved." His RCS Records (Record Company of the South) was run from the offices of his television and radio stations, WVLA-TV, the Baton Rouge NBC affiliate, and WGTE-FM ("The Tiger," after the Louisiana State University mascot). John Fred was the television station's general manager and vice president of RCS Records, for which he managed day-to-day operations. Vetter himself was not a stranger to the music business, having cowritten the much-covered 1966 hit by the Swingin' Medallions, "Double Shot (Of My Baby's Love)."

Vetter had a vision for the title track of Irma's *Safe With Me* album, and he produced it himself. He recalled: "What I tried to do with 'Safe With Me' was to get her into that disco, that whole Casablanca Records feel that was so prominent at the time. I felt that 'Safe With Me,' which was originally a country ballad, could be adapted to that kind of genre. I used [drummer] James Stroud and [keyboardist] Carson Whitsett and the great Malaco rhythm section, and the Jackson Southernaires and the Memphis Horns. I really tried to bring some production values to it. We did a great track and the overdubs went really easy. I just loved working on it. I thought it was the thing that was going to catapult her into the kind of visibility worldwide that she really deserved."

John Fred oversaw the production of the remainder of the record. As Vetter remembers, "John was pretty friendly with Dan Penn, and got him to write a couple of the songs. 'Zero Willpower' and 'Woman Left Lonely' are both great typical Dan Penn kind of bluesy ballads." Penn produced and recorded them at Muscle Shoals Sound in Alabama, with Irma joining him there for her vocals. The remainder of the songs were delivered to John Fred as completed tracks, on which Irma overdubbed her vocals at Sea-Saint Studios.[8]

Irma Thomas and Dan Penn in 2001. (Photograph by Barbara Roberds)

Sea-Saint was part of Sansu Enterprises, the joint venture created by Allen Toussaint and Marshall Sehorn, which included the recording studio at 3809 Clematis Street in the Gentilly neighborhood of New Orleans, and several record labels such as Sansu, Tou-Sea, and Dee-Su. Under the arrangement, Toussaint was free to pursue his creative ideas, while Sehorn ran the business, which included extensive music publishing interests and a variety of master tapes that Sehorn had acquired over the years. Sehorn, who was born in North Carolina, first worked for Bobby Robinson's Fire and Fury labels in New York City, for whom he produced the number one R&B hit "Kansas City" by Wilbert Harrison. After the heyday of Cosimo Matassa's studios, Sea-Saint became the first-choice recording destination in New Orleans.

Danny Jones, who shared engineering duties at Sea-Saint with Roberta Grace and Skip Godwin, remembered recording with Irma and John Fred. "As far as working in the studio together, she was always really nice. But John had this thing that Irma sang her best if she was irritated. She sings better when she gets upset. So John would start singing her how she was supposed to sing the song. Oh, boy, that'll piss her off. She goes, 'John Fred, don't you sing to me.' But he was just always trying to get a little more emotion." In spite of the prickly artist-producer dynamic, Irma's vocals are uniformly excellent. Irma and Danny Jones hit it off, and for years she would tell him that he was her favorite engineer.[9]

Jones remembered that the tapes produced by Dan Penn at Muscle Shoals had been recorded at 30 inches per second, but that Sea-Saint only had a tape machine that played at 15 inches per second, which yielded a slightly lower sound quality. He mentioned this to Allen Toussaint, who told Marshall Sehorn, and within a few days a new Sony MCI tape machine arrived at the studio.[10] Jones also recalled that Fred went to Atlanta to a studio called Web4 to work with the rhythm section there and that other tracks were delivered from Nashville.

Perhaps RCS's most prescient move was to make a video, long before the days of MTV (Music Television), with Irma dancing and lip-synching to the song in the French Quarter and at other iconic New Orleans locations. Vetter said, "The 'Safe With Me' video is an interesting kind of phenomenon because at the time, HBO [then the Home Box Office channel] had nothing to put in between movies. So, 'Safe With Me' was really one of the first music videos and it was in heavy rotation on HBO. They would circulate three-quarter-inch tapes to play the movies, and in between the loading and unloading a tape deck, they would play the 'Safe With Me' video."

The record did not achieve the success that Vetter and Irma had hoped for, although "Safe with Me" was licensed to a London-based disco label for distribution in Europe. Vetter recalled: "We basically were just schlepping around from market to market by ourselves. I honestly don't know how it ended up on that London based disco label. I think it was pretty broadly accepted in the Brit disco scene when it was released, and it got some airplay and some action in the disco clubs in the States. Had we done 'Safe With Me' in London or in New York, I think it would have been a lot bigger, but that's maybe some of my prejudice."[11] RCS may have lacked the infrastructure and resources that could have made it a success, but it was nonetheless a quality production that brought Irma forward as a contemporary recording artist. After our interview, Vetter humbly wrote, "She wasn't promoted properly because I didn't do my job. She deserved better!"

In 1977, Irma and Emile purchased their first home together, on the corner of General Ogden and Peach Streets. Concurrently, they decided to make a change in terms of her show and the musicians with whom they were working.

She said, "We were using a lot of bands that were already together as a band, and we were having trouble with them showing up on time. If they weren't showing up on time, you had somebody in the group who was complaining about what was going on in terms of the situations we're getting to and from jobs. Some of them were being arrogant, and some of them were being negative and hard to deal with. So he [Emile] said, 'I'm going to put together my own band.' He'd been in a lot of clubs and he was seeing a lot of live music. So he started picking musicians that he saw that he thought would be a good part of the band. And it worked out for the better. Oh, I know, because most of the guys that have been with me have been with me for over thirty years. I know."

Now, Irma had her own band, the Professionals (an appropriate name for an organization with a dress code and penalties for lateness), who learned the sometimes-complex chord changes and arrangements of her songs. Emile had assembled a dependable group of musicians who worked as a team without the distraction of individual egos. Irma said that Emile had one firm rule for the band: "No drinking because whenever something happens, you're representing me. I don't indulge in any kind of things that's gonna make me not be clear-headed when I'm performing. I don't drink, I don't smoke, I don't do any kind of drugs, and these are the kind of musicians I want. Otherwise, I don't need them."[12]

Keyboardist Kim Phillips, who still performs with Irma, was one of the first musicians that Emile recruited. Phillips recalled: "My mom knew Emile when he was a kid, and she told him that she had a son that played keyboards. I happened to be at Colt 38, where Emile used to hang out, but I didn't know that was Irma's husband. I was maybe like twenty or twenty-one when I met him, and when I got with Irma, I had to be twenty-two or twenty-three." Phillips thought the gig would entail learning a few blues tunes, he said, "But I was rudely awakened. I mean, all the pretty chords, all the chord changes. You got to take it home and sit down and work with it.

"When I first got with her, I went to the audition. I think they had about fifteen guys to audition for the keyboard, but I didn't know that. I thought she just wanted me to play a song for her at her house. About a week, two weeks later, she said, 'You want the job? It's yours.' The first time I ever flew was with them. My very first trip was going to Japan." He also remembers getting into trouble with Emile when he and several other band members rented motor scooters in Switzerland, and one of them bumped into a parked car.[13] Irma remembers getting a bill for the accident, and taking it out of their pay. Phillips said he never did that again, a lesson learned that earned him a position as the member of her band with the longest tenure.

The Professionals horn section in 2009: Frank Parker (trumpet), Charles Elam III (tenor saxophone), Emile Hall (tenor saxophone). (Photograph courtesy of the Audubon Nature Institute)

The late drummer Wilbert Widow was another early band member. He proved invaluable in helping Emile find many of the other musicians, including trumpet player Frank Parker (who still plays with Irma at Jazz Fest). In 2024, guitarist Arthur Bell had been part of the band for thirty-five years; saxophonist Emile Hall and trumpeter Percy Williams had been in the band for twenty-five years each. The late keyboardist/saxophonist Warner Williams was also with her for decades. The newest members were bassist Ted Long and drummer Larry "Choo" Campbell. Irma comments, "We all go on stage and we say our mistakes sound better than some of the original records. We just go up and have a good time. You know, it's none of 'This got to be exactly right.' And I'll tell my audience, if you want it perfect, buy the record. We're having fun. We're enjoying entertaining you, and that's what it turns out to be."

Having your husband manage the business has its ups and downs. In 1983, Irma said, "Emile takes care of all the business. He fires and hires all the musicians. He bawls me out if I give a half-assed show. If I get up on the stage and don't give an hour of Irma Thomas, I get two or three hours of Emile Jackson! And it's paid off. We're getting more bookings, and I think people are really getting their money's worth when they come see us. We've got a great band too. He rehearses them twice a week."[14]

Emile attributes the band's longevity to the simple fact that he pays them well. He has also refused to sell Irma as less than a premium act. He asked venues and promoters for what he thought was a fair price, and if they balked, he did not take the job. If that meant that Irma did not play many of the local clubs, so be it. He also felt that, except for overseas shows, he did better negotiating on his own than by going through a booking agent.

In 1982, they bought a brick ranch-style home in a neighborhood in the newly developed area called New Orleans East, located between the old city center and Lake Pontchartrain. Unlike the relatively high land elevation of the French Quarter and most of old New Orleans (the "sliver by the river"), the New Orleans East developments sat on low-lying marshland. These suburban neighborhoods were attractive, but also prone to flooding. Yet, they fulfilled an important perceived need, as they catered to a general exodus from urban New Orleans by residents who sought to escape the deteriorating neighborhoods and crime that were increasingly becoming a hallmark of the inner city.

Irma and Emile took pride in their home, and they have lived there ever since (except for the year after Hurricane Katrina when they lived in a home they bought in Emile's hometown of Gonzales, Louisiana). Still working together as a business team, they kept their home on General Ogden as a rental property. Their garage became their rehearsal space, even as they worried about bothering neighbors. Irma mentioned, "I thought we were upsetting the neighbors, but they were happy to have us rehearsing. They were tailgating, putting chairs out. They weren't that obvious, but they were listening." Darell recalled meeting a young Harry Connick Jr. in the garage, when his father, the New Orleans District Attorney Harry Connick Sr., stopped by one day. She said, "When I saw Harry Connick perform later in life, I didn't remember him as being that little boy. I didn't even put the two of them together. Irma told me who he was."[15]

Another business opportunity soon presented itself. Emile often frequented a club near the intersection of Tulane Avenue and North Broad Street, across from the Orleans Parish Criminal District Court. When a friend expressed interest in buying the club, Emile loaned him the money to do so, but when his friend reneged on the debt, Emile ended up as the owner and proprietor. "I had no club on my mind at all,"[16] he said, but he was now in the bar business. Irma remembered, "Emile was looking for a name [for the club]. I said, 'Well, you're a Leo. Why don't you call it the Lion's Den?'" For several years, Emile operated the Lion's Den strictly as a bar, and it remained a comfortable place for a group of friends to hang out. However,

Irma Thomas at the Lion's Den, early 1990s. L-R: Percy Williams (trumpet), Frank Parker (trumpet), Emile Hall (tenor saxophone), Irma Thomas. (Photograph by Daniel Untermyer, Ice Cube Slim Collection, courtesy of the New Orleans Jazz and Heritage Foundation)

when the adjacent business, a company called Irma's Bail Bonds (no relation), moved out after buying its own building around the corner, he leased the additional space. The new room was large enough for a stage, which soon replaced the garage as the band's rehearsal facility.

"That's how we wound up getting into the entertainment business in that building at that time," said Irma. "I was rehearsing there during Jazz Fest and people who were in the neighborhood started coming in, sitting down, and listening to the rehearsal. So of course, Emile with his mind monetarily thinking, said, 'Here we go.'" In addition to shows throughout the year, the club became an essential stop for out-of-town Jazz Fest fans, with Irma and the band performing one long set or two shorter sets each night for twelve days straight.

Admission was twenty dollars at the door, which came with a serving of hot sausage or Irma's red beans and rice. Irma said, "People would get what they wanted to get at Jazz Fest, and would save their stomachs for the red beans." She would prepare the red beans in large quantities, sometimes after she finished a show at night, and freeze portions so she didn't have to cook every day. Emile remembers that people lined up each evening to get in. It was a Jazz Fest tradition that endured for decades. Guests at the club included celebrities and musicians such as newsman Ed Bradley (who sat in on tambourine), pianist/

singer Marcia Ball, director Francis Ford Coppola, guitarist/singer Bonnie Raitt, guitarist/singer Boz Scaggs, and singer Tracy Nelson.

The late 1970s and early 1980s were good years for Irma and Emile. She maintained a full schedule of bookings, and again began appearing in local television commercials, about which Jeff Hannusch asked, "Who can forget her flashing through an enormous stack of bills for Gulf States Coin Exchange?"[17] Allen Toussaint was occasionally hiring her as a backup singer, most notably on Lee Dorsey's *Night People* album. She was becoming increasingly visible as a performer and celebrity at fundraisers, such as a 1984 Arthritis Foundation benefit at which Betty Ford was the featured speaker.[18]

In 1983, Irma began an unbroken yearly tradition of performing a Mother's Day concert at the Audubon Zoo on Magazine Street. It was a major event for her local fan club, whose many members remembered her from her days at Germania Hall and the F&M Patio Bar. Fan club president Linda Boudreaux and her team began a tradition of making handkerchiefs embroidered with Irma's signature logo, which were distributed and used during the second line medley that was always a highlight of each show. Irma was back in full swing. It was good to be home.

DISCOGRAPHY

Singles

Breakaway (J. DeShannon)/Don't Blame Him (Kim Morrison) Maison De Soul 1012, 1978.

It's Raining (N. Neville)/Wish Someone Would Care (Irma Thomas) Jin Records 1028, 1978.

Safe With Me (Lewis Anderson). Produced by Cyril E. Vetter/Zero Willpower (Dan Penn-Spooner Oldham). Produced by Dan Penn, RCS Records 1006, 1979.

Take What You Find (C. Kelly-J. Didier). Producers: John Fred and Casey Kelly/I Can't Help Myself (Sugar Pie-Honey Bunch). Produced by John Fred, RCS Records 1008, 1980.

Dance Me Down Easy (Billy Burnette, Larry Henley)/Woman Left Lonely (Dan Penn, Spooner Oldham). Produced by Dan Penn, RCS Records 1010, 1981.

Looking Back (Otis-Benton-Hendricks). Producers: C. E. Vetter and John Fred/ Don't Stop (L. Anderson). Produced by C. E. Vetter and John Fred, RCS Records 1013, 1981.

I Can't Help Myself (Holland-Dozier-Holland)/What's the Matter Baby (Otis Byers) Paula 456, 1981.

Cocktail New Orleans (T. P. Gordon)/Louisiana U.S.A. (T. P. Gordon). Produced by John Autin, Doubloon 2012, 1984.

LPs

Live (Island Records Help 29), 1977.

Side A

1. You Can Have My Husband (But Please Don't Mess With My Man) (Dorothy LaBostrie) 2. Cry On (Naomi Neville) 3. I Did My Part (Naomi Neville) 4. Ruler of My Heart (Naomi Neville) 5. I Done Got Over (Ernest Kador) 6. It's Raining (Naomi Neville)

Side B

1. Shame, Shame, Shame (Sylvia Robinson) 2. Hip Shakin' Mama (Marshall Sehorn-Irma Thomas) 3. Lady Marmalade (Bob Crewe-Kenny Nolan) 4. Wish Someone Would Care (Irma Thomas)

With Tommy Ridgley's New Orleans Band

Recorded at the New Orleans Jazz and Heritage Festival, 1976

Soul Queen of New Orleans (Maison de Soul LP 1005), 1978.

Side A

1. Breakaway (Jackie DeShannon) 2. Ruler of My Heart (Naomi Neville) 3. Hittin' On Nothin' (Naomi Neville) 4. Hip Shakin' Mama (writer unknown) 5. For the Good Times (Kris Kristofferson)

Side B

1. Don't Blame Him (Kim Morrison) 2. Friendly (Dan Penn) 3. It's Raining (Naomi Neville) 4. Wish Someone Would Care (Irma Thomas)

Produced by John Fred

Engineered by John Fred, Jack Adams, and Joe Avants Jr.

Recorded at Deep South Studios, Baton Rouge, and Swallow Studios, Ville Platte, Louisiana

Freddy Wall, Joey Mucia guitar; Art Riffel, Rod Antoon, keyboards, strings; Randy Jackson, bass; Harold Cowart, bass, strings; Mike Thomas, Stan Kemper, drums; Pete Verbois, saxophone; Alice Jackson, Cora Jefferson, backing vocals

Safe With Me (RCS Records RCS 1004), 1979.

Side A

1. Safe With Me (L. Anderson) 2. Woman Left Lonely (Dan Penn-Spooner Oldham) 3. What's the Matter Baby (Otis-Byers) 4. Zero Will Power (Dan Penn-Spooner Oldham) 5. Dance Me Down Easy (L. Henley-B. Burnette)

Side B

1. Take What You Find (C. Kelly-J. Didier) 2. Princess La-La (C. Kelly-J. Didier) 3. Sugar Pie Honey Bunch (Can't Help Myself) (Holland-Dozier-Holland) 4. Don't Stop (L. Anderson) 5. Looking Back (Otis-Benton-Hendricks) 6. Safe With Me Reprise (L. Anderson)

Produced by John Fred (tracks A3, B3, B6), Dan Penn (tracks A2, A4, A5), Cyril E. Vetter and John Fred (A1, B4, B5), Casey Kelly and John Fred (B1, B2)

Recorded at Muscle Shoals Sound Studios, Web IV Studios, Malaco Studios, Sea-Saint Studio, Sound Stage Studios

Engineered by Danny Jones and John Fred

Mixed by John Fred

Casey Kelly, Jimmy Johnson, guitar; Al Feingold, Carson Whitsett, Randy McCormick, keyboards; Terry McMillan, harmonica; Mike Rhodes, David Hood, Randy Jackson, bass; Buster Phillip, James Stroud, Roger Hawkins, drums; Julie Didier, Courtney Westbrook, backing vocals

Cassette Tape

Live at the Kingfish (RCS Records RCS C-1005), 1980.

Side A:

1. Cry On (Naomi Neville) 2. Two Winters Long (Naomi Neville) 3. Ruler of My Heart (Naomi Neville) 4. I Did My Part 5. I'm Gone (Naomi Neville)

Side B:

1. I Done Got Over (E. Kador) 2. It's Raining (Naomi Neville) 3. Friendly (Dan Penn) 4. Don't Blame Him (Kim Morrison) 5. Breakaway (Jackie DeShannon)

CHAPTER TEN

The New Rules

(1985–1991)

By 1985, Irma's prestige as a New Orleans entertainer had grown to the point that she was invited to headline at The Blue Room, the upscale venue at the Fairmont Hotel (or the Roosevelt Hotel, as it was originally and currently named) that once was advertised as "New Orleans' smartest supper-dance room." Since its opening on New Years Eve in 1936, the Blue Room had hosted artists that included Louis Armstrong, Frank Sinatra, Ella Fitzgerald, Lena Horne, Ethel Merman, Carol Channing, Ray Charles, Marlene Dietrich, Lily Tomlin, Bette Midler, and Joel Grey. Irma told John Pope of *The Times-Picayune*, "When you step into the Blue Room, you feel like you have to act so dignified! It's hard to get loose in the Blue Room, but we're going to turn all that around because we must remember that The Blue Room belongs to the people of New Orleans."[1]

The same year, she signed a recording contract with Massachusetts-based Rounder Records, beginning a professional relationship with producer Scott Billington that would endure for over thirty years. Rounder was different from the other labels for which Irma had recorded because it catered to the same fans who were traveling to New Orleans each year to hear Irma at Jazz Fest. While the prospect of a hit record was not out of the question (it happened with Irma's labelmate Alison Krauss), Rounder was interested in achieving steady, long-term sales by career roots music artists who made music that reflected an aesthetic, however subjective, of authenticity and connection to community.

Founded in 1970 by three college friends in the Boston area—Ken Irwin, Marian Leighton-Levy, and Bill Nowlin—Rounder Records was an unlikely

(1987 photograph courtesy of the New Orleans Jazz Museum, David Kunian, Curator)

success story, established as an anarchist collective that was partially modeled on Folkways Records, the New York label that helped fuel the folk boom of the 1960s. Rounder's 1973 "manifesto" stated:

> Rounder Records is an anti-profit collective that produces records and concerts, and distributes other very small record labels. It is dedicated to remaining an anti-profit service group to make available important traditions of American culture that are largely non-commercial: traditional American string band and bluegrass music, black country blues, and protest music both past and present.

> Our form of work organization is worker-controlled, with no bosses and with all finances in common. All money received from records sold is re-used to make future records. We envision our function as that of a service organization, an alternative to commercial record companies with implications of this alternative structure to continue serving people's culture ethically and in an anti-profit mode in the new world we are all working toward.[2]

By the late 1970s, necessity had forced much of that idealism to adapt to commercial success due to the fact that Rounder found itself with a hit record by George Thorogood and the Destroyers, a Delaware-based roots rock band whose "Move It On Over" and "Who Do You Love" are still heard on classic rock oldies stations. In reality, the success of George Thorogood almost put the company out of business since pressing plants and printers demanded to be paid quickly, while Rounder's network of independent distributors sometimes took months to pay for the records they ordered and sold, leaving the label with a cash flow dilemma. Yet, Rounder pulled through, now with a staff of some twenty salaried people who provided many of the services of a major label: promotion, marketing, and sales. For a time, Rounder would release over 100 albums per year.

Scott Billington began working for Rounder in 1976, first as a part-time salesperson (his full-time job at the time was as a musician who played harmonica with a series of bands in bars and clubs around New England). Scott was a passionate roots music, blues, and rhythm and blues fan who had known the three founders of Rounder since they had started the label. With his friend, the writer Peter Guralnick, he brought Rounder an album by Johnny Shines, the exceptional blues guitarist and singer who had known and worked with the Mississippi bluesman Robert Johnson in the 1930s, which had been recorded at a Boston Blues Society concert. The album was successful enough to lead to new projects with Shines and Robert Jr. Lockwood (another Mississippi blues guitar legend), and a new album with rockabilly artist Sleepy LaBeef—the first to credit Scott as the sole producer.

In the blues world at large, George Thorogood's success had not gone unnoticed, and a great many blues-oriented artists began approaching Rounder, believing that the label had hit upon a way to market blues as popular music, even if the magic it had discovered was really Thorogood himself. One of these musicians was the iconoclastic Texas/Louisiana guitarist/violinist Clarence "Gatemouth" Brown (whom Irma had met at the Sugar Bowl in Thibodaux). Brown's manager, Jim Bateman, made a deal with

Rounder, which now had the financial resources to reach beyond documentary-style folk recordings. Jim and Scott would coproduce Brown at Studio in the Country in Bogalusa, Louisiana, aiming for a sound that expanded on the swinging, big-band blues direction of his 1950s recordings for Houston's Peacock Records. The record they made, *Alright Again!*, won a Grammy Award®, the first for Gatemouth, Scott, and Rounder.

The implications for Scott were huge, as he now began to explore other recording opportunities in Louisiana for Rounder, concurrent with his spending more time in New Orleans, especially as he visited friends during Jazz Fest. He subsequently produced or coproduced records with pianists Tuts Washington and James Booker, and with the virtuosic singer Johnny Adams, before developing a concept that he called Modern New Orleans Masters, which he envisioned as a series of records that would document the contemporary New Orleans music scene. He became friends with the like-minded brothers Hammond and Nauman Scott, who had just founded the Black Top Records label, for which he arranged distribution through Rounder. Black Top would go on to record New Orleans icons such as Snooks Eaglin and Earl King. Then, following an introduction by music journalist Jeff "Almost Slim" Hannusch, Scott met Irma Thomas.

She remembered, "It was actually surprising to me that there was still an audience out there because I had really given up on recording. And there's a local writer named Jeff Hannusch, who's a Canadian transplant, who was a magazine writer, and he wanted to do a story on me. And during his story he was asking, 'Who was I recording with? Are you looking for a contract?' I said, if they want me, but I'm not going to pursue them. I said, if someone comes to me with a valid contract and it makes sense and they're going to stick to what they say, then I'll record for them. So he sent Scott Billington to me. I wasn't a total stranger to Scott. He'd heard of me. He'd heard my voice. And he'd even seen me perform at Jazz Fest. But he never had any idea that I was not signed to anyone."[3] She later added, "Well, it was different when Scott came to me and my husband and talked to us about signing up with Rounder Records. They were doing what they call music legends or something of that nature . . . and it was funny because I told myself I didn't realize I was a music legend."[4]

Scott had unknowingly been introduced to Irma's music by the versions of her songs recorded by Tracy Nelson and the band Mother Earth in the late 1960s. After seeing Irma at Jazz Fest, and experiencing the power of both her voice and her connection with her audience, he believed that her career as a recording artist was far from over. At the time she signed on with Rounder, Irma was 44 years old, and Scott was 34. He said, "I had just made my first album with Johnny Adams, and I could not believe my luck—how fortunate I was to be working with two of the greatest New Orleans singers ever."

Scott and Irma began looking for songs for her debut Rounder album. Through his budding relationships with songwriters, prompted by his experience with Adams, Scott suggested the new Paul Kelly song "The New Rules," and a song that Doc Pomus sent to him called "There Is Always One More Time." Irma revived several songs from her Chess sessions that had yet to be released, including "Yours Until Tomorrow," "I Gave You Everything," and "Good Things Don't Come Easy," along with a reprise of a song from her Imperial days, "I'm Gonna Cry Till My Tears Run Dry." Irma also brought covers of the Etta James song "The Love of My Man" and Bette Midler's "The Wind Beneath My Wings (Hero)." Scott suggested a cover of Ann Peebles's "I Needed Somebody."

Based on his experiences with Gatemouth Brown and Johnny Adams, Scott hired arranger Bill Samuel to write arrangements for the horns, a creative job that needed to be done in advance of the recording sessions. However, when Irma, Scott, Bill, and the Professionals convened in her garage for a pre-production run-through of the songs, Scott was in for a surprise. The songs were rehearsed and ready to go, with keys, tempos, grooves, and endings all tightly in place. Irma's alto sax player Joe Saulsbury Jr. had already written horn arrangements, so Bill joined the band as a baritone and tenor sax player, and helped to refine arrangements on a few songs. Irma said, "I had done the whole nine yards, the band, and I knew everything. So all [Scott] had to do was go in the studio and record. So when I got the album, I saw my name [as coproducer]. I said, 'Oh, that's what I just did.'" Scott had credited her as coproducer for the work she had done.

You can hear her voice bristling with confidence on the album. The songs were all recorded in two or three takes each at Studio Solo in Slidell, located about half an hour east of New Orleans. The studio was chosen because David Farrell, who had previously worked with Scott at Studio in the Country on two Gatemouth Brown albums, was now chief engineer there. Based on the recommendation of keyboardist Craig Wroten, Scott hired the vocal trio of ELS (Elaine, Lisa, and Sharon Foster), who overdubbed background vocals. Both David and ELS would work with Irma and Scott on almost all her recordings for the next twenty years. The album was recorded on a budget that was tiny compared to what most pop albums were commanding. However, the time in the studio was sufficient since the band performed live, using overdub technology only to patch up mistakes, to add another horn part, or to give Irma another pass at her lead vocal.

Engineer David Farrell and arranger Bill Samuel at Studio Solo, Slidell, Louisiana, July 1985. (Photograph by Scott Billington)

The New Rules was released simultaneously by Rounder in the US, Demon/Rounder Europa for England and most of Europe, Zensor in Germany, and Rounder Australia (a remarkable accomplishment, considering Rounder's anti-business beginnings). The cover image was taken by the up-and-coming New Orleans photographer Lee Crum, who captured a vibrant portrait of Irma. Scott designed the cover, and Jeff Hannusch wrote the liner notes.

The Rounder promotion and publicity team succeeded in getting the word out, and the album was greeted with great enthusiasm, with articles or reviews in *The New York Times*, *Philadelphia Inquirer*, *Los Angeles Times*, *New York Daily News*, *Cosmopolitan*, and hundreds of others. The *Los Angeles Times* review summed up the album's reception: "There's nothing flashy about the record, no gimmicks or dance-club mixes—just good songs, great singing and a snappy horn section. Thomas shines best on the title cut and a gut-wrenching essay on guilt and regret called 'I Needed Somebody.' It's unlikely that Thomas will turn up on MTV—nothing of much worth ever does." Kris Kirk wrote in England's *Melody Maker*, "Just the best contemporary R&B. And I mean the best." In *The Austin Chronicle*, John Morthland wrote, "The woman's got guts. And class. Lots of class." *The Village Voice* ran a Lynda Barry cartoon about the album, in which Barry comments, "You're hearing a phoenix rising out of the ashes of what soul singing has become."

This review of *The New Rules* was created by the renowned cartoonist Lynda Barry for the *Village Voice* in August 1986. (Courtesy of Lynda Barry, used by permission)

Locally, Irma was the homecoming queen. She launched the record before eight hundred fans on the riverboat *President*, dressed in a gold-sequined blouse.[5] In the New Orleans *Times-Picayune*, Vincent Fumar wrote, "*New Rules* confirms that Irma Thomas is back on track . . . the album's songs showcase her complete vocal talents rather than using her voice as a mere feature on a fleeing pop vehicle. Planned obsolescence-type pop never suited Thomas well. *New Rules* does."[6]

Jeff Hannusch weighed in on the success of the record: ". . . her most successful album since the '60s." In the same article, Hannusch noted that Irma was delighted with her recent recording success with Rounder, which she felt helped promote New Orleans music nationally. Irma told him, "The album came out at a good time. Locally our bookings started falling off because of

The New Rules (Photograph courtesy of the Concord Music Group)

the economy, but the record gave us a boost. We started getting solid offers from other cities so we started doing some touring again. I did some dates in Europe and I hadn't been there since 1965. Rounder lets me have a hand in producing my records, which no other company has let me do. I think we've been able to balance the real sound of Irma Thomas with a contemporary feel and not sound like we sold out."[7]

While the prediction about MTV was accurate, and while there was not much radio airplay apart from college and public radio stations, *The New Rules* was the kind of triumphant comeback that the print media loved—the story of an artist overcoming the ephemeral nature of of the music business (because, at least nationally, Irma had perhaps been relegated to memory as an oldies artist), and coming back with an identity that was stronger than ever.

There was one notable exception in radio. The New Orleans community radio station WWOZ, founded by brothers Jerry and Walter Brock, who were aided by a team of like-minded supporters, began broadcasting from a small studio in a beer storage room above the Tipitina's nightclub in 1980. WWOZ featured almost exclusively local music, with deejays who included singers Ernie K-Doe and Bobby Mitchell. The result was that 'OZ became a constant soundtrack in the homes of local music fans and in businesses around town, and that every WWOZ fan knew about Irma's new record. The New Orleans Jazz and Heritage Foundation eventually assumed responsibility for the station's operations, and in the internet era the station grew to become a worldwide beacon of New Orleans culture.[8] In 2024, with support from the Helis Foundation, the station moved into modern new studios at the top of the Jax Brewery, along the Mississippi River in the French Quarter. Irma has been a constant supporter of WWOZ, participating in fundraisers, benefit concerts, and on-air live broadcasts. Further, she was among the artists in their 2013 "Guardians of the Groove" campaign intended to highlight musicians, business owners, and community leaders who played a significant role in preserving and enhancing the culture of New Orleans.

Just before *The New Rules* was released, Irma had decided to go back to school. She recalled, "I then felt that the time was right to complete my education. I had watched some of my children graduate and noticed their joy during graduation ceremonies. I was so happy for them, but a little jealous, for I had never known the experience of graduating." Since she had obtained her GED in California, she decided to take a placement exam at Delgado University in New Orleans. "Between gigs, I was going to school and taking a couple of courses, developmental math and English. Completing homework assignments on an airplane was rough; nevertheless, I did it and it paid off. After passing those courses, I qualified for enrollment in English 101 and Math 118." However, she began to get so much work that she again had to put her fledgling academic life on hold. She said, "To try to attend school and tour at the same time is next to impossible." She didn't abandon her studies, but it would take another fifteen or so years to reach her goal.

New Orleans music and Louisiana music in general got another boost in 1987 with the release of the film *The Big Easy*, a romantic detective story starring Dennis Quaid and Ellen Barkin, set in New Orleans and replete with forced Cajun and Southern accents. Even though Irma did not appear on the best-selling soundtrack album, which included tracks by Professor Longhair, the Dixie Cups, Terrance Simien, BeauSoleil, Buckwheat Zydeco, Dewey Balfa, Aaron Neville, and The Neville Brothers, she played a small part as

Scott Billington and Irma Thomas at Studio Solo, Slidell, Louisiana, July 1985. (Photograph courtesy of Scott Billington)

the character Marceline. Her ex-touring mate Solomon Burke had a role as Daddy Mention. The album helped fuel the fire that Jazz Fest had ignited, spreading the word about New Orleans culture and music far and wide.

Irma and Scott both realized, as they went forward, that finding songs would be their greatest challenge. For their second album, Scott recalled, "I began reaching out to more writers and publishers, including Irma's past collaborators such as Allen Toussaint and Paul Kelly, and to various publishing companies. On a trip to New York, I met Jerry Ragovoy at his home. I even asked for song submissions in the free listings in various professional songwriter's magazines, which usually meant a deluge of cassette tape demos, and only occasionally a usable song. However, that was how I made the connection with people such as Clyde Otis, the songwriter and producer who had been behind the success of Dinah Washington and Brook Benton."

Irma said, "[Scott] seems to have a good grasp of what songs fit my vocal ability, and he also knows which songs I will probably gravitate towards. I like those songs that tell good stories. I'm not a gimmick song person. I don't think I've ever really sung a gimmick song, meaning songs that have a lot of repetition and not very much to say. And so we've had a very good working relationship when it comes to choosing material for my recording sessions. There was only one occasion, in fact, that worked out, even in spite of that, when he sent me a song [David Egan's 'If You Knew How Much'] and I said, 'You've got to be joking. You want me to sing that?' He said, 'Yeah, give it a try.' So I just gave it a try. And as it turned out, it did work out because once I started singing and then paying attention to the lyrics, it wasn't a bad song after all."[9] She elaborated, "They are all, to various degrees, about being in love and out of love. That's the ability of the artist to be able to put themselves in any predicament that they need to do to get the job done."[10]

For their second album, Scott wanted to try for a slightly more ambitious sound, with the perhaps naïve hope that Irma could again receive airplay on pop radio stations, at least in New Orleans. He had just completed an album with soul music icon Solomon Burke using a New Orleans rhythm section of musicians associated with Allen Toussaint and Dr. John—drummer Herman Ernest III (who had played on the LaBelle hit "Lady Marmalade"), bassist David Barard, keyboardist Craig Wroten, and guitarist Renard Poché—and suggested them to Irma. Ultimately, they decided to record six songs with the session musicians, and four with Irma's band. The sessions began in April 1987 at Southlake Studio in Metairie, a neighboring town to New Orleans where David Farrell was now working. Bill Samuel wrote the horn arrangements, and ELS provided backing vocals.

Perhaps the greatest song on the album, *The Way I Feel*, was the new Allen Toussaint composition "Old Records," with its gently loping New Orleans groove and wistful lyrics. It became a staple in Irma's set, and Irma and Allen performed it every time they had the opportunity to work together. The record is orchestrated in the manner of one of Scott's inspirations, Thom Bell (who worked with the Spinners and many others), with Wroten providing a lush synth bed on the bridge, and Samuel utilizing a French horn as part of the brass arrangement. Scott played a Stevie Wonder–like harmonica solo. Both Irma and Scott thought she might benefit from a different take on her lead vocal, and they recorded several more passes over the next few weeks, but they ultimately decided to use the original vocal she had recorded with the track which, in retrospect, was in the moment and just right.

Jerry Ragovoy provided the outstanding new song "Sorry, Wrong Number" (which inspired some of Irma's most passionate and forceful singing on record), and "All I Know Is the Way I Feel," which was recorded almost simultaneously by the Pointer Sisters. Clyde Otis proposed that they cut his "Sit Down and Cry," which Aretha Franklin had recorded, and he was right because Irma's take on the song is an emotional powerhouse, even if the arrangement did little to update Aretha's. However, two of the cover songs chosen by Irma and Scott, Aretha's "Baby I Love You" and Martha and the Vandellas' "Dancing in the Street," may have been too iconic to warrant another interpretation, even by a talent as formidable as Irma's, and even with the added funkiness of the New Orleans musicians. "After that," commented Scott, "we were more careful about recording such well-known songs, trying instead to find new material that suited the present-day world."

Scott's file folder for the album includes his correspondence with Irma, with photocopies of the steady stream of cassettes on which he sent songs, which included another new Allen Toussaint song called "Can I Be the One" and John Hiatt's "If I Can Love Somebody." Perhaps these songs would have been better choices than the covers, but Irma chose her repertoire carefully. She felt if she could not put herself inside the story of each song as she performed it, that she could not authentically bring the lyrics to life, then it was not worth considering. As writer Ben Sandmel noted, it is the secret of both her approach and her appeal: "Thomas is a remarkably expressive and affecting singer with a great sense of drama and dynamics. Her appeal is not based on vocal pyrotechnics or adventurous phrasing but rather on her compelling power to inhabit a song's lyrics and communicate them in a completely convincing manner."[11]

Reviews of the album strengthened the momentum created by *The New Rules*. London's *New Musical Express* noted, "Never has her voice sounded maturer or richer than on songs from this album. . . . She's not just one of New Orleans' premier contemporary vocalists, she's one of the world's, and it's about time people woke up to the fact."[12] Perhaps the album's most accurate evaluation came from James Hopkins who wrote in *Option*, "Thomas keeps on demonstrating the difference between recycling younger sounds as if you never grew older, and maturing with the ageless qualities of sweet soul music."[13] Many reviewers, however, commented on "Baby I Love You" and "Dancing in the Street," not always in a positive light.

In between recording sessions, the 1987 Jazz Fest was under way. *The Times-Picayune* took note: "Irma Thomas, whose first job in New Orleans was as a waitress, had fans waiting in mile-long lines to get to her stage at last Sunday's jazz fest. The Ponchatoula-born entertainer, who can put more punch in a song than Sugar Ray Leonard can in the ring, has been signed for her third engagement in as many years at the Blue Room. The singer, who rocked the charts 25 years ago with her first R&B hit, 'You Can Have My Husband,' opens in the Fairmont's swank supper club May 19."[14]

During these years, the relative success of roots-oriented labels such as Rounder and Black Top Records and other smaller companies such as

Alligator Records, did not go unnoticed. In 1988, Virgin Records' deputy head of A&R, John Wooler, started a new blues label called Point Blank, which would sign artists such as Walter "Wolfman" Washington, Duke Robillard, and Solomon Burke (each of whom had recorded for Rounder), Albert Collins (who had recorded for Alligator), John Lee Hooker, and Van Morrison. It wasn't exactly big business, but a new era of recording opportunities for legacy rhythm and blues artists was beginning to blossom. The result was that artists who had survived the end of the commercial era of classic blues and R&B were finding new audiences around the world.

The outlier among all of these record labels was Malaco Records, which had managed to consolidate the traditional rhythm and blues market by signing artists such as Bobby "Blue" Bland, Little Milton, Denise LaSalle, and Z.Z. Hill, cultivating a top-flight songwriting team, and promoting the records to radio stations that catered to older Black listeners. Their hits such as Z.Z. Hill's "Down Home Blues" and Bobby Bland's "Members Only" can still be heard on jukeboxes across the South. Yet, this was not Irma's demographic because her most successful records had leaned as much toward pop as R&B, and her audience was far more diverse.

She was now beginning to perform for her fans in other cities, almost always touring with the Professionals and refusing to use a local pickup band. On February 11 and 12, 1988, she appeared at the Club Lingerie on Sunset Boulevard in Los Angeles, a show promoted by writer and producer Bill Bentley. The connection between New Orleans and Los Angeles remained strong. Several years earlier, Bentley had booked a series of concerts featuring Johnny Adams, Ernie K-Doe, Art and Aaron Neville, and others at the Club Lingerie, with an all-star band of Louisiana expatriates who he dubbed the New Orleans Natives. Assembled by saxophonist Harold Battiste Jr., the band included, at different times, pianist Henry Butler, keyboard player Ivan Neville, drummer Johnny Boudreaux, drummer Brother John Goines, guitarist Leo Nocentelli, vocalist Tami Lynn, bassist Hutch Hutchinson, bassist Lenny McDaniel, saxophonist Jerry Jumonville, and trumpet player Ike "Diz" Williams.[15]

A week later, on February 18, she performed with the Professionals at New York's Lone Star Café, receiving a very positive review in *Cash Box* that noted, "Two minutes on stage and it's clear that Irma Thomas has got it: the combination of awesome pipes and personal expression that most folks associate with deep soul, the down home stuff, what Roland Barnes once called 'the body in the voice as it sings.' And what a voice . . ."[16] In *The New York Times*, Jon Pareles commented, "In fact, she sounds better now; her voice is fuller, her approach more knowing yet more playful."[17] On May 27, just after Jazz Fest, she made her Boston-area debut at Cambridge's Nightstage.

In an article about her appearance at the Benson and Hedges Blues Festival at the Pacific Amphitheatre in Costa Mesa, California, she said, "In the last five years my career has taken an upturn, which is certainly a reason to be happy. I mean, you sing in this business for 30-some years and you begin to wonder if you'll ever get the recognition you think you deserve. Now I have been getting some. I don't feel so bad now about not having had a major hit record in over 20 years because I'm working steadily. I think just being visible is very important to an artist, more-so than having a major record because you can have a hit this year and be totally out of sight and mind the next year, whereas I have been visible the last few years. Just knowing that some people are hearing me and enjoying it is a degree of success in itself."[18]

In early 1989, the CBS News journalist Charles Kuralt produced a segment on Irma for his On the Road series, which meant that a camera crew followed her for several weeks. The culmination of the taping was to be an event that officially recognized Irma as The Soul Queen of New Orleans.

The title was originally bestowed upon her by her longtime drummer, "Sir" Wilbert Widow, who served as her announcer. She recalled, "He would bring me on and he said he got tired of just the 'Ladies and gentlemen, here's Irma Thomas.' He decided to call me the soul queen, and that stayed with me until 1989 on February the 17th, when the mayor and the powers that be of the city decided to dub me, officially. I have to give credit to Kalamu Ya Salaam, who works with the Jazz and Heritage Foundation. He decided to make it a night to honor me and they officially gave me that title on paper, The Soul Queen of New Orleans. And it has stuck."[19]

Larry McKinley, the deejay and one-time co-owner of Minit Records, was the emcee. Mayor Sidney J. Barthelemy presided over "The Coronation of Irma Thomas Musical Queen of New Orleans" at the Saenger Theatre, with Allen Toussaint providing reminiscences, before Irma and her band performed a set.[20]

Sadly, on the same day, Irma's father died of mesothelioma at the age of seventy-five, at his home in Avondale. When she was asked if the event should be postponed, Irma said, "No, you all have put all this work into the event, and nothing will change the fact that my father is gone."

She remembered, "Somehow, I got through it. I realize we draw strength from the strangest places. All of my children were present, and they kept asking me if I was going to be alright. I told them, 'Yes, I am going to be fine.' And I was.

"The finality of death takes a few days to settle in, and my father's passing didn't really hit me until I returned to the mortuary to view his body. I wanted to make sure preparations represented the way my father truly looked in a photograph I had provided. Although I was generally pleased with his appearance, his gaunt body once again reminded me of his tremendous weight loss. I remembered the times I watched him slowly making his way to the kitchen, determined to force himself to eat. His hunger was quite evident because by then he was unable to swallow anything, not even prescribed medicine, so excruciating was the pain. Still, he tried, though unsuccessfully, to gain more strength.

"As I studied the features of his now serene face, my thoughts traveled back to the night before he died. He wanted a bath, so I went over to help him. He was so thin and fragile due to cancer's progression. Doctors had sent him home in September with the prognosis that within two weeks, he would be dead. However, my father did not die until February. He was always a stubborn old guy. Making death wait until he was ready and not one minute sooner was so very typical of my dad. He was the kind of person who just did not give up. We all do what we have to do to get along in this world, and we usually gather strength from places we least expect." Percy Lee's *Times-Picayune* obituary made note that he was the father of Irma Thomas, and listed his occupation as retired longshoreman. Services were held in New Orleans, and he was buried in the cemetery at Mount Everett Methodist Church in Greensburg. He had been a steadfast presence in her life.

Much like her father, Irma never gave up. She had become such a key figure in New Orleans music that she was now being chosen to be the Jazz Fest closer on one of the two main stages, on either of the two weekends. In 1989, she was joined onstage by multi-Grammy®-winning singer Rita Coolidge, who had become a good friend. Irma noted that the festival was a meeting place for artists who seldom had the opportunity to hear one another: ". . . you can always see other singers and musicians out in the audience. A lot of those who perform there also stick around to listen to the others."[21]

For her next Rounder album, Irma and Scott decided to do a live concert recording. The current version of the Professionals was strong, with the talented brothers Harold and George Scott on bass and guitar, and a horn section of New Orleans veterans. They had become a well-tuned unit. The band knew her hand signals, which she used behind her back. Keyboardist Kim Phillips said, "You learn that when you play with her often, you get the hand signals [to let you know] what song she might want to do next, or sometimes she'll lean over and tell you the song." If she said "Let's drip" everyone knew to play "It's Raining." The band followed her as she tailored her shows to each audience, often deviating from any predetermined set list and taking requests from the audience to better accommodate the collective mood. While it might have made sense to record the album at a well-known New Orleans venue, Irma chose the club called Slim's in San Francisco, which was co-owned by the musician and Irma Thomas fan Boz Scaggs. The decision was made partly because she was appreciating her growing audiences away from home, and perhaps partly because she wanted her hometown to know that she was not only a local artist. Scott hired the Phil Edwards mobile recording truck, which ran two 24-track analog machines—before one of them ran out of tape, the other one was started. Both sets on August 30 and 31 were recorded.

Irma remembered a humorous snag. "I'm in San Francisco, California, at Slim's club doing a live recording and the audience was there. We told the audience what was going on, but we told them to be normal. If you like it, applaud. If you don't, don't applaud, which I knew they would. But anyway, I wanted the audience to be comfortable, and that's what we achieved. . . . We did two nights of recording. The second night I was so busy trying to get together to get to the club, I forgot my shoes. So the second night I recorded barefooted and I think that was the most comfortable night I had out. I didn't have any shoes. But the total recording, when I listened back to it, was what I wanted in terms of being able to present my music to a live audience and actually capture that feeling on record . . . I even gave some instructions on how to do the second line and all that good stuff. Well, you wouldn't be from New Orleans if you didn't do that."[22]

Darell Stokes Jackson, who was at the show, said, "She really put her soul into that album. She gave it all. When she was doing that live album, she didn't care when the song ended. It did end, but you could feel that she was just so into each of those songs that you couldn't feel an ending coming. And that room was just electric. People were just so excited to be there and really having a good time with her. When she sings 'I've Been Loving You Too Long,' it just goes through her into the audience and just lights everybody up. You understand that her life experience is coming through her at that point and reaching other people."[23]

Scott did a small amount of touch-up recording at Ultrasonic Studio in New Orleans (for instance, having the horn players re-sing their background vocals, which were too off-mic in the concert recording to use), and then he mixed the record at Blue Jay Recording Studio in Massachusetts with engineer Mark Wessell. It was released in 1991 as *Live! Simply The Best* (after the Holly Knight/Mike Chapman song made popular by Tina Turner), and it became her most successful Rounder release to date. The recording favored

Live! Simply the Best (Photograph courtesy of the Concord Music Group)

her earlier repertoire, but her dynamic versions of the title track, along with the Jim Doris song "Oh Me Oh My (I'm a Fool for You)" (made popular by Lulu) and the Michael Bolton/Eric Kaz song "That's What Love Is All About," were new to her fans. She also finally recorded her popular "second line medley" of "I Done Got Over It" / "Iko Iko" / "Hey Pocky Way," in which her observations about New Orleans culture ("As you know, in New Orleans, we celebrate anything and everything. We celebrate frogs, roaches, mosquitos, alligators, red beans and rice, gumbo, okra, corn, a headache, divorce, separation, and when your pregnancy test comes back negative") and instructions to "put your backfield in motion" never failed to get the crowd on its feet. Many fans brought handkerchiefs to wave in the air as they danced.

To everyone's great delight, and perhaps surprise, *Live! Simply The Best* won Irma's first Grammy® nomination for Best Contemporary Blues Album. Irma had always been more than a blues singer, and she never thought of herself as such, but she recorded several blues songs, including "Don't Mess with My Man." Yet, the word "blues" had come to represent something larger than the pure form of the genre, as it became a catch-all for the sounds of soul music and traditional rhythm and blues, which, in a world in which music composed with samples and beats was dominating the charts, were clearly becoming a part of the American roots music world.

Anticipation was high at the thirty-fourth annual Grammy Awards® at Radio City Music Hall in New York, on a chilly February 25. It was Irma's and Scott's first time at the ceremony. Scott's 1981 recording *Alright Again!* by Clarence "Gatemouth" Brown had won a Grammy Award®, but Scott had not been present. The competition was strong: Buddy Guy (*Damn Right, I've Got The Blues*), Charlie Musselwhite (*Signature*), Johnny Winter (*Let Me In*), and Albert Collins (*Albert Collins*). As fellow attendees kept saying to Irma, it was an honor just to be nominated, but when the winner was announced, it was Buddy Guy who took home the trophy. While she was clearly disappointed, it was another step forward in terms of national recognition. There was a unique highlight of the event for Irma. She met her childhood idol Roy Rogers, the cowboy movie star and recording artist, who posed for a photograph with her.

The nomination was a welcome development, and an advantage in booking new shows, because the New Orleans and Gulf Coast nightclub scenes that had thrived in the 1960s had now all but disappeared. Even the package shows that included touring artists such as Bobby "Blue" Bland, Tyrone Davis, or Denise LaSalle at venues such as the ILA Hall and the Municipal Auditorium were becoming less frequent, while colleges and teen dances now sought other entertainment options. Perhaps it was simply that the generation that had grown up with New Orleans rhythm and blues was aging. What remained were several jazz clubs; a few venues such as Jimmy's and Jed's, patronized mostly by college students and locals; clubs that catered to tourists, especially in the French Quarter; and venues that reflected the Jazz Fest demographic such as Tipitina's and the Maple Leaf Bar (and, soon, the House of Blues), which attracted a coterie of dedicated local and international fans who knew and venerated New Orleans music. Tipitina's had been founded in 1977 as an act of cultural preservation by a group of friends who were inspired to create a venue where their idol Professor Longhair could play, naming it after one of his best-known songs. However, in the New Orleans area, Irma was now performing almost exclusively at festivals and as a star attraction at local conventions. With the nomination, Irma's celebrity had risen. Even the local Schwegmann's grocery chain celebrated her fiftieth birthday by printing her photograph on their brown paper grocery bags, with the words, "Everybody loves Irma Thomas."

DISCOGRAPHY

Singles

The New Rules (Paul Kelly)/The Love of My Man (Ed Townsend) (Rounder 4555). Produced by Scott Billington and Irma Thomas, 1986.

Old Records (Allen Toussaint)/Sorry Wrong Number (Jerry Ragovoy, Peter Udell) Demon Records 1056P. Produced by Scott Billington and Irma Thomas, 1988.

I Believe Saints Go All the Way (A. Harrison)/Mardi Gras Mambo (Elliot-Welsh-Adams) (Sound of New Orleans 10311). Produced by Gary Edwards, 1988.

Hittin' On Nothin' (N. Neville)/Hip Shakin' Mama (Irma Thomas) Maison de Soul 1058, 1989.

LPs

The New Rules (Rounder 2046), 1986.

Side A

1. The New Rules (Paul Kelly) 2. Gonna Cry 'Til My Tears Run Dry (Doc Pomus-Mort Shuman-Scott Fagan) 3. I Needed Somebody (Don Bryant-Ann Peebles) 4. Good Things Don't Come Easy (Dan Penn-Spooner Oldham) 5. The Love of My Man (Ed Townsend)

Side B

1. One More Time (Doc Pomus-Ken Hirsch) 2. Thinking of You (Leon D. Bonds) 3. The Wind Beneath My Wings (Hero) (Larry Henley-Jeff Silber) 4. I Gave You Everything (Terry Woolford and Terry Hamby) 5. Yours Until Tomorrow (Carole King-Gerry Goffin)

Produced by Scott Billington and Irma Thomas

Engineered by David Farrell and Gragg Lunsford

Recorded at Studio Solo, Slidell, Louisiana

Elaine Foster, Lisa Foster, Sharon Foster, backing vocals; Wilbert J. Widow, drums; Guillermo Ladút, Leroy Aych, guitar; Glenn Carvin, keyboards, Bill "Foots" Samuel, alto saxophone, tenor saxophone, baritone saxophone; Joe Saulsbury Jr., tenor saxophone, soprano saxophone, tambourine; Lawrence J. Weber, Terry Tullos, trumpet

The Way I Feel (Rounder 2058), 1988.

Side A

1. Old Records (Allen Toussaint) 2. Baby I Love You (Ronnie Shannon) 3. Sorry Wrong Number (Jerry Ragovoy, Peter Udell) 4. You Can Think Twice (Michael Garvin-Walter Klocko) 6. Sit Down and Cry (Clyde Otis-Lou Stallman)

Side B

1. All I Know Is the Way I Feel (Estelle Levitt-Jerry Ragovoy) 2. I'm Gonna Hold You to Your Promise (Paul Kelly) 3. I'll Take Care of You (Brook Benton) 4. Dancing in the Street (Marvin Gaye-W. Stevenson) 5. You Don't Know Nothin' About Love (Jerry Ragovoy)

Produced by Scott Billington and Irma Thomas

Engineered by David Farrell and Gragg Lunsford

Recorded at Southlake Studio, Metairie, Louisiana

Elaine Foster, Lisa Foster, Sharon Foster, backing vocals; Chester "Chuck" Henry, Harold J. Scott, bass; Wilbert Widow, Herman Ernest III, drums, percussion; Leroy Aych, Renard Poché, guitar; Craig Wroten, Kim Phillips, keyboards; Scott Billington, harmonica; Bill "Foots" Samuel, alto saxophone, tenor saxophone, baritone saxophone; Joe Saulsbury Jr., tenor saxophone; Lawrence Weber, trumpet; Terry Tullos, trumpet, French horn; Ernie Gautreau, valve trombone

Compact Disc

Live! Simply the Best (Rounder 2110), 1991.

1. Breakaway (Jackie DeShannon-Sharon Sheeley) 2. Time Is on My Side (Norman Meade) 3. Hip Shakin' Mama (public domain) 4. That's What Love Is All About (Eric Kaz-Michael Bolton) 5. Thinking of You (Leon David Bonds) 6. I Needed Somebody (Ann Peebles-Don Bryant) 7. Medley: I've Been Loving You Too Long/Please Please Please (James Brown-Johnny Terry-Otis Redding) 8. Hittin' on Nothin' 9. It's Raining (Naomi Neville) 10. Second Line Medley: I Done Got Over It/Iko Iko/Hey Pocky Way (Art Neville-Ernest Kador-George Porter Jr.-Joseph Modeliste-Leo Nocentelli-Traditional) 11. Wish Someone Would Care (Irma Thomas) 12. You Can Have My Husband (Dorothy LaBostrie) 13. Oh Me Oh My (I'm a Fool for You) (Jim Doris) 14. Simply the Best (Holly Knight, Mike Chapman)

Produced by Scott Billington and Irma Thomas

Engineered by Phil Edwards, David Farrell, and Mark Wessell

Harold J. Scott, bass; Wilbert Widow, drums; George Scott, guitar; Reave "Doc" Watkins, keyboards and backing vocals; Emile Hall, tenor saxophone and backing vocals; Warner Williams, tenor saxophone and backing vocals; Lawrence Weber, trumpet and backing vocals; Frank Parker, trumpet and backing vocals.

Tracks

O Holy Night (Placide Cappeau, Adolphe Adam) on *Creole Christmas, Traditional Christmas Music, New Orleans Style* (album released in New Orleans by Coca Cola and the radio station Q93), 1986, Produced by Charles Brant, Bubby Valentino, and Steve Valentino; reissued as *A Creole Christmas*, Epic CD-47045.

Tomorrow (Jimmy McCracklin), It's Got to Be Love (Jimmy McCracklin), duet with Jimmy McCracklin, *My Story*. Produced by Ron Levy, Bullseye Blues CD-9508.

CHAPTER ELEVEN

Going to School

(1992–2004)

Irma continued with her studies at Delgado University, taking one or two courses at a time, as school became an increasingly important part of her life. She switched her major from general studies to business, which was not only a practical decision, but which also enabled her to deduct her tuition as a business expense. She recalled, "I had some wonderful teachers. Two in particular were Mr. Moore, who taught English 101, and Dr. Sandra Wright, who taught my second course in English. Dr. Wright really opened my eyes about how to write essays. She and I still laugh about a comparative essay I wrote about pots. She wasn't familiar with pots and pans. As a PhD English professor, why would she have time to learn about cooking and pots? On the other hand, raising four kids, I had all the time in the world. She thought my essay was interesting because she didn't know there were so many different kinds of pots. I said, 'Honey, these are just the tip of the iceberg.'

"I also took a humanities class in African American history, where I learned more about the civil rights movement. Interestingly, I wound up being the focus of many of the class discussions. As one of the older students in class, I had lived through that tumultuous period, so I was able to clarify from a personal perspective the way things were during that era. Because of my personal experiences, I became one of Dr. Wright's prize pupils in the class. I had been performing for white audiences for quite some time during the civil rights movement; therefore, I was able to give in detail some of the harsh realities of segregation. As a result, Dr. Wright and I established a close student/teacher relationship built on mutual respect. I have great admiration for her teaching ability. She admired my artistic talent and studiousness.

(Photograph by Rick Olivier)

"I always took my lessons very seriously. For example, on one occasion I had worked the whole weekend on an assignment for her class, which was held at eight o'clock Monday mornings. When I got to the class that morning, there were some students discussing their weekend escapades. They continued their discussions while Dr. Wright was beginning her lecture. I was annoyed, so I politely turned around and said, 'Look, I pay for my classes. You come here on a grant or some kind of state funding/aid. My tax dollars and I want to use my money to learn, not hear about what you did over the weekend. So I would appreciate it if you would cut the conversation so we can get on with the lesson.' I had to bring it home to those students because I wanted to hear what the professor was saying, not about their personal adventures. Dr. Wright was educating us with much more important information. Even now, she laughs about the incident. Perhaps my comments made some enemies, but my attitude was that I went to school to learn, not waste time. Still, I made quite a few friends while attending Delgado, and my enrollment was worth every minute of my time.

"Another one of my favorite professors was Mr. Rodriguez. He was a short, white, wonderful math teacher who taught me a lot. For those of us who did not have algebra in high school, the subject was particularly difficult. We had to really push ourselves to get the hang of it. Mr. Rodriguez was always very patient with me as an older student in the class. When we asked questions or asked him to repeat steps to a problem, he always did without making a big deal about it or making us feel small. I will always give him credit for helping me get through math.

"After earning enough credits to graduate in general studies, I decided to change my major to business. Then I encountered Mr. Mullins, Professor of Business Studies. He's a mess. I took quite a few of his classes. There were several other professors that I also remember, some of whom taught computer science. Even though I never really mastered using a computer, they did help me understand computers a lot better. Overall, my Delgado experience was priceless.

"Graduation day for me was phenomenal. My husband, Emile, had undergone back surgery, so it was quite painful for him to attend. Yet, he was there as well as his sister, my kids and family, friends, and my band. I invited them all because I had gotten approval to sing at the graduation. I was later told that my graduation marked the first time that all of the college's professors attended. It was quite a day.

"After receiving my diploma, I sang 'I Believe I Can Fly.' I was so appreciative, proud, and moved. As I sang, tears streamed down my cheeks, and wrapped under my chin. I couldn't stop crying, so filled with joy was I. In the middle of my song, I collected myself enough to thank everybody who had helped me throughout my years of study: those who had shared notes with me when my singing schedule made it necessary to miss classes, those who had tutored me in math, everyone I could think of who had played some part, large or small, in my getting to that glorious day. Then I went back into my song. The whole audience had the wave going, which lifted my heart even more. They were right there with me in all my joy. I don't know who was happier, they or me. But I was one happy lady, one who was truly flying, a feeling that will stay with me the rest of my life. I strongly recommend that anyone who is thinking about going back to school to do so, no matter at what age. You are never too old to learn or start a new career. Pursuing an education is truly an invaluable endeavor. You simply cannot put a price on its worth."

College graduation was a defining moment in Irma's life, and one that still brings tears to her eyes when she talks about it. Irma said, "On that day, I don't believe anybody could be any higher if he or she were taking all the drugs in the world. My spirit soared. The feeling was spiritually uplifting. After all of those years, I felt as though I was floating as I walked across the stage to receive my degree. It didn't seem like fifteen long years had gone by, that is, not until I sat down and really thought about it. It had really been

Irma Thomas celebrates her graduation from Delgado University, as her long-time tenor saxophonist Emile Hall looks on. (Photograph courtesy of the New Orleans Jazz Museum, David Kunian, Curator)

fifteen years, but I had finally earned my degree, and I felt good about all of those years. If I had to do it again, I definitely would. My education was well worth the time and effort."

In 1991, Irma participated in a Jazz Fest–sponsored concert called Dew Drop Inn Revisited at the Riverboat Hallelujah Dance Hall, an event that would be repeated (at the Praline Connection Gospel and Blues Hall) in 1995 and 1999. The first event was also billed as The Toussaint Legacy, featuring many of the singers he had worked with at Minit Records and other labels early in his career: Jessie Hill, Ernie K-Doe, Earl King, Art Neville, Irma Thomas, and Chuck Carbo, all backed by Allen and his orchestra. Irma performed "It's Raining," "Ruler of My Heart," "Breakaway," "Old Records," and "Gonna Cry Till My Tears Run Dry." The evening was filmed and recorded by New Orleans filmmaker Michael Murphy.

Irma's career continued to gain steady momentum. She was growing into the role of a legacy American artist, now mentioned alongside iconic blues and R&B performers such as B.B. King and Etta James. At Jazz Fest in 1992, she performed a nighttime concert at the Municipal Auditorium with Gladys Knight and Lou Rawls, and in 1993, she recorded a duet of the

Little Milton hit "We're Gonna Make It" with B.B. King for his *Blues Summit* album, which featured a roster of top blues and soul artists such as Etta James, Robert Cray, Ruth Brown, and John Lee Hooker.

Around this time, Irma appeared on "Angela" (the *Angela Hill Talk Show*) on WWL-TV Channel 4, New Orleans. Angela Hill was a beloved journalist and the first female anchor at WWL. Her weekday show, billed as "the talk of the town," aired between 1989 and 1996, and hosted local and national guests such as Barbara Bush, Bill Clinton, and Oprah Winfrey. The talk show covered a variety of topics. On this particular episode, Angela and Irma discussed alopecia, the condition that causes patchy to total hair loss on the scalp, body, and/or face. During the interview, Irma, who has never been shy about telling it like it is, told the audience that she was bald, and she removed her wig. Irma has often used her celebrity to promote awareness and to nurture open dialogue about health issues.

Later, during the photo session for her album *My Heart's in Memphis*, photographer Rick Olivier had a spontaneous idea for a different kind of Irma Thomas photograph, without a wig. His wardrobe stylist had arrived at the studio with a large bolt of white satin at the same time Irma was changing wigs between poses. Rick said, "For twenty or thirty years, Irving Penn's portraits were my touchstone on portraiture with one big light source, noble pose, black and white, etc. So I just followed the muse, and said to Irma, 'It would be great,' and she said 'Great, let's do it,' which kinda shocked me at the time, but boy, was I down with it!" Irma said, "Rick has a way of making you feel comfortable. He took that photo of me with no hair. When I took off my wig, he wrapped me in fabric."[1] The image was published in the 2012 book *A Unique Slant of Light: The Bicentennial History of Art in Louisiana* (University Press of Mississippi).

As Irma and Scott made plans for a new record, the search for songs began anew. This time, Scott was able to cast an even wider net, both because songwriters were eager to have Irma record their songs, and because his network of writers and publishers had grown. The resulting ten-track album, *True Believer*, is a songwriters' showcase, and especially, as it turned out, for songs about rain and tears. Dan Penn was becoming a constant songwriting presence on Irma's records, and his "Trying to Catch a Cab in the Rain" (written with Jon and Sally Tiven) and "Smoke Filled Room" (written with Jonnie Barnett and Carson Whitsett) rank with his best work. Allman Brothers alumnus Johnny Neel contributed "Can't You Hear It in My Tears" (written with Tommy Polk), while Tony Joe White (known for his hit "Polk Salad Annie") and Michael Dan Ehmig provided "Heart Full of Rain." Other

(Photograph by Rick Olivier)

writers included Doc Pomus and Dr. John ("I Never Fool Nobody But Me") and Doc's frequent writing partner Ken Hirsch ("Big Talk"). The production approach was perhaps more mellow than on Irma's first two Rounder albums, as Scott and Irma explored a sound that might have found airplay on the "quiet storm" or smooth jazz radio formats, although, in retrospect, the music was still not glossy enough for that.

The backing musicians included many of the best New Orleans players of the 1990s, including keyboardists Sammy Berfect and David Torkanowsky, guitarist Cranston Clements, bass player Chris Severin, and drummer Herman Ernest III. Yet, Scott made one call that did not work out as planned. The veteran saxophonist Alvin "Red" Tyler was contracted to write several arrangements for the band and horn section, as he had just done on the brilliant Johnny Adams album, *The Real Me*. But when the ensemble began running through the charts in the studio, they seemed too "jazzy" and light

An alternate shot from the photo sessions for *True Believer.* (Photograph by Rick Olivier)

for Irma. Tyler's chart for "Heart Full of Rain" made it onto the record, but the others were ultimately abandoned. Scott and Irma both felt that she had made enough records with unsympathetic arrangements, and did not need to force Red's charts on this one. It was a disappointment because Irma and Red were friends and New Orleans icons who had known one another for years. Instead, on the songs that used horns, Bill Samuel again wrote the charts.

Irma told *Grammy®* Magazine, "When I'm in the studio, I blot out the walls, and to me there's an audience there. So I'm still singing with that perspective, and we still do it the old way I did back in the old days, with the band being there and going for live takes." The article continues, ". . . as ever, Thomas remains unsurpassed when it comes to ballads, proving it here with a gorgeous version of Tony Joe White's "Heart Full of Rain" as well as two new songs ("Can't You Hear It in My Tears" and "Smoke Filled Room") that literally brought the singer to tears in the studio.[2]

She recalled the story of recording the emotive vocal on "Smoke Filled Room," in which the protagonist blames her tears on the smoke in her eyes. "Well, the song is a story about a woman who walked into a smoke-filled room and she saw her significant other sharing time with someone else and, yeah, for some reason I was doing the song and I started crying and everybody else started crying. And that was the first time that happened and it happened again at another recording session. But that time was so poignant because nobody knew what I was crying about and I couldn't tell them either. It just got welled up and I let it go. But it's a very good story. And I guess I was living the part."[3] Dan Penn later remarked that he wished that Irma had recorded the song again, sans tears, but Irma and Scott chose to go with the feeling in her live-with-the-track vocal.

David Farrell, who was the engineer or co-engineer on all of Irma's Rounder albums, commented on her approach: "You've got to tell the story and you've got to live the story. And she does that. She's not just singing words and singing notes. She's emotional about what she does, and it comes across. I remember Fats Domino told me one time, 'I always smile when I sing because people can hear me smiling on the radio.' I thought that was an interesting way of putting it. But it's that way of transferring that emotion into what you're singing, and that's what grabs, catches people. That's what sets a great singer apart from somebody just going through the motions."

David also became adept at recording her performances in the studio. Her powerful voice could overwhelm the recording equipment, even with her practiced microphone technique (for instance, she would lean back from the microphone when she sang at full volume). He said, "She has a wide dynamic range. Back in the analog days, you had to be careful about overloading the tape. Digital was a little more forgiving, but still, I always like to try to record something that, when I play it back, sounds good from top to bottom. So, when she's singing low, I'm riding it up [manually adjusting her sound level, in sync with her performance]. But when she goes in those really big ranges, you've got to control that as well." He also appreciated the thought that Irma put into each session. "I always found that she came prepared. She wasn't trying to figure it out on the spot. She'd give you multiple performances, of course, but it's not like she would walk into the session cold. She always seemed like she had studied the song, studied the words, knew what she wanted to say, knew how she wanted to sing it." With regard to the Rounder sessions, he added, "I think she knew that she was surrounded by everybody who wanted her to be good. You know, Scott and me and all the musicians. She wasn't ever put on the spot to do something. She was there to do her part."[4]

True Believer was well-received by the media. *The Washington Post* stated, "When Thomas sings Penn's 'Smoke Filled Room' or Pomus's 'I Never Fool Nobody But Me' or Johnny Neel's 'Can't You Hear It in My Tears,' the anguish and self-doubt she feels is nearly palpable—a sharp contrast to the songs of love, affirmation and inspiration that dot the album as well and reveal another side of Thomas's compelling vocal personality."[5] A *Chicago Tribune* review speculated that Thomas "apparently wants to be taken seriously as a pop diva, and such carefully polished material as 'Trying to Catch a Cab in the Rain' and 'Smoke Filled Room,' with their meticulously crafted choruses and slickly cascading arrangements, might do the trick."[6] The *Toronto Star* gave a nod to the "tight band, strong pianist David Torkanowsky, and a blasting horn section."[7] For Rounder, the album was a modest success. It was not easy to sustain the buzz of her first three Rounder releases.

During this time, when Irma and the Professionals were traveling home from a European tour, Emile agreed to perform a show at New York's famed Bottom Line nightclub at a reduced rate since the Japanese television network NHK wanted to film Irma's performance. NHK offered to grant Rounder and Irma the rights to use the high-resolution digital footage for promotion. However, when Emile saw the packed house, and calculated the sum of the collective cover charges, he realized that the club was about to pocket a huge profit. He and Scott went to the office of club owner Allan Pepper, where Emile demanded to be paid a fair price for the show. Barely containing his anger at being exploited under the pretense of a free video, Emile's New Orleans accent became increasingly impenetrable as his ire rose. Emile finally placed his hand firmly on Pepper's desk, looked him in the eye, and then walked out. Pepper turned to Scott and said, in his streetwise New York intonation, "I know he's pissed, but what the f*** did he say?" In the end, Pepper paid Emile his asking price, and Emile was satisfied that he received what he felt his artist was worth.

In 1993, Irma realized a longtime dream when she made her first gospel album, *Walk Around Heaven: New Orleans Gospel Soul*, for Rounder Records at Ultrasonic Studio in New Orleans. The ten-track album was produced by Scott Billington and Irma Thomas, abetted by associate producers Sammy Berfect and Dwight Franklin, who were both revered arrangers and keyboardists in the New Orleans gospel world. Berfect, whose nickname was "The Bishop," was a virtuoso on the Hammond B-3 organ who also performed jazz and R&B. He is still revered by his fellow musicians many years after his death. By 2025, Franklin was still active in the New Orleans gospel scene. An exceptional component of the album is the background vocals by Tara Darnell, Pamela Landrum, Earl Smith Jr., and Charles Elam III. The liner notes to the album were written by The Reverend E. Darnell Jones of the First African Baptist Church of New Orleans, which Irma still attends every Sunday when she is in town, and where she remains a member of the choir. Founded in 1817, "Old Baptist" is the oldest continuous African American church in North America.[8]

Gospel music and the church have always been part of Irma's life. She said: "In the South, if you were a child in the family and church was going on, you went to church, that wasn't an option. It was part of the social gathering. Everybody in the household dressed and went to church. It's funny because I can remember that in the country, we wanted to look nice when we got to the church. So we didn't put our socks and shoes on until we got [there]. There was a little creek that was near the church, and we would go down to the creek and wash the dirt off our feet and put our shoes and socks on so we would look neat going into the church house. We would go to Sunday school and spend the entire day at church up until the late evening services, which started at five o'clock. They would end somewhere between, say, eight or nine o'clock at night—it was dark when we finished. So my aunt would bring a basket of food and we would have our lunch there and even have our dinner at church, and then we would walk back home.

"Even when we moved back to New Orleans, church was almost an all day thing. But I did have a choice there. If I had something to say, a little speech to do, I would stay for the main service, or I would go home. It was just a part of our social gathering, a part of our social life."[9]

Irma had once met her biggest gospel music influence, Mahalia Jackson, if only to shake her hand, but she recalled her pervasive presence. "My dad had his blues records and he had his gospel records. Mahalia Jackson was one of the persons whose records and music he had in the house. Also, I can remember I must have been about maybe eleven or twelve when he bought the first black-and-white television. And I used to watch shows that may have featured Mahalia. Any gospel show that was ever played on the radio, you're going to hear at least one or two gospel songs by Mahalia Jackson."[10] Irma admired Jackson's refusal to sing anything but gospel music, and never "crossing over" to the world of popular music as many of her contemporaries had. It is a practice that Irma follows as well. She will not sing gospel music in her R&B sets or albums, and vice versa.

Irma recalled, "I wanted to do a gospel album as my way of saying and showing people how grateful I am for my faith and in the faith I have in Jesus Christ as being my mentor throughout my life. I always tell people I didn't know that I was supposed to sing. He was guiding me. That was the reason I lost two jobs. I have been quite successful in spite of some of the things that people call hard times. I didn't look at them as hard times and because of my faith, I'm still doing what I love to do. There have been times when I didn't know what the next job was coming from and all of a sudden the phone would ring. That has to be Christ, it had to be Jesus because who else would be in my life to be able to pull those kinds of strings?"

A review in the United Kingdom's *Cross Rhythms* lauded the album:

> If you're a serious follower of 60s R&B you'll know Irma. She cut the original of the Stones' "Time Is On My Side" and a dozen other soul classics. Now she's "gone gospel" and what a joy this is—probably the best of its kind since Mahalia Jackson soared to Heaven with those massive outpourings of controlled emotion. Irma is a member of the historic First African Baptist Church Of New Orleans, where most Sundays find her in the church choir. All of her experience and expertise have been brought to this her first gospel album. There are definitive versions of standards such as "No, Not One," and "Just A Little While To Stay Here," Bessie Griffin's gem "Careful Hands," the Christmas song "O Holy Night," and some newer material. The restrained careful backing allows the voice to do its devastating work. As though anything could stop it! Destined to be a classic album.[11]

Yet, she was unhappy with the gospel world's perception of her as a secular artist working in the gospel field. Irma said, "The gospel deejays who were supposed to be Christian deejays questioned my faith. And so when I was told that, I said, 'I don't think I'll be doing another gospel album,' and I said, 'Now I see why I didn't want to be a gospel performer, because if that's what they have to deal with, it's more cliquish than the rhythm and blues field.' And so that was my only disappointment."[12] She would not make another gospel album until 2024.

In 1994, Irma received the Rhythm and Blues Foundation's Pioneer Award, which came with a $15,000 prize. Other honorees that year were Otis Blackwell, Jerry Butler, The Coasters/The Robins, Clarence Carter, Don Covay, Bill Doggett, Mable John, Ben E. King, Little Richard (who received the Lifetime Achievement Award), Johnny Otis, Earl Palmer, and The Shirelles, with whom she celebrated at the awards ceremony at the Roseland Ballroom in New York City. During a subsequent short tour on which many of these artists performed, Irma noticed that she was the only one who still had an active recording career. Then, as an affirmation of her popularity with the blues community, she won the 1995 W.C. Handy Blues Award for Best Soul Blues Female. In fact, she would either win or be nominated for a W.C. Handy Blues Award (or Blues Music Award, as they came to be called) most every year for the next two decades.

The same year, Irma was invited to sit on the advisory commission that led to the establishment of the New Orleans Jazz National Historical Park. In 1995, the United States Congress passed legislation to create the first and only national park dedicated to an art form. Its two locations in New Orleans continue to be a source of information about jazz and other regional music, and to offer live music performances.[13] This was a physical manifestation of a resolution passed in 1987, "expressing the sense of Congress respecting the designation of jazz as a rare and valuable national American treasure,"[14] in the city where jazz was born, and a further coalescence of the idea that New Orleans music was a valuable part of America's cultural heritage.

During this time, Rounder Records was still largely perceived as a folk, bluegrass, and old time music label, but the importance of its Louisiana R&B and zydeco roster was brought home at the 1995 South by Southwest music conference in Austin, Texas. To celebrate Rounder's twenty-fifth anniversary, the label's promotion director Brad Paul staged a free block party concert in front of the city's iconic Driskill Hotel, at the intersection of Sixth Street and Brazos. Billed as Mardi Gras in March, the event began with an unauthorized second line parade down Sixth Street with the ReBirth Brass Band. Then, Irma, Johnny Adams, and Beau Jocque and the Zydeco Hi-Rollers each performed a set.

Paul remembered, "As the sponsor of the Sixth Street Stage, Rounder was given the Governor's Suite [at the Driskill] and this palatial, large event room/party room. We had a huge press and radio party before the concert, and we were giving out Mardi Gras beads. The room had a big balcony overlooking the stage. All the VIP press and radio people that we invited came out onto the balcony and were throwing Mardi Gras beads out at the audience. That was a great show. I think we got a lot of good write-ups." It was a crucial moment for both the label and the artists, as Louisiana roots music in general was being embraced as part of the South by Southwest aesthetic of alternative music. It was one of the highlights of that year's conference.

A month later, the second Dew Drop Inn Revisited show was held during Jazz Fest, this time with Wardell Quezergue and his orchestra backing Irma, Johnny Adams, and Eddie Bo, along with two artists who were too young to have performed at the original Dew Drop, Kermit Ruffins and Marva Wright. The singer and drag performer Bobby Marchan (the lead vocalist of Huey Smith and the Clowns, whose own song "There Is Something on Your Mind" reached #5 on the *Billboard* pop chart in 1959) was the emcee, just as he had often been at the Dew Drop. His company, Manicure Productions, did not miss a beat in the 1980s and 1990s, when he was involved with Juvenile and

L-R: Andrea Thomas Gibbs, Irma Thomas, Tina Thomas, Jean Marie Thomas, and James Thomas, circa 1990s. (Photograph courtesy of Tina Thomas)

other bounce (the New Orleans party-driven hip hop genre also described as twerking) and hip-hop artists.

As Irma and Scott looked at possible directions and concepts for future recordings, Scott had the idea to approach two well-known musicians/producers as collaborators. Scott would still act as Irma's A&R person, but he proposed to hand over actual production duties. The first was Allen Toussaint, who was writing new songs, and who still had an indelible connection with Irma. Irma and Scott met with Allen at Sea-Saint Studios, in his red-wallpapered second floor office, where they gathered around the white grand piano in the middle of the room. Allen began playing some of his new material, and she began singing along as she listened. Scott remembers that it seemed as if they had gone back in time, to a very familiar place, as they laughed while they worked through the lyrics and phrasing. Even if not every song had resonated with Irma, the time for the new collaboration seemed right and natural.

Yet, it was not to be. Allen's son and business manager Clarence "Reginald" Toussaint called Scott with a proposed budget, which to Scott and Rounder Records was high enough to be jaw-dropping. Irma was selling records, but not on the scale of a major pop artist. Scott commented, "To be fair, Allen deserved to be paid at the level of a major label producer, and maybe he had gotten an equivalent amount in the hit-making days of Sea-Saint, but it was just not something we could do, even if I couldn't fault Reginald for asking." There was never a counteroffer from either side, and that was the end of the project.

In 1996, Allen and his new partner Josh Feigenbaum started their own label, called NYNO (for New York-New Orleans), and began signing the kinds of artists with which Rounder, Black Top, and other smaller New Orleans–focused labels were working. The first release was Allen's own album, *Connected*—his first in nearly twenty years—followed by records by saxophonist Amadée Castenel (a frequent Toussaint sideman), trumpeter James Andrews, soul singers Wallace Johnson and Larry Hamilton, and the New Birth Brass Band. Allen had found a new creative outlet, and Sea-Saint was again humming along as a record-making center. Surprisingly, he never approached Irma to ask about her joining the fold. Her Rounder Records contracts were for two or three albums each, so the opportunity was there. However, Allen would never make another record with his professed muse.

The idea for the second prospective producer was Rolling Stones guitarist Keith Richards, who had been recording and touring with his own band, the X-Pensive Winos. It was impossible to know if he was ever able to consider the idea because his manager was clearly not interested in presenting it to him. Scott tried reaching Richards through several of the musicians who had worked with him, but to no avail.

Thus, Irma and Scott got busy producing their sixth album together, *The Story of My Life*, which was released on Rounder in 1997. As Scott began reaching out for songs, an intriguing prospect presented itself. Dan Penn offered to travel to New Orleans for the sessions, bringing with him his songwriting partners Carson Whitsett (the Malaco house band keyboardist, originally from Jackson, Mississippi) and Jonnie Barnett (from Nashville), to write songs during the sessions. It was perhaps an audacious idea, but everyone welcomed the possibilities.

Scott recalled, "For several days in a row, the songwriting team would check in at Ultrasonic Studio in the morning. Then, they would retire to their quarters at the Parkview Hotel on Audubon Park, and just before our dinner break, they would show up with a completed song." After dinner, Irma and the backing band (keyboardist David Torkanowsky, guitarist Michael Toles [whom Scott had met on a Charlie Rich session in Memphis], bassist George Porter Jr. [from the iconic New Orleans funk band the Meters], and drummer Raymond Weber) would record the song. On several songs, Irma's band members Warner Williams (keyboard) and Charles Elam III (tenor sax and vocals), as well as Dan Penn (acoustic guitar) and Carson Whitsett (keyboards) also contributed. Scott continued, "It was a magical, spontaneous

The crew behind *The Story of My Life*: guitarist Michael Toles, liner note writer Michael Goodwin, engineer David Farrell, Scott Billington, bassist George Porter Jr., Irma Thomas, drummer Raymond Weber, Dan Penn, keyboardist David Torkanowsky, songwriter Jonnie Barnett, songwriter/keyboardist Carson Whitsett. (Photograph by Rick Olivier)

Irma Thomas, Dan Penn and George Porter Jr. share a laugh at Ultrasonic Studio in New Orleans. (Photograph by Rick Olivier)

Michael Toles listens to a playback at Ultrasonic. (Photograph by Rick Olivier)

process." While listening to the playback of a take of "I Count the Teardrops," Weber began playing a drum pattern with his hands on the five-gallon water cooler bottle in the studio. "Nobody take a drink!" exclaimed Scott because the pitch exactly complemented the song. Engineer David Farrell immediately set up mics around the bottle, and the part was added to the track.

The remainder of the album comprised covers such as John Ellison's "Love Don't Get No Better Than This," and new songs that included Allen Toussaint's "We All Need Love," (which suited Irma to a T, as his compositions always did) and Dawn Thomas's "The Story of My Life" (characterized by *Jazz Times* as "a contemporary power pop ballad"),[15] on which Irma delivers a sublimely controlled vocal that veers into operatic territory, occupying the lyric about perpetual heartbreak as if it truly were the story of her life. Scott and the musicians aimed for a modern soundscape, with layered keyboard sounds. There is also a vocal duet with Charles Elam III (her ofttimes sax player, and a frequently employed session background singer) on a cover of the Oleta Adams hit "Get Here." They had been performing this song in Irma's shows for many years, and the closeness of their harmonies is remarkable—one of the few times she shared a lead vocal with another artist. Yet, it was the songs written during the sessions by Dan Penn and his team that were the album's strongest, and one wonders what the album would have been like if all the songs on the album had been created in the same way, in that moment.

The album was generally well received. The *Times Colonist* noted that "Thomas is singing better than ever and lovingly caresses these wonderful songs with a rare intelligence and passion."[16] Irma and Scott may have been settling into a groove that had more to do with a 1970s soul sensibility than with classic New Orleans R&B, but it was a sound into which Irma transitioned naturally, especially when the songs were emotionally authentic to her.

During this time, Emile's daughter Darell visited New Orleans for Jazz Fest. As an admirer of fine art, she took Irma gallery-hopping in the French Quarter. As they walked into a certain gallery, Darell recalled, "It was just Irma and me and maybe one or two other people. We noticed that the lady that worked there was giving a lot of attention to this lady, who was sort of incognito. Well, it was Cicely Tyson." The three women talked for a while, and Tyson then bought one of Irma's Jazz Fest posters, in addition to her other purchases. "Irma and the lady took it apart, because it was in a frame, and Irma signed it for her. Oh, that was such a great day. Irma introduced me to so much in New Orleans, and took me to so many places and so many sites. She is generous to a fault. When I am at her home, she'll share what's in her closet with me because we kind of have the same body type. It's just so much fun being around her."[17]

In September 1998, singer Johnny Adams passed away at the age of sixty-six, after a long battle with cancer. Even though he was a few years older than Irma, Johnny was her artistic contemporary, and their careers had followed similar paths, from making their debut recordings for Joe Ruffino, to touring for Percy Stovall, to having long tenures with Rounder Records. In the months before his death, three benefit concerts were held for him at the Mid-City Lanes Rock'n'Bowl (the bowling alley and music venue at which he often performed), the Palm Court Jazz Café, and Tipitina's (a concert organized by Scott Billington that included Irma, Alvin "Red" Tyler, Aaron Neville, and Walter "Wolfman" Washington). When Irma sang Johnny's first hit, "I Won't Cry," he came down from the balcony to join her, even though he was not supposed to perform that night. It was an emotional moment for all present.

The 1999 edition of the Dew Drop Inn Revisited program during Jazz Fest, in which Irma again participated, was a poignant occasion because it was also billed as a Tribute to Johnny Adams. New Orleans rhythm and blues was savoring a new heyday, but the majority of the artists now in the spotlight were those who had been part of the popular music scene in the 1950s and 1960s. There were few younger artists who were continuing the tradition, especially as traditional R&B was displaced by hip hop and bounce.

That same year, the promotion director of Rounder Records, Brad Paul, arranged a performance during Jazz Fest at the Maple Leaf Bar with Irma and her label mates (and fans) Marcia Ball and Tracy Nelson. All three had recent Rounder releases. Paul recalled, "It was at a time in Rounder history when I was promoting Tracy Nelson, Marcia Ball, and Irma Thomas. As a result of conversations with Marcia and Tracy, I realized that they were both huge Irma fans. While they both obviously knew and had many times interacted with Irma, somehow the two of them, Marcia and Tracy, had never met. Concurrent with that, I was talking with the program director at WWOZ. As head of radio promotion at Rounder, the preeminent New Orleans label at the time, I worked very closely with the radio station. It was always, what can we do together? What can we do to help you guys? What you got coming up fundraiser-wise? We were always going back and forth. So I said, well, how about we do a benefit show for WWOZ and see if I can bring in Marcia, Irma, and Tracy? Of course they were like, yeah, that would be amazing. Do you think you can do it? And I did—all three of them liked the idea."[18] The show was a great success, and the singers enjoyed themselves so much that they asked if Rounder might like to make a record of the three of them together.

Pianist, singer, and songwriter Marcia Ball, born Marcia Mouton in Vinton, Louisiana, first heard Irma at the New Orleans Municipal Auditorium when Marcia was only thirteen years old. She noticed that Irma was visibly pregnant (with her fourth child Andrea) at the time. While Marcia has lived in Austin, Texas, for most of her professional career, her incorporation of the piano styles of musicians such as Professor Longhair and Fats Domino, as well as the influence of singers and songwriters such as Carol Fran and Barbara Lynn, have made her an adopted New Orleans music icon, with multiple Jazz Fest gigs each year, including WWOZ's piano night. Her soprano voice contrasted well with Irma's alto.

Tracy Nelson first came onto the national scene with the San Francisco band Mother Earth in the late 1960s, with whom she covered several Irma Thomas songs. Following the success of her composition "Down So Low," which was covered by Linda Ronstadt, Etta James, Cyndi Lauper, Maria Muldaur, and many others, she bought a small farm outside Nashville, where she has lived ever since. Her big voice was as powerful as Irma's.

The trio gathered at Ultrasonic Studio, with Scott and engineer David Farrell, and the same rhythm section used on Irma's *The Story of My Life* (with the exception of George Porter Jr., who was out of town, and who was replaced by Buckwheat Zydeco bassist Lee Allen Zeno). The horns were arranged by Wardell Quezergue, who had produced Irma's Atlantic Records single almost two decades earlier, and by Victor Goines, the young New Orleans saxophonist who was a member of the Lincoln Center orchestra and who had once been a member of Ruth Brown's touring band. The singers swapped vocal parts with one another, while providing harmony background parts as they exchanged leads.

The singers and Scott each brought ideas for songs and songwriters to the table. Dan Penn and Carson Whitsett transformed Irma's idea of "Woman on the Move" into a feminist R&B anthem, and Lafayette-based David Egan wrote the title song, "Sing It!," the humorous "People Will Be People," and the simmering "Please No More." David had initially become known as a member of the Shreveport R&B band A Train, and subsequently with the Lafayette progressive Cajun band Filé. Over the years, his songs were recorded by Joe Cocker, John Mayall, Etta James, Solomon Burke, Percy Sledge, and others. He would be an important part of Irma's future. Marcia brought "If I Know You," her collaboration with Austin bassist Sarah Brown, and Tracy brought the devastatingly sad Rory Michael Bourke-Mike Reid ballad, "In Tears." The last song on the record is an earth-shaking duet by Irma and Tracy on Jerry Ragovoy's "You Don't

An alternate cover shot from *Sing It!* L-R: Irma Thomas, Marcia Ball, Tracy Nelson. (Photograph by Rick Olivier)

Know Nothin' About Love," on which the two singers achieved a remarkable symbiosis of intensity.

During these sessions, another of Irma's interests became apparent because she and Marcia were both big fans of the television game show *Jeopardy*, and would try to schedule breaks so they could tune in. She said, "I'm a game show fanatic. I love *Jeopardy*, *The Price Is Right*, *Split Second*. I like game shows because, ironically, you learn a lot because they use a lot of everyday circumstances and everyday current events. So I pick up on a lot of that."

Roots music fans loved *Sing It!*, and it was a great success—it was by far the best-selling album that any of the three artists had achieved individually, reaching #6 on the *Billboard* blues chart and eventually topping 100,000 worldwide sales (a high figure for any roots-based, non-hit record). Music journalist Mike Joyce commented, "The trio's chemistry is hardly surprising. Marcia Ball and Tracy Nelson have long been disciples of Thomas's Crescent City soul, and all three singers are well versed in southern blues, country, and gospel styles. To find them in the studio collaborating after all these years would be a treat even if they were merely sharing harmonies and trading lead vocals on old songs. But several new tunes and a seasoned cast of musicians prevent *Sing It!* from becoming a purely sentimental exercise."[19]

In the spring and early summer of 1998, Rounder's Brad Paul oversaw a major US tour, on which the three singers were backed by the Professionals, with everyone traveling in two buses. Paul commented, "I remember that I felt I should have gotten some kind of bonus pay or combat pay for having to negotiate with Emile. And, you know, that's good. Any good manager is always looking out for his artist or her artist's best interest."[20]

The tour was booked by Jack Randall of Ted Kurland Associates, who recalled that the tour played almost every important festival and venue available at the time for a high-level roots-oriented act. Randall commented, "It was a really nice [tour], and Irma's band got the job done." Tour manager Ellen Karas had previously worked with Brad and Jack on a tour of Rounder folk artists. They began in the Southeast, performing at festivals such as City Stages in Birmingham, Alabama, working their way north to the Berklee Performance Center in Boston, then west to Fitzgerald's in Chicago, the Minnesota Zoo, and Jazz Aspen in Colorado. In fall 1998, the tour continued with two fly-in weekend runs with venues that included San Diego Street Scene, Bumbershoot in Seattle, the Long Beach Blues Festival, and the Monterey Jazz Festival.[21]

Irma said, "The tour was fun. We were on a tour bus—the ladies were in the back and the guys were up front." She recalled a humorous incident. "There was a time when Tracy came on stage with her dress inside out. She didn't realize it. I mean, Marcia and I were looking, and we kept saying, something's not right with that dress. So finally, when the set was over, we said, Tracy, did you realize you put your dress on the inside out?"

Almost each show involved an advance interview or two, but some journalists seemed only interested in stories that offered a touch of gossip or dirt. Irma said, "We didn't have any dirt to give them. We were three grown women, and we had respect for each other, so there was no trash among us. Then they didn't want to interview us because they didn't have anything bad to write."

Following the tour and sustained attention from the press, the record received both the W.C. Handy Blues Award for Best Contemporary Blues Album, and a Grammy® nomination. The three singers traveled to Los Angeles, when the Grammys® were held at the Shrine Auditorium on February 4, 1999.

Irma recounted, "That was my second Grammy® nomination, the CD that we did together. It started really from an appearance we did to promote our individual CDs on Rounder Records. We had so much fun together, we said, why don't we do this and put it on a CD? Just the three of us, you know. Of course, next thing we know, we're in the studio. And the irony of it, we're in the studio having this great time doing this recording and we were deciding what we're going to wear to the Grammys®, in jest, of course, and how are we going to act when we receive a Grammy®. And lo and behold, we got nominated. We were all shocked, but, you know, we didn't get it. But we had a great time having done that project together. Hopefully we'll do another one in the future."[22]

After returning home from the Grammys®, Irma reigned as queen of the irreverent Krewe du Vieux parade during Mardi Gras, riding on a mule-drawn carriage with duchesses Marcia Ball and Tracy Nelson as her court. This walking parade through the French Quarter, with its brass bands and mule-drawn floats, remains a hipsters' Carnival favorite, noted both for its excellent taste in music and its sophomoric humor (sub-krewes, responsible for individual floats, include the Krewe of Drips and Discharges and the Krewe of Underwear). Scott went to the ensuing ball as a member of the Mystic Krewe of Comatose, dressed as a zombie with white and purple face paint, and a black wig. Not surprisingly, Irma did not recognize him.

In the summer of 1998, Irma was invited to perform at the Porretta Soul Festival in Porretta Terme, Italy, where she was backed by an all-star Memphis band that included guitarist Michael Toles, keyboardist Marvell Thomas, drummer James Robertson, and a horn section that featured saxophonist Jim Spake and trumpet player Scott Thompson. The festival was organized as a tribute to Otis Redding, and most singers were asked by artistic director Graziano Uliani to perform one Redding song. Irma chose "I've Been Loving You Too Long," which brought the crowd of Italian soul music fans to its feet.

Uliani recalled:

> It was the first week of January 1997. I had decided to celebrate my birthday in Memphis, before flying to New Orleans. The mood in the Crescent City wasn't great in those days. There were rumors that some tourists visiting the monumental cemeteries had been murdered. But I had a goal: I wanted to bring Irma Thomas to the twentieth edition of my Porretta Soul Festival.
>
> Scott Billington had given me the phone number of Emile Jackson, Irma's husband and manager. I called him, and he set up a meeting for 12 p.m. at the Lion's Den, the club he ran with Irma. I booked a place in the French Quarter, then asked a taxi to take me to 2655 Gravier Street, in the heart of Mid-City.
>
> "Are you sure?" the driver asked me. "It's an odd time to go to that place."
>
> When I arrived, I knocked on the door of a small building, but no one answered. I insisted. After a while, a man peered through the peephole and asked who I was. I told him I had an appointment with Emile Jackson. I heard him talking to someone, who told him to let me in.
>
> I entered. In the center of the room, a barber was cutting the hair of a man who I assumed was Emile Jackson. He had the young man offer me a drink. I

> didn't want anything, but under the bar I spotted a revolver. A bit worried, I thought it would be better to accept. I took a Coke.
>
> When the barber finished, he stepped outside and shook the towel full of hair directly onto the sidewalk, not even bothering to sweep the floor. Maybe Irma would take care of it later.
>
> Emile got up, walked over to me, and, introducing himself, said: "I'm ready!"
>
> The negotiation wasn't easy. My shaky English struggled to keep up with Emile's accent. In Porretta, I had the Memphis All Star Band, led by Michael Toles, but the idea of inviting Irma without her band annoyed him. I left without being sure I'd have her at the festival.

Probably Scott Billington's intervention was a blessing. Irma Thomas did make it to Porretta. Uliani added:

> The show was unforgettable. After a ride through both old and new classics—including "It's Raining"—Irma earned a standing ovation with a soul-stirring version of "I've Been Loving You Too Long," a heartfelt tribute to Otis Redding, to whom that year's festival was dedicated. Her performance was perfectly in sync with the spirit of the place and the accompaniment of the Memphis musicians.

It was a hot evening, so Emile found the next best seat in the house. He listened to the concert live on the radio while sipping a beer in the gelato shop run by Graziano's son. Uliani continued: "A few years later, Scott Billington had the idea of having her record an album with that same band. In 2000, *My Heart's in Memphis* was released, a huge success. All of the songs had been co-written by Dan Penn, who had made his European debut in Porretta in 1994."[23]

A passionate soul music fan, Uliani has created his own "Soulsville" in this small town in the foothills of the Apennine Mountains. The local citizens have caught his infectious enthusiasm, to the degree that there is even a very good local gospel choir.

At the festival, Irma showed her curious side when she went on a hike with Scott. At home in New Orleans, she often joined a small group of women for morning walks, both for exercise and socializing. At Porretta, Irma and Scott somehow ended up at a trailhead, with a sign pointing the way downward to a church or shrine. Emile stayed behind as they walked the mile-long trail, past carefully maintained stations of the cross, until they came to a small white chapel that was flooded with sunlight and filled with

Irma at the 2006 Porretta Soul Festival. (Photograph courtesy of the Porretta Soul Festival archive)

fresh flowers. It was like stumbling into a dream. There was no one else there, and no apparent way for the flowers to have been placed there. When Scott tried to locate the trail again several years later, he could not find it.

Scott had previously made two "songbook" albums that showcased the work of writers Percy Mayfield and Doc Pomus, performed by singer Johnny Adams. Since Dan Penn had been such an integral part of Irma's recordings for so long, he thought, "Why not make an album of all Dan Penn songs?" Penn's repertoire was certainly deep enough, and he was steadily writing new songs. Scott and Irma approached him, and Penn agreed to coproduce an album of new and old material, all written or cowritten by him. Penn was clearly excited, with the primary request that his cowriters be present to be part of the studio band on the songs they had written or would write with him.

The album was recorded at Sounds Unreel Studio in Memphis in 1999, with musicians who included bassist James Kinard, drummer Steve Potts, and keyboardist Spooner Oldham augmenting the band that Scott had heard at the Porretta Soul Festival. The repertoire was mostly created for the project, but a few old songs such as the Penn and Oldham classic "I'm Your Puppet" were given fresh arrangements. Dan's cowriters, in addition to Oldham, were Marvell Thomas, Bobby Emmons, and Carson Whitsett. Irma sang live with the rhythm section in the studio, but her final vocals, as well as background vocals by ELS, were recorded at Ultrasonic Studio in New Orleans.

Dan Penn and Irma Thomas. (Photograph by Rick Olivier)

Dan had spent nine years in Memphis in the 1960s and 1970s, and he was enthusiastic about recording there. In the liner notes to *My Heart's in Memphis*, he told Robert Gordon, "I always said, and I still believe, that Memphis has the best recording air of anywhere in the world. It's a touch of the musicians. That's one part of it, but the other—I always put it down to the sea level of where it's at. Things sound different as you move around from sea level up into the mountains, and Memphis has always been down in that low bottoms. It's always sounded a little more soulful than anywhere else and that's the way this record sounds to me, a little more soulful." Irma was less mystical about the recording location, stating, "We could be in the middle of a cow pasture and it wouldn't matter. It's still Irma."[24]

By most accounts, the album was an artistic success, and it won the 2001 W. C. Handy Blues Award for Best Soul Blues Album that year. In his extensive review in *Offbeat*, Roger Hahn gave Dan Penn due credit for providing Irma with a fresh platform, writing that the "feeling of majesty and accomplishment establishes plenty of moments where it's easy to believe the Soul Queen of New Orleans may be in the best voice she's ever been, that she may be singing with more conviction, with more wisdom, more *chops*, than anyone in the business today, at least as far as *this* kind of music goes." He concluded by saying, "*My Heart's in Memphis* offers the chance to experience one of America's great artists working at the height of her powers."

Songwriter Hoy "Bucky" Lindsey, engineer David Farrell, Dan Penn, Irma Thomas, and Scott Billington, Ultrasonic Studio, New Orleans, circa 2001. (Photograph by Barbara Roberds)

But what was "this" kind of music? With its Memphis-style R&B horns, surging Hammond organ fills, Wurlitzer piano, and churchy background vocals, it might have been received as an exercise in nostalgia. Perhaps it was something else. Scott called it "part of our ongoing quest for a contemporary space where Irma could go creatively—honoring the musical roots that nourished her without being confined by them." It reflected an aesthetic shared by Irma, Dan, and Scott—a fusion of R&B, country, and pop that according to Scott, "aimed to let Irma be Irma. Maybe you could call it in this instance 'Great American Songbook, Memphis Style.'" It was a wistful sound. The songs, which were mostly ballads, embraced an adult sensibility that fit Irma, and she sang them directly, without irony. There was little chance of the album becoming a big hit, with radio increasingly dominated by hip-hop and machine-sequenced pop tracks. It certainly might have been easier for Irma and her team to have made a retro New Orleans R&B record that was aimed at her baby boomer-generation fans, much as the singer Sharon Jones was reviving a mid-1960s soul sound for a similar audience.

Hahn reiterated the paradox of the album: "When all is said and done, the truth is it's hard to describe exactly what kind of music this is, hard to

An alternate shot from the photo sessions for *My Heart's in Memphis*. (Photograph by Rick Olivier)

imagine what the audience for it is, and equally hard to defend it against charges that *My Heart's in Memphis* may be less than absolutely perfect. It's hard, even, to know what to compare this music to. And in that regard, you could say that Irma Thomas remains absolutely true to the path she chose early in life, exploring exactly what her feelings—her heart and her soul—tell her she should be exploring."[25] *My Heart's in Memphis* may have been a beautifully crafted work, but the critical momentum of Irma's earlier Rounder Records and *Sing It!* seemed to have quietly slipped away, and it was not a great commercial success. Scott mused, "Perhaps if this album were to be released today, twenty-five years later, it would have been better received. Both Irma and Dan are living legends. Irma's singing is breathtaking, and the songs are so good."

It would be five years before Irma would record again, but it was not for lack of desire on her part. Rounder Records was being cautious. Perhaps the market had reached its saturation point as the number of New Orleans recordings and roots music releases in general grew each year, all aimed at the same niche audience, however large it might have been. Coveted media spots such as a review in the *New York Times*, the late-night television shows, or a spot on National Public Radio required a big story. Just as *The Big Easy* film had been a catalyst for interest in New Orleans roots music, so had 1996's *Buena Vista Social Club* album jump started a craze for traditional Cuban music, and 2000's *O Brother, Where Art Thou?* film brought about renewed interest in bluegrass and old-time American music. Focus on one genre or another came in waves, after which general interest would wane—the very nature of popular culture.

On August 11, 1999, Thomas "Tommy" Herman Ridgley died of lung cancer at East Jefferson Hospital in Metairie, Louisiana. A performer during the golden era of New Orleans rhythm and blues, his catalog included over seventy recordings with several record labels. After his passing, Irma performed for a benefit for Ridgley's family at Tipitina's along with other artists such as Allen Toussaint, Ernie K-Doe, Marva Wright, George Porter Jr., and the Untouchables. Irma said, "He was the wind beneath my wings. He goes back to my beginning and I feel good that I was able to express my gratitude. If he hadn't brought me to the places where the talent could be heard, I could be washing dishes or waiting tables."[26] "He was responsible for my being in the business."[27]

Irma continued to tour, as she established a number of regular gigs at venues such as The Regattabar in Cambridge, Massachusetts, where she packed the house each time. She had taken to carrying a large notebook of the lyrics to all the songs she had ever recorded (later replaced by an iPad), so she could satisfy even the most obscure request, even if the band did not know the song and she had to sing it *a cappella*, as she had as a young woman in England. Sometimes, she would base most of her show on audience requests, which gave her fans what they wanted, but sometimes at the expense of a thoughtfully paced set. Irma commented, "I allow my fans to make requests so usually by the end of the night, I'm assured that I've at least pleased 95 percent of the crowd that has come to visit me. I love what I do and that's the joy I get out of it. And seeing the faces of those who've paid the price to come catch my performance and requested a song that they wanted to hear and got it."[28]

Irma's shows at the Regattabar marked the beginning of her relationship with booking agent Paul Kahn, the director of the Massachusetts-based agency Concerted Efforts, as he followed up on the venue's inquiry to Rounder's Brad Paul. Kahn remembered, "I learned early on that one of the keys [for being a successful agent] is to be able to think like the artist and understand their needs. What is the magic number to get bookings consummated?" All the numbers at the Regattabar worked because it provided first-class air tickets for Irma and Emile, along with a comfortable hotel suite. It became an annual gig. "The Regattabar was four or five nights, and I would tack on a New York City date, usually Saturday going into the Tuesday through Saturday at the Regattabar, or maybe a date after it. She would play the Lone Star Roadhouse in Midtown, or B.B. King's."[29] As Irma and Emile grew older, the first-class air tickets became a prerequisite, especially to accommodate Emile's tall frame and recurring back issues on long overseas trips.

There were a few snags along the way. Mort Cooperman, who booked the Lone Star Café and later the Lone Star Roadhouse in New York, became involved in an offer for Irma to perform on the popular Italian television show called *Doc*, which was broadcast on RAI Channel 2. Kahn recounted, "It was a multi-night, multi-day engagement. I was familiar with the TV show because I had booked Matt "Guitar" Murphy there on his first European tour with his band, which led to the reunion of the Blues Brothers Band and was a major tipping point for me as a booking agent.

"Anyway, they [Irma and Emile] missed the flight and they didn't make the gig. When I finally caught up with them and spoke with them, I said, 'What happened?' 'Well, we got to the airport and our flights were coach. So, we turned around and went home.' The other previous lesson I had learned from shows in Europe is that contracts are fairly worthless. You get a contract back signed and it states, 'We're providing this amount in cash and first-class flights,' and it's not followed. I kind of had it out with Emile and Irma. I said, 'You have my home number, why didn't you call me?' In any case, I had some other business in Europe with the Blues Brothers band the following spring, and we reinstated the booking. So, Irma did go with her band and play the *Doc* show. I was in Rome with them. So it had a happy ending."[30]

Kahn continued to represent Irma on a nonexclusive basis over the years. Along with a partner in France, he made an effort to book her for a summer on the European jazz festival circuit, targeting events such as the Montreux Jazz Festival in Switzerland and the North Sea Jazz Festival in the Netherlands, but it never happened. At one point, Irma asked if she could sign an exclusive booking agreement with him. Kahn said, "I think Irma was at a point where she was frustrated and she thought, 'Maybe if I give Paul an exclusive, it'll improve my business.' They wanted to work. They wanted to keep the Professionals working." As their relationship evolved, the exclusive part of the agreement did not work out, but Kahn continued to book her "when I'd get an offer that met her magic number," which included major gigs such as the Detroit Jazz Festival. At the Tanglewood Jazz Festival in Massachusetts in 2006, Irma participated in a Johnny Mercer tribute as a guest of Dr. John (who was promoting his *Mercernary* album), along with guitarist/singer John

Pizzarelli, singer Anne Hampton Calloway, and singer Catherine Russell (who is also Paul's wife). On this and other occasions, Paul, Catherine, Irma, and Emile had the opportunity to spend leisure, nonbusiness time together.

In 2003, Irma appeared on the DVD *Dancing to New Orleans*, a set of live performances of Louisiana music produced by Michael Murphy and Cilista Eberle, who were becoming the primary video documentarians of the New Orleans music revival. Murphy's initial experience was in radio, with a résumé that included the Blues Stage radio program and a stint at Boston public radio station WGBH, which sent him to New Orleans in the late 1980s to help record their Jazz Fest broadcasts. Eberle had a background in the world of narrative feature films. As the couple became ever more involved in the New Orleans music scene, they slowly built Michael Murphy Productions into a major producer of music-related video content, including hundreds of hours of live performances recorded at the New Orleans Jazz and Heritage Festival. Much of their early work at Jazz Fest was funded by the Japanese television network NHK (the equivalent of America's National Public Radio), while later productions would appear on the networks A&E, BET, and VH1.

In 2003 and 2004, Murphy and Eberle began preproduction of their film about New Orleans music, *Make It Funky* (transcripts of their interviews with Irma Thomas for the film were made available for this book), which was funded by Sony Pictures. Sony's only stipulation was that a major artist be added to the bill, which, after careful negotiation, turned out to be Keith Richards of the Rolling Stones.[31]

On April 27, 2004, between the two weekends of Jazz Fest, they staged and filmed a concert at the Saenger Theatre that seemed a summation of everything that adherents had come to appreciate about New Orleans music, and a celebration of its new "golden age." Among the artists interviewed were Troy "Trombone Shorty" Andrews, Jon Cleary, Cosimo Matassa, Aaron Neville, Art Neville, Earl Palmer, Bonnie Raitt, Kermit Ruffins, Irma Thomas, and Allen Toussaint. A number of outstanding musical performances were presented, including The Neville Brothers' "Fiyo on the Bayou" and Snooks Eaglin and George Porter Jr.'s "Come On (Let the Good Times Roll)." Allen and his band performed three of his own songs, as well as providing accompaniment for Jon Cleary and Lloyd Price. The film would eventually be broadcast on the BET, VH1, and Showtime networks, and released on DVD.

Irma was already booked on the day of the show, and she could not appear, so Murphy filmed a short set by Allen and Irma performing as a duo, separate from the live concert, in the otherwise empty Saenger Theatre. For many fans, it was a highlight of the film. Their new versions of "It's Raining," "Old

Records," and "Gonna Cry Till My Tears Run Dry," with an added reprise of "Old Records," show that their chemistry was intact and even quite magical. It is interesting that one of Allen's favorite songs in Irma's repertoire was not one that he had written, but the Doc Pomus-Mort Shuman-Scott Fagan song "Gonna Cry Till My Tears Run Dry." After this taping, these are the three songs they would perform together almost every time they shared the stage.

Irma also found time for a new nonmusical endeavor. After she received her diploma, she continued her involvement with Delgado University. At her graduation, she was asked by Melanie Deffendall, Professor of Sociology and College and Career Success Skills, if the college could start a program bearing Irma's name that would seek to encourage young women to enroll in college and finish their degrees. Irma, knowing how difficult it was to be a mother, performer, and wife while attending classes, thought it was a good idea, and she agreed. The Irma Thomas Center for W.I.S.E. (Women in Search of Excellence) Women program was established in 2002 with the mission of empowering women to fulfill their academic, personal, and professional potential.

Deffendall would coordinate times with Irma to offer mentoring sessions, usually on Saturdays between 10:00 a.m. and noon. "We would call, put out fliers, and let them know that I was going to be there. I would talk to all the young ladies who had children and who were contemplating quitting and not going and getting their degrees for whatever reason, and try to inspire them to continue their education. I said, 'Look, I did it, you can do it.'"[32] Tragically, Deffendall passed away due to COVID in the pandemic's early days.

In 2005, the W.I.S.E. program won the mentoring program of the year award from the American Association of Community Colleges. After Hurricane Katrina, the mining and metals company Freeport-McMoRan donated $50,000 to assist in the establishment of an official Irma Thomas Center for W.I.S.E. Women. In 2007, a physical location on Delgado's City Park campus was designated for the center, which made it possible for the program to offer a variety of support services such as lectures, workshops, career opportunities, women's health information, counseling, resource library, computer lab, use of office supplies, and a quiet space for students to study, relax, and network. Additionally, Irma made frequent guest lecture appearances to motivate the students.[33]

Irma said that hearing from women that she had been an inspiration to them to finish their degrees made all of the work in college and at the center worth it. Irma has also been an inspiration to her own children. Irma and her youngest daughter Andrea attended Delgado at the same time, but Irma was enrolled ahead of Andrea and graduated first. Andrea said, "One of the real memorable things for me was when I was attending Delgado, and I graduated from there. I was blessed to actually have my mother to be the guest speaker at my graduation, so that was awesome." Irma said, "I spoke at her graduation at Delgado, and instead of writing out a speech, I told my story to the graduating class."[34] Andrea furthered her education and graduated with honors from Southern University of New Orleans. Irma received an accolade for her academic career and service in 2010, when she was inducted into the Phi Theta Kappa Honor Society.

DISCOGRAPHY

Compact Discs

True Believer (Rounder 2110), 1992.

1. Trying to Catch a Cab in the Rain (Dan Penn-Jon Tiven-Sally Tiven) 2. Can't You Hear It in My Tears (Johnny Neel-Tommy Polk) 3. I Never Fool Nobody But Me (Doc Pomus-Mac Rebennack) 4. Smoke Filled Room (Dan Penn-Jonnie Barnett-Carson Whitsett) 5. Big Talk (Ken Hirsch-Mark Mueller) 6. Chains of Love (Henry Van Walls) 7. Heart Full of Rain (Michael Dan Ehmig-Tony Joe White) 8. Sweet Touch of Love (Allen Toussaint) 9. I'll Be Satisfied (B. Gordy-T. Carlo) 10. True Believer (Daryl Burgess)

Pamela Landrum, Earl J. Smith Jr., Charles Elam III, backing vocals; Cranston Clements, guitar; David Torkanowsky, keyboards; Sammy Berfect, Hammond B3 organ and piano; Chris Severin, bass; Herman V. Ernest III, drums; Amadee Castenell, tenor saxophone; Bill "Foots" Samuel, tenor and baritone saxophones; Alvin "Red" Tyler, baritone saxophone; A. J. Pittman and Frank Parker, trumpets; Chris Belleau, trombone

Produced by Scott Billington and Irma Thomas

Recorded and mixed by David Farrell

Recorded at Ultrasonic Studio, New Orleans

Walk Around Heaven: New Orleans Gospel Soul (Rounder 2128), 1993.

1. Ask What You Will (Doris Akers) 2. I Know Prayer Changes Things (Robert Anderson) 3. Careful Hands (Bessie Griffin) 4. Hold to God's Unchanging Hand (F. L. Eiland-Jennie Wilson) 5. No, Not One (Johnson Oatman Jr.) 6. I Will Say Yes Lord (unknown) 7. Walk Around Heaven All Day (Cassietta George) 8. Oh, Holy Night (Adolphe C. Adam) 9. Just a Little While to Stay Here (Albert E. Brumley-Eugene M. Bartlett) 10. Where We'll Never Grow Old (James C. Moore)

Donald Ramsey, Lawrence Baulden, bass; Herman Ernest III, drums; Anthony R. Brown, guitar; Sammy Berfect, organ; Dwight Franklin, piano, organ, vocals; David Farrell, tambourine; Charles Elam III, Earl Smith Jr., Pamela Landrum, Tara Darnell, backing vocals

Produced by Scott Billington and Irma Thomas

Associate Producers: Dwight Franklin and Sammy Berfect

Recorded and mixed by David Farrell

Recorded at Ultrasonic Studio, New Orleans

The Story of My Life (Rounder 2149), 1997.

1. No Use Talkin' (Cindy Bullens-Francesca Beghe) 2. The Story of My Life (Dawn Thomas) 3. I Count the Teardrops (Carson Whitsett-Dan Penn-Jonnie Barnett) 4. Cried Too Long (Lisa Mednick-Sarah Brown) 5. Love Don't Get No Better Than This (John Ellison) 6. Hold Me While I Cry (Carson Whitsett-Dan Penn-Irma Thomas, Jonnie Barnett) 7. I Won't Cry for You (Dan Penn-Carson Whitsett-Jonnie Barnett) 8. We All Need Love (Allen Toussaint) 9. Get Here (Brenda Gordon Russell) 10. Keep the Faith (Jeff Franzel-Nina Ossoff-Porter Carroll) 11. Dr. Feelgood (Aretha Franklin, Ted Lewis)

Charles Elam, III, Elaine Foster, backing vocals; Michael Toles, Dan Penn, guitars; David Torkanowsky, Carson Whitsett, Warner Williams, keyboards; George Porter Jr., bass; Raymond Weber, drums; Jamil Sharif, trumpet; Chris Belleau, trombone; Bill Samuel, baritone saxophone; Charles Elam III, tenor saxophone; Jack Williams, valve trombone, trumpet

Produced by Scott Billington and Irma Thomas

Recorded and mixed by David Farrell

Recorded at Ultrasonic Studio, New Orleans

Sing It! (Rounder 2152) with Marcia Ball and Tracy Nelson, 1998.

1. Sing It! (David Egan) 2. I Want to Do Everything for You (Joe Tex) 3. In Tears (Mike Reid,-Michael Bourke) 4. Love Maker (Gary Nicholson-Steve Cropper) 5. Yield Not to Temptation (Deadric Malone) 6. Heart to Heart (Sarah E. Campbell-Donnie Fritts) 7. People Will Be People (David Egan) 8. Please No More (David Egan-Greg Hansen) 9. If I Know You (Sarah Brown-Marcia Ball) 10. Woman on the Move (Irma Thomas-Dan Penn-Carson Whitsett) 11. He's Mine (Gary Nicholson-John Jarvis) 12. Shouldn't I Love Him (Homer Banks-Steve Cropper) 13. You Don't Know Nothin' About Love (Jerry Ragovoy)

Dave Torkanowsky, keyboards; Michael Toles, guitars; Marcia Ball, piano; Davell Crawford, organ; Lee Allen Zeno, bass; Raymond Weber, drums, percussion; Victor Goines, baritone saxophone; Ed Petersen, Derek Houston,

Joe Cabral, tenor saxophone; Barney Floyd, Jamil Sharif, trumpet; Scott Billington, tambourine

Produced by Scott Billington

Recorded and mixed by David Farrell

Recorded at Ultrasonic Studio, New Orleans

My Heart's in Memphis: The Songs of Dan Penn (Rounder 2163), 2000.

1. My Heart's in Memphis (Bobby Emmons-Dan Penn) 2. Keep It Simple (Carson Whitsett-Dan Penn-Irma Thomas) 3. Not Enough Time to Change (Carson Whitsett-Dan Penn-Hoy Lindsey) 4. If You Want It, Come and Get It (Dan Penn-Marvell Thomas) 5. Blue in the Heart (Carson Whitsett-Dan Penn-Jonnie Barnett) 6. I'm Your Puppet (Dan Penn-Spooner Oldham) 7. Irma's Song (Dan Penn-Irma Thomas-Spooner Oldham) 8. Life at the End of the Road (Carson Whitsett-Dan Penn) 9. I Do (Dan Penn-Spooner Oldham) 10. Woman Left Lonely (Dan Penn-Spooner Oldham) 11. Hurtin' for Certain (Dan Penn-Swain Schaefer) 12. The Joke Is on You (Carson Whitsett-Dan Penn-Jonnie Barnett) 13. Zero Will Power (Dan Penn-Donnie Fritts-Spooner Oldham)

Dan Penn, Elaine Foster, Erica Falls, Lisa Foster, backing vocals; Michael Toles, guitars; Spooner Oldham, Bobby Emmons, Marvell Thomas, Carson Whitsett, keyboards; James Kinard, bass; James Robertson, Steve Potts, drums; Scott Billington, percussion; Jim Spake, saxophones; Howard Lamb, trombone; Scott Thompson, trumpet

Produced by Scott Billington and Dan Penn

Recorded and mixed by David Farrell

Recorded at Sounds Unreel Studio, Memphis, and Ultrasonic Studio, New Orleans

Tracks

We're Gonna Make It (Gene Barge-Billy Davis-Raynard Miner-Carl William Smith) with B.B. King on his *Blues Summit* album (MCA Records 10710), 1993. Produced by Dennis Walker and Deny Diante.

There Must Be a Better World Somewhere (Doc Pomus-Mac Rebennack) on *Till the Night Is Gone: Tribute to Doc Pomus* (Forward/Rhino Records 71878), 1995. Produced by Scott Billington and Irma Thomas.

CHAPTER TWELVE

After the Storm

(2005–2006)

At Jazz Fest in 2005, Irma's position as a New Orleans music icon was more visible than ever. She performed at a New Orleans All-Star Musical Tribute with Dave Malone, Ivan Neville, Leo Nocentelli, Big Sam, and Allen Toussaint, as well as a tribute to the pioneering guitarist and gospel singer Sister Rosetta Tharpe, with Maria Muldaur, Marcia Ball, Tracy Nelson, Lana Del Ray, and Angela Strehli.

During the early part of the year, Scott Billington presented a concept for a new album to both Irma and Rounder Records, and he was finally given a green light from Rounder to proceed. Irma's reemergence as an artist had been news in 1986, but it was going to take something new to get people to pay attention again in the new millennium. He said, "We seemed stuck in that we were making rhythm and blues records in a style that was already decades old. The records were wonderful, but I think a listener who knew our work could imagine what a new record was going to sound like before even listening to it."

In his memoir, Scott wrote:

> I started imagining a different kind of Irma Thomas record, with acoustic instruments, with her voice front and center, and with songs chosen only because they would come to life when she sang them—songs that would sound good when inhabited by her voice. The producer and composer Allen Toussaint once told me that he often heard Irma's voice when he wrote, and now I was hearing Irma's voice singing new songs by Eleni Mandell and Kevin Gordon, and old songs by Blind Willie Johnson and Mississippi John Hurt. I called Irma and told her what I was thinking.

Irma Thomas at the Porretta Soul Festival, 2006. (Photograph courtesy of the Porretta Soul Festival archive)

"Well, that sounds interesting," she said. "Why don't you send me some of the songs?"

"I'll overnight [mail] them to you tomorrow," I replied. "You may think I'm crazy, but I can hear this so clearly."

A few days after she received the compact disc I had sent, she called.

"Scott, have you lost your mind? What am I going to do with this material?" she laughed.

Then, she changed her tone to something more serious and said, "But you know me pretty well, and I guess you really are hearing something, so I'll give it a shot."[1]

Still, she was not completely convinced. She said, "There were maybe one or two songs in the whole bunch that I really wanted to sing, the rest of them I just wasn't getting it. And he said, 'No, you're going to do all right. Stick with it. We're going to be fine.'" Irma said, "So I finally picked out some that I could live with, we'll put it that way." Sessions were planned for September 2005 at Ultrasonic Studio in New Orleans, with a core band of keyboardist David Torkanowsky, bassist James Singleton, guitarist Corey Harris, and drummer Stanton Moore. Irma and Scott continued to work on the song selection, which now included two new David Egan compositions, a vintage Doc Pomus song, Mississippi John Hurt's version of "Make Me a Pallet on Your Floor," and the Billy Taylor-Richard Lamb civil rights anthem, "I Wish I Knew How It Would Feel to Be Free." Everything was in place.

Then, in August 2005, Hurricane Katrina struck New Orleans. After multiple levees breached in the aftermath of the storm, Irma's home, the Lion's Den, and Ultrasonic Studio were all submerged. Everything in them was ruined. Initially, Irma was feared missing in the storm,[2] but she and the band had been working that weekend at Antone's Club in Austin, Texas. While in Austin and watching the televised news reports about the heavy flooding near their home in New Orleans East, Irma told Emile, "Honey, you know we don't have a home." The problem was that no one could go home because home was not there anymore.

Irma's friend Marcia Ball helped find hotels and longer-term housing in Austin for Irma and her band, until Irma and Emile left to stay with his relatives in Gonzales, Louisiana, about an hour upriver from New Orleans. Irma commented, "I call Marcia my sister, because she was there for me when we were stranded." Eventually, they bought a small home in Gonzales, where they would live for the next year and a half. Emile was the first to go back to New Orleans to survey the damage. He told Irma that he didn't want her to see the house, and he waited until he had visited several times before she finally accompanied him. The water had risen to the ceiling, and the back wall of the house was gone. Everything they owned was lost.

To many people, the idea of going to a recording studio to make a record might seem like a low priority under these circumstances, but that is exactly what Irma did. The team that Scott had assembled, along with engineers David Farrell and Steve Reynolds from Ultrasonic Studio, converged on Dockside Studio (where cell phone service was not to be taken for granted) in rural Maurice, Louisiana, in December 2005. Irma remembered, "We went to the studio in the country called Dockside, outside of Lafayette, Louisiana. And they had these living quarters. It was a nice setup—a little studio apartment. It was interesting because all of us had cell phones trying to keep in touch with the family and what have you. But you couldn't use the cell phones inside the studio. You had to go outside and stand underneath this tree."[3]

It was an emotional reunion because the musicians had not seen one another since the storm. Now, everyone was staying at the studio, sharing meals, and sharing stories.

After everyone settled in, Scott decided to start the first session with the Arthur Alexander song "In the Middle of It All." Irma recalled, "We weren't

Stanton Moore and Irma Thomas at Dockside Studio, Maurice, Louisiana, December 2005. (Photograph by Scott Billington)

sure which direction musically we wanted to go with, tempo wise, so Stanton Moore said, 'Irma this is where I hear it.' And he started playing the beat. And then each musician chimed in with what they could feel from what he was doing. And while he was doing that, David Farrell started recording and I just started singing. By the time we got to the end of it, I think everybody was crying because all we could think about was what we had been through. In the middle of it all, we were still doing what we loved to do. [In fact] all the songs seemed to fit in with what had happened to us. We had one called "Make Me a Pallet on Your Floor." Go figure. Can you imagine how many pallets were laid on the floor after Katrina? That was another one that kind of made us reflect on what we had been through. So it had such a good feeling, I think, because of us coming together. We were all scattered across Louisiana and even across the United States, for that matter. And to come together and come up with those songs the way we did and the feeling that we put into them was like therapy for all of us."[4] And somehow, the choice of songs and the stripped-down musical setting all started making sense. Irma turned to Scott and said, "OK, now I get it."

David Egan, who lived in Lafayette, became an integral part of the sessions. After a personal phone call from Irma to Emile with a list of things that needed to be done on the homefront, Irma gave David her idea for a song called "These Honey Do's" ("Honey do this, honey do that"). Egan came back the next day with a composition that gave the album a moment of humor. He also played piano on the other two songs he had written. At first, Irma did not understand the story of his song called "If You Knew How Much," and she was having a difficult time singing it. "Well," David told her, "Imagine that you're in love with someone you could never be with, a love that could not happen." On the next take, by the middle of her singing the song, tears were again streaming down her cheeks.

A few weeks after the initial tracks were recorded, Irma and Scott returned to Dockside to complete her vocals, now that she was familiar with all the songs, as well as to add background vocals and a few instrumental parts by Lafayette-area musicians (Sonny Landreth on slide guitar and Dirk Powell on fiddle, fretless banjo, and guitar). The background vocals were performed by Charles Elam III and Juanita Brooks, both from New Orleans, and local singer Marc Broussard. As a finishing touch, Scott had the idea to record the Stevie Wonder song "Shelter in the Rain," with just Irma and David Torkanowsky on piano, at Torkanowsky's studio in New Orleans. When it seemed as if the *a cappella* "I Count the Tears" needed something else, James Singleton laid down a bass part in his living room, which engineer Steve Reynolds recorded using portable equipment. The finished record was not like any other Irma Thomas album. In fact, the overall sound might be described as Americana, but with deep blues and jazz overtones.

Steve Reynolds commented that, during these sessions, he learned something important about making records with authentic emotional impact. It is common practice in multi-track record production to correct mistakes in a vocal performance—the wrong lyric, a bad note, or awkward phrasing—by "punching in" the singer as she sings the new lines. She will hear the old performance, then sing the new version of the part to be replaced as the engineer records only the new line. However, with Irma (and other singers that Scott had worked with, such as Johnny Adams), this technique served only to create a disjointed final track. Instead, after listening to her performance and considering changes that might be made, and perhaps talking about her approach with Scott, Irma would sing the song again, in its entirety, so the story and the emotion flowed naturally, even if the final vocal would be a composite. Of course, if a mistake had been made on her earlier records, which were recorded live to tape, the entire performance by the full band would have to be recorded again, but recording complete vocal performances in the multi-track era made an emotional difference.

Gradually, the people of New Orleans began rebuilding their city, including Irma and Emile, who were resolute about staying where they were in New Orleans East. Since their home had gone underwater, almost nothing could be salvaged. Everything except the foundation and brick walls had to be replaced. Irma said, "I felt the loss, but I've never been very materialistic. I like my things. Every woman does. But if it's lost, so be it, and that's the way I feel about the things I lost in Katrina. I'm still alive and I can make more music."[5] When they were finally able to move back, they kept the house in Gonzales. Still, it would be years before the neighborhood in New Orleans East was restored to pre-hurricane condition. Several politicians had advocated that the area be abandoned because of its propensity for flooding, and that housing stock in the inner city be rehabilitated instead, but the residents were having none of it.

Just before the storm, Emile and Irma had made the decision to sell the Lion's Den, and they had a buyer. However, after the sale was complete, the new owner decided that she had jumped into the deal without giving it enough thought. Emile refunded her money. The club was subsequently damaged heavily by the flooding in the aftermath of Katrina. Considering the cost of renovation and the general hard work of operating a bar, Irma and Emile decided not to reopen. She later told journalist Dean Budnick, "The thing I really miss about having a place like that was that it kept my chops up and it kept the band's chops up. We were able to sing a lot of stuff that we normally didn't get the chance to sing onstage. It also had that intimacy, where the audience felt close to us, and we felt close to the audience."[6]

The film *Make It Funky* had been scheduled to debut in theaters in September 2005. However, in the interest of not wanting to seem exploitative of the tragedy of Hurricane Katrina, Sony held back the general release, with subdued one-day premieres in Los Angeles and New York. Reviews were uniformly positive, if wistful. *The New York Times* wrote, "*Make It Funky!* is the most heartbreaking movie I've seen in some time, all the more so because sorrow is the last thing on its mind."[7] However, the film became a rallying cry for New Orleans, and was shown at numerous fund-raisers around the country. The cable channel VH1 aired the film with proceeds going to Mercy Corps and MusiCares. Further broadcasts soon followed on BET.

Then September 20, 2005, producer Ken Ehrlich (the longstanding producer of the Grammy Awards® show) staged and filmed two simultaneous benefit concerts called From the Big Apple to the Big Easy, at Madison Square Garden and Radio City Music Hall in New York, with proceeds going to the Bush Clinton Katrina Fund, Habitat for Humanity, MusiCares, and the Children's Health Fund. It was a star-studded double affair, with performances by pop stars such as Lenny Kravitz, Elvis Costello, Jimmy Buffett, Simon & Garfunkel, Bette Midler, John Fogerty, and Elton John. At the same time, it was a showcase for New Orleans artists, who included Clarence "Frogman" Henry, Allen Toussaint, Aaron Neville, Dave Bartholomew, The Meters, The Neville Brothers, and the Dirty Dozen Brass Band. Irma performed "Time Is on My Side" and the Bessie Smith song "Back Water Blues," in addition to a medley of "Brother John/Iko Iko" with the Dixie Cups and Cyndi Lauper. A year later, Ehrlich and Michael Murphy would produce a two-DVD set drawn from the events, *From the Big Apple to the Big Easy: The Concert for New Orleans*.

In early 2006, Irma and Allen Toussaint were both honored as the first post-Katrina recipients of the *Offbeat* magazine Lifetime Achievement Award. *Offbeat*, like its antecedent, *Wavelength* magazine, was another important element in the New Orleans music revival. Publisher Jan Ramsey and managing editor Joseph Irrera provided a platform for writers who delved into the history of New Orleans music, as well as a valuable promotional tool for contemporary musicians. In *Offbeat*, the world community of New Orleans music fans had a central location for news, as well as thorough listings of every local music event. Irma and Ramsey became good friends over the years.

The Grammy Awards® made time to acknowledge what New Orleans had been through, as well as the importance of the city's music. The ceremony on February 8, 2006, began with presenters Stevie Wonder and Alicia Keys paying tribute to New Orleans. Then, near the end of the program, Allen Toussaint, Bonnie Raitt, The Edge, Dr. John, and Irma Thomas performed Allen's song "Yes We Can Can." Irma stayed onstage to sing "In the Midnight Hour" with Bruce Springsteen, Sam Moore, and a large ensemble. The Recording Academy's MusiCares wing was one of the first organizations to provide financial aid to out-of-work Gulf Coast musicians (the organization hired New Orleans guitarist Reid Wick to oversee distribution of funds to musicians in need), which CEO Neil Portnow spoke about at the end of the show. The New Orleans segment was among the finest "Grammy® moments" created by Ehrlich, whose support for New Orleans music was unwavering.

Irma recalled the event: "We were invited to the Grammys® in 2006, and there was an early party that took place prior to the actual giving out of the Grammy Awards®. I think they were trying to help us earn some cash to try to get back on our feet. Allen and I had performed at this early party and when I got through performing, they called me back out on the stage because earlier that afternoon they had asked me two different times about what I missed and what I lost in the flooding situation. And I said, well, the one thing that I really regret losing was my nomination medals that I couldn't find after the storm because everything kind of floated all over the place. We were just talking in conversation. So after I finished doing my performance that afternoon on stage, they called me back out. I said, 'Uh oh, what have I done wrong now?' So I went back out on stage. Then the gentleman presented me with the medals that I had lost. And I just couldn't do anything but cry because I wasn't expecting that. I thought that was very beautiful of them to do that for me because I didn't ever expect to win a Grammy®. At least I had that I was nominated. And to me, that's just as important as actually winning the Grammy®. Enough that people thought enough of you to nominate you and respect your talent to feel that you deserve an award like that."[8]

On February 27, 2006, Mardi Gras went on, but not as usual. This time, it was not only a ritual, but a gesture of resilience. Tens of thousands of people were still displaced, living in Atlanta or Houston, saddled with mortgages for damaged homes that might never be rebuilt. Yet, the party went on. In the New Orleans tradition of dancing in the face of adversity, floats were decorated with blue tarps, and motifs of broken levees, vermin, and uncollected garbage. Writing in *New Orleans Magazine*, Errol Laborde called it the greatest Mardi Gras ever. He said, "Mardi Gras, the day itself, could not be denied. Celebrating hard was more than an escape—it was a mission."[9]

In the same spirit as Mardi Gras that year, Jazz Fest went on as scheduled in April 2006. In addition to her regular set, Irma was asked to perform the iconic song "Bridge Over Troubled Water" with its author, Paul Simon. Irma said, "We had what they call a soundcheck rehearsal earlier that day, and there weren't any other people out there other than the technicians and the stage people who were getting prepared for everything. And Simon and I were going through the song, and it was weird because when we got through, you could hear a pin drop. Then we did it again in front of the live audience and when we got through the same thing happened. You could hear a pin drop. It was like, Wow. I was just having fun. You never know how your voice will affect people, but I think being the song that it was, it gave you a moment to reflect. And I think everybody was more or less having that moment of reflection on what we had gone through. But yet here we are singing and having as much joy in our life as we possibly can. Once again, the glass is half full."[10]

Before the opening weekend of Jazz Fest, on April 25, the new album was released, with Rick Olivier's striking album cover photograph of Irma in a white headscarf and robe made her appear more regal and strong than ever. Called *After the Rain*, it was an immediate hit with critics and fans. The *Austin Chronicle* summed it up: "*Rain* frames her marvelous and supple voice with relatively spare arrangements provided by mostly acoustic instruments. The result is closer to what one might expect from Delbert McClinton or Marcia Ball: laid-back soul accentuating the rich nuances of her vocals. Drawing from contemporary writers Gwil Owen, Kevin Gordon, and Eleni Mandell, and mixing them with tunes from legends like Arthur Alexander, Blind Willie Johnson, and Doc Pomus, Thomas' willingness to take chances mostly pays off. Stevie Wonder's 'Shelter in the Rain' as the closer is worth the price of the disc alone. Accompanied simply by David Torkanowsky's piano, Thomas torches it up with the consummate grace of someone who's lived it over the course of a career that's exceeded more than 40 years."[11]

Concurrent with the horrible loss of life, the failure of the levees, confused government response, and the havoc of cleaning up and rebuilding, Hurricane Katrina was having the effect of bringing New Orleans culture to the public eye—at least for a short time—along with the realization of how fragile it was. Irma commented, "I think it took the flood to really make the city itself realize how important people like Fats Domino, Allen Toussaint, Aaron Neville, and the Neville Brothers, and those of us who are still around performing, those of us who are still alive are to the city, I think they took us for granted because we all grew up around here. But it made them realize the importance that we are for the city of New Orleans."[12] In the liner notes to Allen Toussaint's *Songbook* album, Ashley Kahn noted, "With a honed sense of dry humor, Toussaint calls 2005's Hurricane Katrina his booking agent, crediting the storm for rebooting his career as a performer after flooding him out of home and studio."[13]

That summer, Irma returned to the Porretta Soul Festival in Italy. Graziano Uliani remembered: "In 2006, a year after Hurricane Katrina, the Porretta Soul Festival paid tribute to the city and music of New Orleans, inviting Irma Thomas, the Neville Brothers, and Davell Crawford back to Rufus Thomas Park. This time, with her band, Irma left an unforgettable mark. In 2021, we created fifteen murals dedicated to the soul greats who had left their mark in Porretta, and among the queens was Irma Thomas. Her image, powerful and unforgettable, reminds us that music, just like life, always finds a way to remain, even when everything else seems to be falling apart."[14]

On September 14, 2006, Irma and Allen Toussaint would again be in the mass-media spotlight. Ken Ehrlich was enlisted by the sports channel ESPN to put together the pregame show for the first ABC-TV Monday Night Football NFL (National Football League) game of the 2006 season, which

Onstage at the Porretta Soul Festival, 2006, L-R: Irma Thomas, Kim Phillips (keyboards), Emile Hall (tenor saxophone), Robert "BJ" Harvey (bass), Arthur Bell (guitar), Larry "Choo" Campbell (drums). (Photograph courtesy of the Porretta Soul Festival archive)

also happened to be the first Saints game in the Superdome in New Orleans since Katrina. He immediately brought in Jazz Fest producer Quint Davis. Ehrlich remembered:

> Fortunately, we got Green Day and U2 to do the song called "Here Come the Saints," which Bono found [the ReBirth Brass Band and Sammie "Big Sam" Williams were part of the performance]. But they wanted someone to do the anthem, and they came to me with a couple of suggestions, not bad names, but they were pop names and nothing to do with New Orleans. It was just so obvious to us that the only way to really do that was to get Allen Toussaint and Irma to do the national anthem, which would be the first sound that people would hear. Forty thousand people at the Dome, you know, and was basically signaling the rebirth of New Orleans, the rebirth of the Saints.
>
> They didn't want Irma and Allen—they wanted this pop star. So at one point, I think I went to someone that probably had a little more influence than me, and I said, "You can't do this. If you open the show with somebody that's not from New Orleans and you have them do the anthem when you have these two national heroes, Irma and Allen, it's a bad mistake." So ultimately, they relented. With very little announcement, they came out. "Ladies and gentlemen, to sing our national anthem," I think they said, "The soul queen of New

Detail of Irma's portrait from a mural depicting women soul singers at Porretta Terme, Italy (Photograph by Johnette Downing)

> Orleans, a national treasure, Irma Thomas and Allen Toussaint." Well, I've been in places where people cried before, you know, cried happy, but that was incredible. I've never forgotten that moment.[15]

Several notable benefit CDs were also produced during this time. Rounder Records released a collection called *A Celebration of New Orleans Music to Benefit MusiCares Hurricane Relief 2005*, using New Orleans tracks drawn from its catalog and those of labels it distributed. All materials, from color separations to booklet printing to CD manufacturing, were donated. Irma's "Second Line Medley," from her live album, was included. She recorded her version of "Backwater Blues" for Nonesuch's benefit album for Habitat for Humanity, *Our New Orleans: A Benefit Album for the Gulf Coast*, which also included new recordings by Allen Toussaint, Dr. John, Eddie Bo, the Preservation Hall Jazz Band, and others.

Before the storm, producer Joe Henry had already recorded an album of songs by several of the great voices from the soul music era (Ann Peebles, Billy Preston, Mavis Staples, Allen Toussaint, and Irma Thomas) called *I Believe to My Soul* at Capitol Studios in Los Angeles in June 2005. When it was released later in the year, a portion of the proceeds were donated to Hurricane Katrina relief.

U2's guitar player, The Edge, was quick to act in providing support for New Orleans with his Music Rising organization, which he founded with music producer Bob Ezrin. The organization assisted over three thousand musicians following Hurricanes Katrina and Rita, in addition to providing tens of thousands of students with instruments. The organization provided one million dollars to endow The New Orleans Center for the Gulf South at Tulane University, and continues its disaster relief efforts today.[16]

In October, Irma gained an important new venue when she signed on for her first Legendary Rhythm and Blues Cruise, the company's first Pacific trip from San Diego to Cabo San Lucas in which she was coheadlining with Taj Mahal and Ike Turner and the Kings of Rhythm. She has continued to perform on either the Caribbean or Pacific leg of the Legendary Rhythm and Blues Cruise excursion at least every other year, often topping the bill. The 2015 Caribbean cruise was billed as Big Easy/Fantasy, and also featured Allen Toussaint.

In December 2006, *After the Rain* was nominated for a Grammy® for Best Contemporary Blues Album. Irma's fellow nominees were a formidable lot: The Robert Cray Band's *Live from Across the Pond*, Dr. John & The Lower 911's *Sippiana Hericane*, Keb' Mo's *Suitcase*, and Susan Tedeschi's *Hope and Desire*. The album had reached #12 on the *Billboard* blues chart on July 29, 2006, and was still selling steadily. It also won the Blues Music Award for Best Soul Blues Album.

The evening before the awards show, Irma, Scott, Emile, and Emile's high school friend Clyde Bailey left a pre-Grammys® party (where Emile's preferred drink of Hennessey was not available) to drive across town to the La Louisiane nightclub and restaurant on Overhill Drive. The club was a throwback to an earlier era, with a feeling of faded faux elegance—dark drapes and small tables—with live music performed on a tinsel-fringed stage surrounded by a wraparound bar. Henry Carbo, who had sung with Irma in junior high school, was the star attraction that night. Everyone stayed up well into the early morning hours.

The next day, at the pre-telecast ceremony of the 49th Annual Grammy Awards®, held at the Staples Center in Los Angeles on February 7, 2007, Irma, Emile, Scott, David Egan, and their friends sat together, waiting for the winner of the Contemporary Blues category to be announced. Irma recalled: "My husband was to my left. Scott was to my right. There were about five of us together sitting there. And when they got to the category where I was nominated, I'm sitting there with my head down and saying, 'Please call my name, please call my name, please call my name.' And so when they actually called my name, I said, 'Did I just hear what I thought I heard?' And I

Emile Jackson, David Egan, Irma Thomas, and Scott Billington backstage at the Staples Center in Los Angeles after Irma's first Grammy® win, February 7, 2007. (Photograph by Danny Clinch. The GRAMMY Awards® statuette is a registered trademark of The Recording Academy® and is used under license.)

still haven't moved. I'm just sitting there, and . . . I just hear what I thought I heard. So my husband stood up and said, 'Baby, you have to get up and go up to the stage to get your Grammy®.' It just never occurred to me that it was actually happening. It was like all of a sudden I was in this wall of no sound and I'm walking to the stage. And when I got there, I asked the young man who was doing the announcements and I said, 'Did you really call Irma Thomas?' He said, 'Yes.' I had nothing written out to say. I had no, nothing in mind to say because I didn't expect to win. This was my third nomination, so I wasn't expecting to win. But when I actually won it, I didn't have sense enough to jump up to go get it. But it was a beautiful experience, and it's just hard to explain. You have to really be there to get it.

"Then you go through a battery of interviews when you're going through the back, when you're going offstage, different magazines, TV cameras, and all that. When I got to one of them, one of the ladies had the audacity to ask me if they gave me my Grammy® because of Katrina. And I looked at her. I counted to 10, four or five times, and I swallowed four or five times and I counted again. I looked at my producer, Scott Billington. I said, 'Should I say what I'm thinking or should I say something nice?' Then he said, 'Irma, be nice.' So I said, 'Well, if that was the reason that they gave it to me, then I will take it back to New Orleans with pride and say thank you.'"[17]

In her acceptance speech, Irma said, "First of all, I want to say, thank you God. And thank you New Orleans. Forty-nine years you believed in me and it finally paid off."

At the age of sixty six, after almost fifty years of recording, touring, and trying to make the right decisions to keep her career afloat, Irma Thomas had won a Grammy®. She was duly feted in New Orleans, and perhaps as an acknowledgment of this achievement, she was inducted into the Louisiana Music Hall of Fame at a Ceremony in Mandeville on April 14, 2007.

DISCOGRAPHY

Compact Discs

After the Rain (Rounder 2186), 2006.

1. In the Middle of It All (Arthur Alexander) 2. Flowers (Kevin Gordon-Gwil Owen) 3. I Count the Tears (Doc Pomus-Mort Shuman) 4. Make Me a Pallet on Your Floor (public domain) 5. I Wish I Knew How It Would Feel to Be Free (Richard Lamb-Billy Taylor) 6. If You Knew How Much (David Egan) 7. Another Man Done Gone (traditional; new lyrics by Irma Thomas-Scott Billington) 8. Till I Can't Take It Anymore (Clyde Otis-Ulysses Burton) 9. These Honey Dos (Irma Thomas-David Egan-Corey Harris) 10. Another Lonely Heart (Eleni Mandell) 11. Soul of a Man (Blind Willie Johnson) 12. Stone Survivor (David Egan) 13. Shelter in the Rain (Stevie Wonder)

Charles "Chuckie C" Elam Jr., Juanita Brooks, Marc Broussard, backing vocals; David Torkanowsky, keyboards; James Singleton, acoustic bass; Stanton Moore, drums; Dirk Powell, electric guitar, fiddle, banjo; Sonny Landreth, guitar; Corey Harris, guitar

Produced by Scott Billington

Recorded by David Farrell and Steve Reynolds

Mixed by Paul Q. Kolderie

Recorded at Dockside Studio, Maurice, Louisiana

Tracks

Back Water Blues (Bessie Smith) on *Our New Orleans: A Benefit Album for the Gulf Coast* (Nonesuch Records 79934-2), 2005.

The Same Love That Made Me Laugh (Bill Withers), Loving Arms (Tom Jans) on *I Believe to My Soul* (Rhino Records 8122-73189-2), 2005. Produced by Joe Henry.

Whenever (Look Up) (Naomi Neville) with the New Orleans Social Club (Ivan Neville, Leo Nocentelli, George Porter Jr., Raymond Weber, with Marcia Ball) (Burgundy CD-80589), 2005.

CHAPTER THIRTEEN

Soul Survivor

(2007–2010)

Contrary to expectations, Emile found that the Grammy® win was detrimental to Irma's bookings. He said, "To me, it hurt us a little bit. Everybody thought we were going to go up [in price], but we weren't." In the post-Grammy® and post-Katrina world, many of Irma's dependable bookings went away, including those at the yearly Carnival balls of Krewes such as Endymion and Bacchus. According to Emile and Irma, the Krewes began bringing in national acts such as Kool and the Gang, and paying them much more than they had paid local acts. Ed Muniz, the founder and captain of Endymion for over fifty years, had known Irma since he was a teenager and had attended her shows at Germania Hall, so it was difficult for them to accept that his organization no longer wanted New Orleans music.

However, there were still new roads to explore. Between 2007 and 2013, following a suggestion from Quint Davis, Irma began performing a set of gospel music at Jazz Fest, billed as a "Tribute to Mahalia Jackson." This afforded her the opportunity to give two distinct performances each year: her secular show on one of the main stages, and her gospel set in the gospel tent. Sometimes she shared the bill in the gospel tent with other artists such as Marva Wright and Raychell Richard (2008); Pamela Landrum and Mavis Staples (2009); and John Boutté (2011). From 2014 until the present day, she has presented her own gospel set, now called The Gospel Soul of Irma Thomas. It was very important to her to perform her gospel set apart from her regular show, out of respect for the sacred nature of the material. For the same reason, she had never performed a gospel song as part of her regular performance in a nightclub or festival. She dedicated the first of these shows to the memory of her mother.

Irma Thomas performing her annual Mother's Day concert at the Audubon Zoo, New Orleans, 2009. (Photograph courtesy of the Audubon Nature Institute)

While she has made her career as a rhythm and blues singer, many of Irma's fans might be surprised to learn that gospel music is her first calling. Kalamu ya Salaam wrote, "In her own ultra-honest way, Thomas shared with the *Tribune* one of her deepest dreams: 'If I could do what I do, which is sing, and at the same time meet all of my financial obligations, I wouldn't sing what I'm singing now. I would sing gospel. When I'm singing gospel, it's a totally different feeling.'"[1]

She elaborated, "People don't realize how close I am to gospel as I am to R&B. When I sing gospel music, it is prayer for me. It's a way of expressing my thoughts, of asking for help or giving thanks for the process that I've been through, that I've been successful at. When I sing gospel, I'm very serious about it. It's nothing that I play with. And I have to remind folks that gospel music is not entertainment. It is prayer set to music. If they pay attention to the lyrics, they would be more mindful of how they react when they hear gospel music. I am very, very close to it because when I'm singing it, I have this special warmth that comes over me that I really enjoy having. I'm at peace. It gives me a peace that you just don't get from other kinds of music. You can get it, but it's not the same."[2]

Reflecting on the dual path of gospel music and rhythm and blues, Irma said, "I knew one thing, I did enjoy singing. I think a lot of that came from being an only child and realizing that if you got up in front of a bunch of folk and you sang, you got attention. I enjoyed getting the attention, and I still enjoy as much as I get while performing. In a round-about way this leads into the gospel side of things—when your steps are ordered by God, whatever it is he has planned for you in your life, it's going to happen whether you like it or not. So I guess God saw something, he gave me something that he wanted me to use in the way that he wanted it to be used. And this was the way it got me into where he wanted me to be—because after I got fired for singing on the job, I did start making a living singing."[3]

With Irma's Grammy® win still resonating, she and Scott were ready to embark upon a new album. The marketing team at Rounder suggested that they make a record with an all-star cast, teaming Irma up with well-known artists who were fans or who had been influenced by her. In theory, it was a good idea because the bigger story of Irma singing with a roster of well-known acolytes would be more likely to generate publicity, airplay, and overall attention than simply another Irma Thomas record. However, to Scott, that kind of record seemed like a career ender—a signal that creative ideas had run out, and a grab for the marketplace. Plus, the nature of records of this kind meant that the singers often had to record their vocals apart from one another, in different studios and in different cities, robbing the ensuing record of the chemistry that might have made the collaboration worthwhile. Then he had an idea.

While the guitar and perhaps the tenor saxophone were the fundamental instruments of rock and roll, in New Orleans it was the piano that held everything else together, from Jelly Roll Morton, through Professor Longhair, to more contemporary players such as Jon Cleary and Davell Crawford. Scott thought, "Why not make a record that features Irma with a different piano player on each song? The song selection could be as broad as it was on *After the Rain*, and we could reach out to the kind of artist/collaborators who would create a story for the marketing." Everyone he asked—Marcia Ball, Henry Butler, Davell Crawford, Jon Cleary, Dr. John, David Egan, Norah Jones, Ellis Marsalis, Tom McDermott, John Medeski, Randy Newman, and David Torkanowsky—said yes. The rhythm section of bassist James Singleton and drummer Raymond Weber would be consistent throughout most of the record, except for songs that would be recorded as solo piano and voice.

Several of the pianists engaged for the album *Simply Grand* brought new songs to the sessions, while Scott found others such as the new Burt Bacharach and Steve Krikorian song, "What Can I Do," which Irma recorded with David Torkanowsky, the rhythm section, and a string quartet. Bacharach himself took great interest in the session, asking for rough mixes and offering feedback as the song evolved. His melody was typically unusual, even tricky, but after living with it for a few weeks after cutting the track, Irma executed it with aplomb. Jon Cleary's "Too Much Thinking" recalled the original New Orleans rhythm and blues era, with background vocals by Elaine Foster, Erica Falls, Charles Elam III, and Earl Smith.

Among the cover songs, the collaboration between Ellis Marsalis and Irma on the Clyde Otis song "This Bitter Earth" showed a different side of her—a mellower, jazzy side that revealed her Pearl Bailey influence shining through. Otis, who had recently passed away, had been advocating that Irma record this song for many years, and it took this setting to make it work. Henry Butler's country/gospel reharmonization of the recent John Fogerty song "River Is Waiting" gave Irma room for one of the album's most joyful vocals, as Raymond Weber and James Singleton hit a groove that inspired Irma to keep ad-libbing at the song's end. When reprising her 1962 record "Somebody Told You" with John Medeski, the team thought that the key of the song would probably have to be adjusted down a notch or two, given that most singers cannot hit the same high notes as they get older, but it stayed right where it had always been, in the key of A.

Erica Falls, who had recently become a member of ELS, recalled the sessions, and how surprised she was that Irma was recording live in the studio. "I learned so much of how everything kind of came together, how you put a record together, because this was all still really new to me at the time as far as being in the studio and recording and how sessions went. I also learned a lot from the give and take of energy in the studio because we were fortunate enough to have her there. Most times we go in, the lead's already done and you just go in and lay down background vocals. But she was there and so we had the exchange of energy and it was really, really great to experience that. So I took a lot away from that session and I learned so much, you know, the bass line goes here and we're going to put this here and we can take this out and we can put this in. All of it was just really mind blowing to me. So I became a sponge and I just absorbed a lot."[4]

Most of the album was recorded at Piety Street Studio in New Orleans, including a session on Mardi Gras day 2008 with Dr. John. However, Irma and Scott also traveled to legendary studios on both coasts: to Sunset Sound in Hollywood to record with Randy Newman, and to Sear Sound in New York to record with Norah Jones and John Medeski. Sunset Sound had been the choice for artists as varied as The Doors, Crosby, Stills and Nash, and

Scott Billington, Irma Thomas, and Mac "Dr. John" Rebennack at Piety Street Studio, New Orleans, Mardi Gras Day, 2008. (Photograph by Rick Olivier)

Aretha Franklin, and also the venue for many Disney recordings. Randy Newman's piano was delivered there before the session. Sear Sound, built by the musician, audio visionary, and tinkerer Walter Sear, was designed as a space for musicians to record live, with a wonderful array of analog gear. It was Norah Jones's preferred recording venue (also a choice made over the years by David Bowie, Lou Reed, and Wayne Shorter).

The album release party for *Simply Grand* was held at Joe's Pub in New York, where Irma performed two shows backed by David Torkanowsky, a local rhythm section, and singers Elaine Foster and Erica Falls, performing the entire repertoire from the album. Tom McDermott was in town, so he was able to reprise his track from the record, the Louis Jordan hit "Early in the Morning." For the audience in the small venue, the shows were a treat. "Irma never sounded better," said Scott. "It was wonderful to hear her with the backing vocalists in an all-acoustic setting. I secretly wished that Irma could have toured with these musicians, and maybe I mentioned it to her. The Professionals had her repertoire down cold, but this sound was fresh, and it got away from the old-school R&B format."

The record was a steady, modest success, reaching #4 on the *Billboard* blues chart on August 30, 2008, and winning Irma's fourth Grammy® nomination. It also won the Blues Music Award for Best Soul Blues Album. Scott commented, "In retrospect, I think the concept might have been too ambitious. There are some wonderful performances from Irma on the album, but every time we settled into a session with one of the pianists, and finished our song, it was time to move on to the next session. We never established the sustained intimacy and vibe that we had with *After the Rain*. It might have made more sense to have collaborated with just a couple of the pianists—maybe Dr. John, Ellis Marsalis, or David Torkanowsky, but then we wouldn't have had the story." Even with the story, and with the efforts of the Rounder marketing team, the record did not generate the buzz of *After the Rain*.

At Jazz Fest in 2008, Irma had the opportunity to perform "Shelter in the Rain" with its composer, Stevie Wonder. Television producer Ken Ehrlich, who was an acquaintance of Stevie Wonder, was in the wings at the Acura Stage when Irma arrived, just before the set began. Ken asked her, "Listen, if I could broker some kind of [situation with] you going out with Stevie and doing 'Shelter in the Rain,' would you do it?" She said she would.

Since Stevie Wonder communicated with the stage crew through his headset, Ehrlich asked for access to the microphone to speak with him directly. Ehrlich reported, "Irma Thomas is here. She recorded 'Shelter in the Rain,' and if you think you could do just a head chart and just put it together on the fly, she would come out and sing it with you." Stevie gave an affirmative reply, and brought Irma to the stage. They performed the song as a duet, just as she recorded it.[5] She remained onstage to join him in singing "Superstition."

One might assume that walking on stage to perform with Stevie Wonder, without a rehearsal, might be a bit unsettling on the nerves. However, Irma took the opportunity in stride. She said, "I don't think I ever equate nerves with what I do because I enjoy it so well. First of all, I never thought I could make a living doing it. And now that I am making a living at it, I don't call it work. I'm having fun. When I tell my husband I'm tired, he'll say, well, how can you be tired? You say you were having fun. I say you can be tired having fun."[6]

Irma had the further distinction that year of being chosen as the subject of the New Orleans Jazz and Heritage Festival poster, which featured a 2006 painting by Douglas Bourgeois that was based on a 1964 publicity photograph. *Times-Picayune* art critic Doug McCash wrote, "It's like a weird dream. Soul siren Irma Thomas, dressed in a golden Jackie Kennedy pantsuit, beckons us into a lush landscape of blue irises, python-like oak limbs, and red-winged black birds that sing along to old-fashioned phonograph records. It's sexy, that's for sure, elegant but a little clumsy too, a touch obsessive, frighteningly fertile, somehow sad, and mildly forbidding. It's the 2008

New Orleans Jazz and Heritage Festival poster. The best the Jazzfest has ever produced, in this critic's opinion. The first in which the singular intensity of the artwork matches the singular intensity of the festival's hometown."[7]

With all the interest Irma was generating, she was approached by the well-regarded booking agent Ted Kurland, who had access to major jazz festivals and other large venues around the world. His agency had booked her before, and he believed he could substantially increase both her income and her visibility. He proposed partnering with New Orleans manager Adam Shipley, the former talent buyer and general manager of Tipitina's, who had always had a good relationship with Emile.

They tentatively began a new relationship when Irma was booked to substitute for an ailing Etta James, who was forced to cancel an appearance at a festival in Vermont. The offer sounded good to Emile until he learned that he would have to pay for the band's travel expenses and the 10 percent booking commission out of the gross receipts—a standard practice. Scott Billington kept encouraging him not to focus on this one gig, but on what the future might hold, especially the festival jobs in Europe that could pay tens of thousands of dollars each. Yet, for Emile and Irma, control over their own business and the importance of setting their own terms for each gig prevailed, and they decided to keep their business to themselves. Scott saw it as a lost opportunity because this move could have placed her on the same stages as artistic peers such as Gladys Knight or Patti LaBelle.

On May 6, 2009, Irma was inducted into the Blues Hall of Fame at the 30th Blues Music Awards at the Memphis Marriott Downtown hotel, reflecting her full acceptance by the blues community. Perhaps, as popular culture marched forward, older musicians who were embraced by niche audiences (in blues, bluegrass, or jazz) were fortunate to still have substantial fan bases, and the blues audience had become Irma's.

New Orleans itself was an outlier because music styles and rituals that were regarded as part of the "roots music" world remained a living part of the city's culture. Sunday morning gospel music, Sunday afternoon second lines, the Mardi Gras Indians, and traditional jazz continued to attract young people, many of whom embraced the culture with passion, without expecting anything beyond the joy of participation, and the satisfaction of being accomplished enough as musicians, singers, or other participants to move the traditions forward. The same rich culture that had nurtured a young Irma Thomas was still more or less there. Even if the nightclubs and record companies were gone, the heart of the music survived; music by and for the people remained in the neighborhoods from which it had originally come.

Allen Toussaint, Irma Thomas, Oliver Morgan, Cosimo Matassa, and Frankie Ford at Tipitina's, 2009. (Photograph by Rick Olivier)

Irma had now spent twenty-three years with Rounder Records, which celebrated its fortieth anniversary with a concert at Nashville's Opryland (the current home of the Grand Ole Opry) on October 12, 2009. Hosted by actress Minnie Driver, the concert included short sets by many of the key Rounder artists over the years, including Irma, Driver, Nathan & the Zydeco Cha Chas (with New Orleans pianist Henry Butler), actor/comedian/banjo player Steve Martin, banjo player Bela Fleck (with fellow banjo player Abigail Washburn and Dobro player Jerry Douglas), and singer-songwriter Mary Chapin Carpenter. Irma performed "River Is Waiting," as well as the first song she had recorded, "Don't Mess with My Man." The concert was released on CD and DVD, with the addition of tracks by bluegrass superstars Alison Krauss and Union Station with Robert Plant, and pop/jazz vocalist Madeleine Peyroux, which had been recorded and filmed elsewhere. The roster of artists represented a certain aesthetic: music that existed on its own terms, apart from the pop music marketplace, all sharing roots in different communities across America. Perhaps Irma most exemplified that connection as she joined the elite club of artists who had performed on the stages of both the Apollo Theater and the Grand Ole Opry.

Despite their long history, Irma and Scott Billington would do just one more session for Rounder Records. In 2009, to celebrate Irma's fifty years as a recording artist, Rounder Records released a compilation called *The Soul Queen Of New Orleans: 50th Anniversary Celebration*. The album brought together many of Irma's best Rounder recordings, along with tracks such as "Back Water Blues" that had appeared on other labels over the years. To make the record unique, Irma and Scott recorded three new songs with the Professionals, which, after over thirty years, still included keyboard player Kim Phillips. They began the recording process with rehearsals in her garage, just as they had on their first collaboration.

The record business was changing again as sales of physical goods—especially compact discs—began a slow and steady decline, a process that was accelerated when the catalog-friendly Tower Records chain went bankrupt in 2006. The coffee shop giant Starbucks, which had been an important outlet for certain Rounder titles, subsequently stopped selling CDs. Younger music fans were increasingly drawn to the free and fast-growing file-sharing sites such as Napster, and it would be a few years before the revenue-generating streaming platforms such as Spotify caught on in a big way, and before the comeback of the vinyl LP. Rounder, which at one time employed over one hundred people, shrank to a staff of thirty-five, and was sold to the Concord Music Group in 2010. It had become a large business (perhaps the antithesis of what the founders of the company had laid out in their early manifesto) that could no longer sustain itself. Scott stayed on as a full-time employee of the Concord-owned company until 2017, and he continued to pitch ideas for a new Irma Thomas album (which included a collaboration with Jon Cleary—a purely retro 1960s-sounding rhythm and blues album, which would have included several new Allen Toussaint songs), but he was never again able to obtain a budget to proceed.

Irma made guest appearances on records with several high-profile New Orleans artists. "Heart of Steel," her 2010 collaboration with the popular band Galactic (which featured drummer Stanton Moore, who had played on *After the Rain*), places her in a modern funk setting, with her voice sampled and layered to dramatic effect. The track demonstrated her openness to making a record in a new, nonlinear way that was not strictly based on a live performance. Producer Ben Ellman remembered, "We recorded her in a different context than the song ended up being, and we ended up taking her *a cappellas* and building the "Heart of Steel" song around them. When she [originally] sang it, it was very much more straightforward, maybe even a one, four, five type blues thing. In the end, we thought, hey, this is cool, but we could do better. Let's try to do something different, a little more modern. We literally just took her *a cappellas* and built around them."[8] Galactic picked up the torch of the New Orleans funk band The Meters, but have since forged a creative path that on record, utilizes sampling and other modern production techniques that have brought the New Orleans rhythm and blues sensibility forward.

For Mardi Gras in February 2010, Irma presided as the Grand Marshal for the Krewe of Grela, the oldest Carnival krewe on the Westbank of the Mississippi River in the town of Gretna, a suburb of New Orleans. In April her touring schedule sent her to Australia, where she performed at the Corner Hotel in Richmond, Victoria. In 2011, she returned to Australia to perform twice at the Byron Bay Bluesfest on Tyagarah Tea Tree Farm in Byron Bay, New South Wales, alongside Mavis Staples, Jethro Tull, and Osibisa.[9]

On August 23, 2010, Irma was selected as one of National Public Radio's 50 Great Voices, a list that includes artists such as Nat "King" Cole, Ella Fitzgerald, Placido Domingo, and Freddie Mercury. Melissa Block interviewed Irma for NPR's show *All Things Considered* during which Block said, "Thomas's voice is a true New Orleans treasure. The soul queen isn't just from the city—she's *of* the city, and her voice reflects that." Irma replied, "It's just something about the way we, as performers from this city, the way we do things. We hear extra sounds in our heads—extra beats, extra backbeats, extra rhythms that people from other parts of the United States just don't understand or get." Allen Toussaint seconded that thought by referencing Irma's phrasing in particular as being part of the New Orleans sound. Pianist David Torkanowsky added, "She is sort of ingrained in the genetics of this place. It's heart-wrenching when she sings. It's dripping with soul." Torkanowsky, who was featured on several of her Rounder Records, said that when he performs with Thomas, it feels like an intimate conversation, which is why he believes people love her. He said, "There's no pretense to her delivery or the sound of her voice or how she renders a lyric, and she won't sing anything that she doesn't believe in." Irma concluded the interview by saying, "I don't think my fan base [cares] about how many notes I can hit. They want me to sing the doggone song. If the song doesn't dictate adding all this other stuff to it, then why do it? Sure, I may be able to hit fifteen notes in one bar, but is it gonna help the song? No."[10]

Concurrently, New Orleans culture received another big boost from the HBO series *Tremé*, which ran for three and half seasons between 2010 and 2013. Produced by David Simon and Eric Overmyer, who had previously worked together on HBO's *The Wire*, the series tells the stories of a variety of New Orleans characters, some based on actual people, in the aftermath of Hurricane Katrina. Most New Orleanians felt that the show provided a sympathetic and largely accurate portrait of their city—the eccentricity, the beauty, and the crime. For people around the world who were captivated by New Orleans culture, it was a validation of what they had come to love, and a reminder of the fragile nature of the Gulf Coast region.

For musicians, it was a small windfall. Many of the lead characters in the show were fictional musicians who interacted with actual New Orleans players such as Tom McDermott, and the New Orleans Jazz Vipers. Almost every episode of the show provided a showcase for legacy New Orleans artists, including trumpeter Kermit Ruffins, the Soul Rebels Brass Band, and singer John Boutté, who performed the title song for the series. Irma made her debut as a television actor when she was given a small role as a backroom poker player, with Emile also sitting at the table, in which the trombone-playing character Antoine Batiste loses the money he had just earned on a gig with Allen Toussaint to Irma. Then, she takes the stage to sing "Time Is on My Side" with Allen Toussaint and a large band. Dave Bartholomew, the trumpet player, producer, and songwriter who was the primary architect of the sound of the first New Orleans rhythm and blues era, was the featured soloist.

Tremé provided a capstone for the worldwide fascination with all things New Orleans, a large-platform appreciation of New Orleans culture in the aftermath of Hurricane Katrina, and perhaps of the sensibility that New Orleans was a place worth saving. Many feared that rebuilding initiatives after the storm would leave New Orleans traditions behind, but the second line parades, satirical Mardi Gras floats, traditional jazz bands, brass bands, neighborhood po' boy sandwich shops, Mardi Gras Indians, and gospel choirs came back stronger than ever. Young musicians who were attracted to traditional New Orleans jazz began arriving from around the world, either playing on the street or gigging on Frenchman Street, which had evolved into a major entertainment district, replacing Bourbon Street as the nexus of New Orleans music for tourists. However, the same vigor did not extend to New Orleans rhythm and blues. No matter how many people loved the old records and the artists who performed at Jazz Fest each year, it was music of a particular time, and there were only a few young musicians willing or able to carry the tradition forward (notably Troy "Trombone Shorty" Andrews, Davell Crawford, Jon Cleary, John Boutté, and the band Galactic).

DISCOGRAPHY

CD

Simply Grand (Rounder 2208), 2008.

1. River Is Waiting (John Fogerty) featuring Henry Butler 2. If I Had Any Sense I'd Go Back Home (Rose Marie McCoy) featuring Dr. John 3. Too Much Thinking (Jon Cleary) featuring Jon Cleary 4. Early in the Morning (Dallas Bertley) featuring Tom McDermott 5. What Can I Do (Burt Bacharach-Steve Krikorian) featuring David Torkanowsky 6. Underground Stream (David Egan) featuring David Egan 7. Thinking About You (Norah Jones) featuring Norah Jones 8. Be You (Doc Pomus-Mac Rebennack) featuring Dr. John 9. This Bitter Earth (Clyde Otis) featuring Ellis Marsalis 10. Cold Rain (Brian King) featuring David Torkanowsky 11. Somebody Told You (Naomi Neville) featuring John Medeski 12. Overrated (L. Juby-S. Howard) featuring Davell Crawford 13. Same Old Blues (Don Nix) featuring Marcia Ball 14. I Think It's Going to Rain Today (Randy Newman) featuring Randy Newman

In addition to the piano players listed above:

Charles Elam III, Earl Smith, Elaine Foster, Erica Falls, backing vocals; James Singleton, Peter Harris, Tim Luntzel, bass; Kristen Miller, cello; Michael Skinkus, congas, bongos; Alfred Roberts, congas, tambourine; Jason Marsalis, Raymond Weber, Steve Jordan, drums; Patricia Doucette, viola; Hannah Thiem, Nathan Cohen, violin

Produced by Scott Billington

Recorded by David Farrell and Steve Reynolds

Mixed by Paul Q. Kolderie

Recorded at Piety Street Studio, New Orleans, Seer Sound, New York, and Sunset Sound Recorders, Hollywood

Tracks

I Just Can't Get New Orleans Off My Mind (Fats Domino) with Marcia Ball, from *Goin' Home: A Tribute to Fats Domino* (Vanguard 225/26-2), 2007.

"Got to Bring It with You (Rick Giles-Chuck Jones-Kim Wilson), "Let It Be Me" (Joe Brucato), "Your Ship Has Sailed" (Irma Thomas-Warner Williams) from *The Soul Queen of New Orleans: 50th Anniversary Celebration* (Rounder Records 11661-2214-2). Produced by Scott Billington and Irma Thomas, 2009.

“Time Is on My Side” (Norman Meade-Jimmy Norman), from *Treme: Music from the HBO Original Series, Season 1* (Geffen Records B0014910-02). Produced by Blake Leyh and Tony Seyler, 2010.

“River Is Waiting” (John Fogerty), “Don’t Mess with My Man” (Dorothy LaBostrie), from *Rounder Records 40th Anniversary Concert* (Rounder Records 11661-3277-2). Executive producer: Brad Paul, 2010.

“Heart of Steel” (Galactic and Jim Greer) with Galactic, from *Ya-Ka-May* (Anti-Records 87002). Produced by Ben Ellman, 2010.

CHAPTER FOURTEEN

The Legacy Years

(2011–2025)

In the third decade of the new century, Irma and Emile were living comfortably and well-positioned, with the luxury of being choosy about which gigs she would accept. She did not need the money since she and Emile had built a secure retirement with their savings and real estate investments. Yet she continued to sing, and her voice was in such good shape that she surprised herself. Ben Sandmel wrote:

> After 55 years in the music business, Thomas' voice has aged like a fine wine. It is slightly deeper and richer than in decades past, yet she has not suffered any loss of range, pitch or nuance. As she told the New Orleans *Times-Picayune* in 2013, "A lot of folks who are in this business at [my] age, their voices are on the way out the door. They're straining to get a halfway decent note out. I'm blessed. I don't have that problem. In fact, I'm finding that my voice seems to be getting a little stronger. I'm able to hit notes that I didn't think I could hit. Maturity helps. I'm thankful that I'm still capable."[1]

The era of classic New Orleans rhythm and blues had now become a sort of mythology for the music's most devoted fans, with artists such as Irma Thomas and Allen Toussaint occupying rarified spots in the pantheon, and others such as the pianist James Booker, who was little celebrated during his lifetime, ascending to sainthood. Among the most important manifestations of this phenomenon were the Ponderosa Stomp concerts, symposiums, and foundation. Organized by the passionate superfan Ira "Dr. Ike" Padnos, the

Irma Thomas at Esplanade Studio, New Orleans, April 2024. (Photograph by Daymon Gardner, courtesy of Newvelle Records)

Ponderosa Stomp sought to bring attention to artists from the past who might otherwise have been forgotten. Irma was a star of the 2015 edition of the event, which also featured fellow 1960s-era singers Mable John, Brenda Holloway, Betty Harris, and Barbara Lynn, held at the Rock'n'Bowl music and bowling venue in New Orleans. Nevertheless, Irma was far from done with her career, and far from forgotten. Retirement was not a word in her vocabulary, and she continued to find the kinds of new platforms that eluded many of her peers.

Sadly, on March 6, 2011, Irma lost her mother, who died of colon cancer at the age of ninety-four. Irma had last visited her mother in California in 2006, where she was living with Jean Marie, but they had stayed in touch by phone. Irma made arrangements for the funeral and cremation (her mother's choice), and she sang at the service. "I had some moments where things were a little rough for me in terms of my position on what I had to do. And I really wasn't able to really grieve until a couple of weeks or so later after I got back to New Orleans." She recalled her mother as a very kind person who would "give you her last dime," a view shared by Irma's children. She laughed when she said that her mother had spoiled James.

In 2012, Irma had another chance to explore her jazz side with a collaboration with the Preservation Hall Jazz Band on "May Ev'ry Day Be Christmas," a swinging Louis Jordan song that was part of a holiday compilation called *Holidays Rule*. The label was Hear Music, a company that had been acquired by Starbucks, and that was now a joint venture between the coffee company and Concord Music. The same year, a life-size statue of Irma was erected in the French Quarter's Legends Park at 311 Bourbon Street as a monument to iconic New Orleans music makers. Sculptures of other artists in the same courtyard are Fats Domino, Ronnie Kole, Pete Fountain, and Al Hirt.

The accolades kept coming, as Irma won the 2013 and 2014 Blues Music Awards for Soul Blues Female Artist. Then, for six nights in November 2015, Irma again had the opportunity to try her hand at acting, playing herself in a musical production at the Anthony Bean Community Theater and Acting School at 1333 South Carrollton Avenue under the direction of Anthony Bean. The theater and school was established in the spring of 2000 to meet the growing demand of New Orleans area residents seeking a quality and culturally diverse performing arts venue.

Simply Irma, A Musical Play, after the title of her live album, *Live! Simply The Best*, documented the pitfalls and success of her dramatic career. According to the theater website, "A large cast of singers/dancers and actors will have you singing and dancing in the aisles to her many hits, such as, 'It's Raining,' 'You Can Have My Husband,' 'Ruler of My Heart,' 'I Wish Someone Would Care,' 'Hip Shakin' Mama,' and many, many more."[2]

It was Bean's first attempt at a musical, and the production was a local success. Although Irma was delighted by the experience, she found it challenging at times. She said, "I'm spontaneous. I like that spontaneity between me and the audience. When you're doing a play as such, you have to stick to the script because other people have to bounce off of your cues, which made it real interesting because one night I forgot to do something. And of course it just kind of screwed up everything. But it went OK. We ironed it out, but it was fun."[3]

Irma's middle daughter Tina, who was assistant director of the play, said the event was memorable because she had the opportunity to sing onstage with her mother. Tina considers herself more a dancer than a singer, and recalled that when the family lived in California, she and her dance partner/brother, James, would open shows for Irma. However, this play offered a rare mother-daughter vocal duet for the Thomas family. Irma's eldest daughter Jean Marie praised her siblings for having their mother's musical talent, something she felt she did not share with them, and said, "Mom gave me her face, but not her voice." During the play's second run, Tina wrote out Irma's lines in a book to make it easier for Irma to remember and to stick to the

Irma Thomas and Tina Thomas performing in *Simply Irma, A Musical Play.* (Photograph courtesy of Tina Thomas)

script. The technique worked because it seemed perfectly natural that Irma would be reading from the book of her own life to the audience.

The year also brought news of the death of Allen Toussaint, who suffered a heart attack at the age of seventy-seven in his hotel room on November 10, 2015, after giving a concert at the Teatro Lara in Madrid, Spain. He had remained a vital creative force, and was relishing his renewed career as a performing artist, especially with the album made with Elvis Costello, *The River in Reverse*. In his later years, Allen had become a symbol of the dignity and resilience of New Orleans, just as Irma had. He was always dressed elegantly in custom-tailored Brioni suits that he bought at Rubenstein Brothers in New Orleans (albeit sometimes worn with Birkenstock sandals and white socks), and his audiences loved his modesty and quiet humor, even if he masked his inherent shyness with a kind of formal politeness as he introduced his songs. His solo album *Songbook* had been released in 2013, and he was working on a new album with producer Joe Henry that included his reimagination of several of Professor Longhair's compositions as slowed-down "classical" pieces. Only a few months before he died, he had sent Irma a CD with ten new songs for her to consider recording. Allen's passing was especially hard

Irma surrounded by her children at her seventy-fifth birthday party at the Irma Thomas Center for W.I.S.E. Women. L-R: Andrea Thomas Gibbs, Jean Marie Thomas, Irma Thomas, Tina Thomas, James Thomas. (Photograph courtesy of Tina Thomas)

on the New Orleans music community because he had been a fulcrum for so many other artists. Among many tributes was "Yes We Can Can: An Allen Toussaint Salute" on July 20, 2016, at the Hollywood Bowl amphitheater in Los Angeles, at which Irma performed.

Irma celebrated her seventy-fifth birthday at the W.I.S.E. Women Center on February 13, 2016. "Irma's 75th Birthday Bash" was written on mock 45 RPM records that hung from the ceiling, and the space was filled with photographs of Irma throughout the years. Music was provided by Bobby Cure and the Summertime Blues, Meters guitarist Leo Nocentelli, and the Professionals, with her son James Thomas providing vocals after a short set by Irma herself.[4]

Between September and November 2017, Irma embarked on the Heart and Soul Tour, playing thirty-eight venues in twenty-four states, plus Washington, DC, with the gospel group The Blind Boys of Alabama and the Preservation Hall Legacy Quintet (a group of Hall-associated players assembled for the occasion when the actual Preservation Hall Jazz Band had too many conflicts to join the tour). The Preservation Hall group opened the show, after which they were joined by the Blind Boys and their own band. After intermission,

Irma sang a set backed by a hybrid of both bands. In keeping with her principle of not mixing gospel and secular music, she sang only her rhythm and blues material. Chris Goldsmith, who put together the concept and booked the tour, commented, "It was a great wonderful show, especially the one I saw at the Belly Up [Tavern, in Solana Beach, California]."[5]

Irma also tried something different in 2017, when she collaborated on a children's song with the coauthors of this book—the children's musician and author Johnette Downing and producer Scott Billington. At Johnette's 2016 concert for children in the Kids Tent at Jazz Fest, Irma and her daughter Tina, a preschool teacher who uses Johnette's music and books in her classroom, could be seen dancing in the audience. After the concert, Irma commented that she would like to work on a song together. Johnette's 1950s-style doo-wop song "Poor Worry Anna" seemed like an ideal opportunity for a duet, and the resulting harmonized performance was a highlight of Johnette's 2019 *Swamp Romp* children's album, which included a variety of Louisiana roots music styles.

The song was recorded on September 19, 2017, at the Rhythm Shack in the Riverbend neighborhood of New Orleans by engineer and owner Jake Eckert, and produced by Downing and Billington. The minimalist instrumentation of two ukuleles played by Johnette and Scott, arco and pizzicato bass by James Singleton, and drums by Doug Belote lays the gentle bed for the vocals. On the first take, Irma sang the song flawlessly, but the producers asked her to sing it one more time for good measure. After the second take, Irma listened to the playback, and said that it sounded good to her, if it sounded good to them. When she left the studio, Jake looked at Johnette and said, "You just recorded a duet with Irma Thomas, and that's forever." The realization that children would hear Irma Thomas singing on a children's album filled the room with joy.

After the recording was released, Irma performed the song with Johnette and Scott at Jazz Fest in April 2019 in the Kids Tent—one of the few Jazz Fest stages on which she had not previously appeared. It was a poignant moment for all as Irma connected with yet another generation. Two of Irma's own children, Tina and Andrea, were in the audience dancing with the parents and students from Tina's class.

On May 19, 2018, Irma was bestowed with an Honorary Doctorate of Letters degree from Tulane University in New Orleans. During the commencement ceremony at the Mercedes-Benz Superdome, Dr. Thomas sang her 1962 hit "It's Raining" with Dr. Michael White's Original Liberty Jazz Band. Irma told Eve Abrams of NPR's *Morning Edition* about how it felt to earn her undergraduate degree at Delgado Community College: ". . . when

Irma Thomas and Johnette Downing at the Rhythm Shack Studio, New Orleans, September 2017. (Photograph by Scott Billington)

you go get your education, you've *earned* that. You don't have to depend on nobody, but you."[6] Tulane University president Mike Fitts remarked about the four honorary degree recipients that year (James H. Clark, Steve Gleason, Dr. Paul E. Farmer, and Irma Thomas), "Each of these individuals reflect the best of humanity through their achievements, their triumphs over adversity and their service to others."[7]

In September 2018, at the Ryman Auditorium in Nashville, Irma was presented with the Americana Music Association's Lifetime Achievement Award for Performance. Under the leadership of the association's director Jed Hilly, the term "Americana" had become expansive, embracing more than the tradition-leaning "alternative country" music that the term had first described. The organization began recognizing all the diverse roots music genres that were a part of the American musical identity, which that year were represented by Rosanne Cash (the Spirit of Americana Free Speech Award); k. d. lang (the Americana Trailblazer Award); Buddy Guy (Lifetime Achievement Award for Instrumentalist); Irma Thomas (Lifetime Achievement Award for Performance); and Olivia Records founders Cris Williamson and Judy Dlugacz (Jack Emerson Lifetime Achievement Award for Executive).

After receiving her award, Irma sang "Time Is on My Side," backed by Buddy Miller's all-star band, with the Nashville gospel quartet The McCrary Sisters providing background vocals. Just as Irma began singing, there was a malfunction with the house sound system and her vocal microphone went silent. Since she could still hear herself in the stage monitors, she didn't stop. Remarkably, the power of her voice filled the Ryman, audible above the amplified band. At the end of the song, she received a standing ovation. However, the applause would not stop, and once the sound system was repaired, it was clear that the clamor would not end until she sang the song again, with full amplification. She then gave what was likely among the most impassioned performances ever to resonate within the venue's hallowed walls. The audience was on its feet again, having been transported to a place that only a singer of Irma's communicative skill could take them.

The same year, Irma's relationship with guitarist and singer Walter "Wolfman" Washington came full circle when she recorded a vocal duet with him on his album *My Future Is My Past*, which was produced by Galactic's Ben Ellman. Walter chose the David Egan song "Even Now," which he had learned when performing as a sideman on Johnny Adams's final album, *Man of My Word*, in 1998. Ellman chose a stripped-down sound for the track, with only pianist David Torkanowsky, bassist James Singleton, and drummer Stanton Moore supporting the duo's emotive performance. Irma liked the song enough to add it to her live set.

During this time, Irma and Emile developed a closer bond with their grandson Isaiah Gibbs, Andrea's son (whom they affectionately call Emile Jr.). Isaiah said, "I was with my grandma a lot because she would pick me up from school almost every day. Sometimes they'd do rehearsals in the garage, and I would sit up in there and listen, and just be around them and be in the music environment because that's what I do now. I'm a producer and an artist, and I feel like I got my musical gift from her.

"One thing I respect the most about my grandma is that she never looked at herself in the mirror and thought she was a superstar. She was always humble, and she would always treat people with respect. Every time she would see a fan or a supporter, she would actually have a conversation with them. It was always a very wholesome moment, and it always makes me smile when I see that happen. But yeah, I love my grandma to death. I'd do anything for her."

With firm direction from Irma that the lyrics had to be clean, Isaiah wrote a rap to go along with Irma's version of "Simply the Best," and he performed it with her for two consecutive years at Jazz Fest. He said, "Being on stage with her was a surreal feeling because at that time I was just starting my rap career. But when I got on that stage for the first time and saw all those people, it was kind of gut-wrenching because how do you get over this fear of being in front of all these people? That's not even the most amount of people she's sung in front of, so I know it's a crazy skill to have—to be composed like that and still be able to entertain. That's some good energy. It was fun being able to perform next to her."[8] In 2025, Isaiah enrolled in the Music Business program at Loyola University in New Orleans.

In January 2020, the filmmaker Ben Chace approached the French boutique record label Newvelle Records, which specializes in audiophile-quality vinyl LPs, about backing a new film/recording project that would include performances by several New Orleans music legends. He was already working with the label, making films of sessions with its jazz artists such as Jack DeJohnette, Bill Frisell, and Billy Lester, and he had recently moved to New Orleans. The project resulted in the film *Music Pictures: New Orleans*, as well as a boxed set of vinyl LPs, with one disc each by Little Freddie King, Jon Cleary, Ellis Marsalis Jr., and Irma called *New Orleans Collection: Complete Set*. Irma's eleven-song album, *Love Is the Foundation*, was her first full album since her Grammy®-nominated *Simply Grand*. Irma said, "I picked through the ones [songs] I liked and we decided on how many, and went into Esplanade Studios [New Orleans], and did it just before the COVID thing started."[9]

The album features New Orleans favorites Johnny Vidacovich on drums; Kyle Roussel on piano, Wurlitzer, and B3 organ; and Alfred "Uganda" Roberts on congas, as well as Stephen Daly on electric and pedal steel guitar; Paul Defiglia on electric and upright bass; Andrew Baham on trumpet; Roderick Paulin on saxophone; Terrence Taplin on trombone; and Paggy Prine, Sierra Green, and Kyshona Armstrong on backing vocals. Most of Irma's vocal performances were recorded live in the studio.

Irma said, "I always choose songs that have good storylines, and, on this particular session, they all had great storylines. May not have been some that I would do or say personally, but you don't always look at it from a personal standpoint. You look at it like a script, and you are playing a role and telling a story and you want it to be believable. So you have to picture yourself in that. What would you do if you were in that position? It makes it easier to sing because in your head while you're singing it, you are that person in that position. Since I've been around since mud, I've had a lot of life and living under my belt, so it's not hard for me to put myself in a lot of those positions."[10]

New Orleans jazz pianist Ellis Marsalis Jr. often said that when he listened to his earlier records, he wondered why he sounded like he was in a hurry. As he aged, he learned to slow it down and not be in such a rush—that it was as much about what not to play as it was what to play and when. In his later music, we hear the space between the notes. Irma, at the age of eighty, seems

Irma Thomas and Ben Chace at Esplanade Studio, New Orleans. (Photograph by Daymon Gardner, courtesy of Newvelle Records)

to have taken this approach on songs such as Freddie McKay's "Picture on the Wall," where she settles in and takes her time with the delivery.

The album was released in 2020, both as part of the boxed set of vinyl LPs and as a separate disc. The film (which also includes performances by the Tremé Brass Band), *Music Pictures: New Orleans*, premiered on June 12, 2022, at the Tribeca Film Festival in New York, with Irma and Little Freddie King performing live at the screening. Chace had produced only one previous documentary short, but his live footage from the recording sessions, paired with interviews with the musicians, give the film a compelling immediacy.

Audiophile Audition called the album a "masterpiece." A review in *Offbeat* stated: "Thomas sounds like a precious jewel placed in an exquisite setting. The whole package is a work of art, from the striking black and white cover photograph by Daymon Gardner, a headshot portrait in meticulous detail that seems to reveal something deep and essential in Thomas's character; to the art museum quality graphic design and the opaque pearl vinyl disc that graces your turntable like a designer outfit."[11]

When writer Keith Spera complimented Irma on the ultra-close-up album cover photograph, she said, with her typical dry wit, "It looks like me." He also asked her about the inside photograph, but she admitted that she had not yet opened the album even though she had a record player. When asked why not, she replied, "I was on the recording session, so I know what it sounds like," and then she laughed.[12]

In 2021, Cilista Eberle and Michael Murphy were approached by Peggy Scott Laborde of WYES-TV in New Orleans with the idea of producing a documentary film about Irma Thomas, on the occasion of Irma's eightieth birthday. The film would be cofunded by WYES and the Jazz and Heritage Foundation. Eberle and Murphy's first call was to Irma, who affirmed her confidence in their work. She told them, "I trust you completely, but here's what I want you to do. I want you to make a program so that when I'm gone, when I've passed on, my grandchildren and my great-grandchildren can look at that show and have a really good idea who I was as a person, who I was as an artist. Can you make that?" Michael replied, "Yes, we can do this."[13]

My Life in Music is a triumph of documentary filmmaking, built around interviews with Irma and associates such as Ken Ehrlich, Bonnie Raitt, Alison Toussaint-LeBeaux, Ledisi, and Scott Billington. Since Eberle and Murphy had filmed and recorded many of Irma's musical performances over the years, they were able to include live versions of a broad cross-section of her repertoire. With distribution through American Public Television, the documentary was eventually broadcast on 90 to 95 percent of public television stations in the United States, and it won a Suncoast Regional Emmy Award. Murphy, at the time of this writing, was still hoping for a worldwide commercial release. Irma won her own Emmy award for the program.

Commenting on his long working relationship with Irma, Murphy said, "You meet Irma, you talk to Irma, and I guess what comes to mind is that sometimes you can meet somebody and you kind of wonder, the person I just met, is he or she really like that? Or was that like a façade? Is there another agenda?"[14] Michael, as well as Irma's friends and acquaintances, will tell you there never is. She truly is just Irma.

Part of being "just Irma" is her direct, honest, and open approach to talking about her life, career, and her health. When she was in her late seventies, Irma went to her doctor for her annual checkup. The doctor asked how she felt, and she told him she felt fine. Then he asked, "But how do you really feel?" Irma told him that she felt tired now and then, but that she attributed it to old age. Her doctor told her that it was not from old age, but that she was suffering atrial fibrillation (AFib), a common heart condition that causes an irregular and often rapid heartbeat in the upper chambers of the heart. He sent her to a heart specialist at Ochsner Hospital who performed two separate ablation procedures, the second one lasting for seven hours. As a result,

Irma's heart rate was stabilized, never going below eighty beats per minute. She recalled, "I'm blessed because all my doctors are fans, and when your doctors are fans, they tend to want to take good care of you."

During that same period, while she was working on a Blues Cruise, her doctor contacted her to say that he had good news and bad news. The bad news was that he suspected she had breast cancer, but the good news was that she was fortunate because they had caught it early. She underwent a program of radiation therapy, driving to all but one of her twenty-four appointments at the Touro Cancer Center on her own. At the hospital, she was finally given a cancer-free diagnosis, which was celebrated by the ringing of a bell. With Emile and Tina by her side, Irma said, "Before I ring this bell, I want to say thank you to all of you nurses and doctors who have been very kind in your giving spirit taking care of me. I have been putting it off, but thank you all." As part of her shows, she now reminds the women in her audience to have their yearly mammogram, and the men to have annual checkups, stressing the importance of early detection.

An advocate of early prevention that likely saved her life, Irma recorded a voice-over for her character in an animated short for Tulane University Medicine. The video, *Clinical Trials: The Heart and Soul of Science*, "addresses the history of structural racism in medicine . . . [and] the underrepresentation of minority communities, an imbalance which can lead to negative health outcomes."[15]

Throughout the 2000s, The Preservation Hall Foundation, an adjunct of the historic venue and the band, had become an increasingly important focal point for traditional New Orleans music, especially through its education outreach. Irma had become a part of the organization's wide-reaching orbit. On Friday, May 6, 2022, the Preservation Hall Jazz Band celebrated its sixtieth anniversary with a concert at the Orpheum Theatre in New Orleans, with guests that included Irma, Big Freedia, and Nathaniel Rateliff. She was also part of each year's Midnight Ramble series during Jazz Fest, an exclusive series of late-night concerts that were a hot ticket for New Orleans music fans, often selling out immediately. Ticket holders are often not privy to the musical lineup for the Rambles, and part of the excitement is the unusual matchups that seemingly magically take place as guest artists drop in for jam sessions. In 2024, following her performance with the Rolling Stones at the Jazz Fest fairgrounds, Stones guitarist Ron Wood performed with Irma during her night at the Ramble. The pairing set off a flurry of social media posts from audience members delighted to share the news and their experience at this exclusive event.

Among the many homemade tributes to Irma around New Orleans is this painted utility box on Canal Street. (Art by Robin Daning, used by permission of Community Visions Unlimited, cvunola.org. Photograph by Johnette Downing)

Another historic venue was also celebrating a milestone event. Defying all expectations, especially considering the decrepit state of the building as recently as 2022, the historic Dew Drop Inn reopened on March 1, 2024. Developer Curtis Doucette Jr., working with Frank Painia's grandson Kenneth Jackson and others, oversaw an $11 million restoration of the nightclub and seventeen-room hotel, which now includes a small museum. With each room named for a musician who had once performed there, including Irma, it quickly became a destination for New Orleans music fans. Irma headlined the reopened venue's first show in the comfortable performance space, supported by Deacon John and his band. Half a century had passed since the sounds of New Orleans rhythm and blues had resonated in these walls. Doucette said, "I have to say, this is the very first time that I've fallen in love with a building. Before I fell in love with the building itself, I fell in love with the history that was made in this building."[16] After the closing of many historic dance halls and clubs throughout Louisiana over the years, it was refreshing to see one venue emerge from the ashes to reclaim its stature in the musical heritage of the State.

The same year, Irma embarked on two exciting new projects, including the surprising *Audience with the Queen*, made with the band Galactic and produced by band members Ben Ellman and Robert Mercurio. The team began recording the album at the band's Number C studio in New Orleans in 2023, but not in the way to which Irma was accustomed. The producers made demo versions of the songs with their dynamic singer, Angelika "Jelly" Joseph, so Irma could learn them. Then, she came to the studio to sing along with the basic tracks. Mercurio recalled, "She didn't really love the process. She would show up pretty much every session and be like, when are we going to do it with the band? And we'd be like, oh, maybe next time." Irma would sing multiple takes of each song, giving Ellman and Mercurio plenty of material to edit into a final performance. While Scott Billington had utilized this process on her Rounder recordings, she had always started by performing live with a band, and she did not have to sing the songs quite so many times. This was different. It was the exact opposite approach taken on her sessions for Newvelle, which were primarily a snapshot of a live performance.

There was, however, a recurring theme: her relationships with record producers who felt that she sang better when she became aggravated. Ellman commented, "That was the hard part for me. I felt like she got better and better the more takes we took, but she would also get more annoyed. But that was actually making it better." Mercurio added, "We were upstairs in a crow's nest, and she's downstairs in a booth, so we didn't have a visual on her. We would say, well, that was really great, Miss Irma. Can we take another take? And we would just hear radio silence." However, when Irma listened to what Ellman and Mercurio had done with her performances from their previous session, it was difficult for her to argue with the results. Mercurio added, "She would hear a finished vocal and say, 'My God, is that me?' You know, she didn't like the process, but she liked the outcome." Irma began telling interviewers that Ellman and Mercurio made her sound like she was twenty years old again.[17]

One of the nine songs on the album was cowritten by the New Orleans artists Boyfriend and Princess Shaw, while all others were collaborations between lyricist Sean Carey and the band. Carey would begin the process by attending a vocal session, having a conversation with Irma, and then going home to write. The songs are built around classic rhythm and blues structures, but the stories in the lyrics and the melodic twists give them a modern spin.

Audience with the Queen is not a Galactic album that features Irma Thomas, but a fully realized statement from Irma with the band in support. The album begins with the gospelly "How Glad I Am," on which Irma may sing falsetto for the first time on record. It is a dramatic piece with choir-like background vocals that ease into the album. "Where I Belong" sums up Irma's remarkably long career and vitality—"I guess I'm right here / where

Galactic and Irma Thomas. L-R seated: Jeff Raines, Irma Thomas, Stanton Moore, Robert Mercurio, Ben Ellman. L-R standing: Rich Vogel, Eric Gordon, Angelika "Jelly" Joseph. (Photograph by Katie Sikora, courtesy of Galactic)

I belong / still doing my thing / still singing my song"—against a fanfare of horns and a big vocal chorus. "Lady Liberty" recalls a Staples Singers civil rights–era protest song, perhaps a reminder that some things have not changed, while "Love's Gonna Find a Way" and "Over You" strike a bluesy tonality. "Puppet on a String" is a ballad with a sing-along hook. The songs seem especially well tailored to Irma's own stories, and she sings them like she means them. The album is a modern take on her classic sound. As far as recording was concerned, she had reached another creative peak. Ellman and Mercurio had given Irma a vital, modern, and fully realized sound.

In the meantime, Ben Chace had moved to Paris. He began imagining a new film/recording project for Irma, this time focusing on her gospel repertoire, and he was soon able to obtain funding from the small Belgian company Capitane Records, Positive Vibrations Foundation, and several private sources. He commented, "It makes sense, in a way, for an eighty-three-year-old woman to be singing about God and existence more than singing about falling in love." Irma added, "Most of the songs that I'm doing are songs that I've sung at the gospel tent at Jazz Fest. But he had a couple of songs that he wanted me to do." Chace was pitching several songs that were outside of the traditional gospel oeuvre. One of them was George Harrison's "My Sweet Lord," and another was Brazilian samba and bossa nova pioneer Jorge Ben's "Brother." Irma was not thrilled with either one. Of "Brother" in particular, she told Chace, "I don't know—it doesn't sound like gospel to me. When you get to New Orleans, we are going to have a lot of work to do on the songs."

Chace booked four days of sessions at Esplanade Studio, from April 8 through 11, and began assembling the supporting cast, which included the Belgian band/rhythm section The Soldiers of Love (Nicolas Michaux on guitar and keyboards, Clement Nourry on lead guitar, Edgar C. Clark on bass, and Yannick Dupont on drums), along with New Orleans pianist Kyle Roussel. Singer Diane T. Peterson (an old friend of Emile and Irma's) did the vocal arrangements. Guests on the record would include the gospel group The Blind Boys of Alabama; Trombone Shorty; singers Lauren Daigle, Valerie June, and Cyril Neville; and bluesman Little Freddie King.

Ironically, while he was driving in his rental car down Esplanade Avenue two days before the sessions, Chace heard Jorge Ben on Dean Ellis's Brazilian music show on WWOZ. He said to himself, "'Oh, this is a sign.' Then this old voice comes in singing along with the pre-recorded tracks, and I'm like, 'What is this?' Then Dean said, 'We're so honored and privileged to have Jorge Ben in the studio with us.'"

Chace texted WWOZ station manager Dave Ankers, who replied (a day later) that Jorge Ben was indeed in New Orleans, and staying with the filmmaker T. G. Herrington, who had produced, with Danny Clinch, the film *Tuba to Cuba* with the Preservation Hall Jazz Band. Chace subsequently contacted Herrington, who asked Jorge Ben if it might be possible for him to attend Irma's first day of sessions on Monday (he was scheduled to leave New Orleans on Tuesday). Herrington's reply was, "He's down—he'll be there tomorrow."

Chace continued, "I put ['Brother'] at the end of the day, so we could at least get into the rhythm [of the sessions], and we did a few very traditional gospel songs to make sure Irma was feeling like we were doing the right thing." Chace told Irma that the composer of the song he had been trying to convince her to record was in New Orleans, and that he would soon come by the sessions. Five hours later, Jorge Ben finally arrived, but with the expectation that he would simply be present for the recording of his song. He did not know who Irma was, and, of course, Irma did not know who he was, but all were impressed with his star-quality presence. Irma said, "All right, let's do it."

The rhythm section began playing the song, abetted by the percussion of two Mardi Gras Indians, which gave the music a Brazilian-leaning vibe. Except for the drummer and the percussionists, who were in sound-isolation booths, Irma and the band were positioned around the large main recording room at Esplanade Studio, with Irma positioned across from Jorge Ben. Chace said, "He was sitting there and she had a direct eyeline to him and she

Irma Thomas and Jorge Ben at Esplanade Studio, New Orleans. (Photograph by Giancarlo D'Agostaro, courtesy of ISG Film LLC)

just started singing to him. He had his headphones on, but she's just nailing him with a big performance. And he just starts singing, you know? I'm in the control room, and I could hear something through one of the other microphones. Then my other producer was down there and he's texting me, 'Jorge is singing.' So we yell at Misha (engineer and studio owner Misha Kachkachishvili) 'Get a microphone on him!'"

"They just start going back and forth, and the thing went on for like thirty minutes—it was like improv call and response. It was like ecstatic music, you know? It was truly like the spirit descended down, and Jorge, at the end of it, he's weeping. He's in Portuguese saying, 'Obrigado, Dios,' and weeping, and Irma [is saying] 'It's incredible, what happened.'" The next day, Troy "Trombone Shorty" Andrews came to the studio to add a vocal track and a trombone track to the performance, responding to the interaction between Irma and Jorge Ben. Finally, Chace edited the performance down to "a nice, healthy six-minute jam."

All the sessions were filmed. Like many of Irma's producers before him, Chace was in awe of Irma's ability to transcend the studio and to deliver a performance that could move listeners to tears. It's not a quality that is often heard on contemporary records, when vocals may be so processed and saturated with effects that every human flaw is either obscured or removed.

There were other highlights of the sessions: Irma's duets with Cyril Neville on "Every Grain of Sand," and with Valerie June on the Clark Sisters song "Is My Living in Vain?" Lauren Daigle sang with her on "My Sweet Lord." "They tried a few takes of it, and they did one take that was really good, and Irma did that amazing roots gospel thing where the song ends, but then they all start clapping and just do an *a cappella* thing and pull it back up, and it was stunning. Lauren was weeping at the end of that one." Chace said, "She didn't hold anything back. You know, she just gave it so much on every track from the first take. It was really inspiring, [with Irma] at eighty-three to see that."[18]

A few days later, Irma gave a live performance of the full program from the album at St. Luke's Episcopal Church, before a packed audience of invited friends and family, with all four of her children present.

Irma continued to have a very active year. With Galactic, she made appearances at the Newport Jazz Festival in Rhode Island on August 2, 2024, and at the Summerstage Festival in New York's Central Park on August 4. Ben Ellman commented, "She just knows how to light up a room. We got to perform a couple of our original tunes, and then we did maybe four or five of her tunes."

2024 was a year of more accolades, notably when she was selected as one of the first fifty inductees in the NOLA Walk of Fame, commemorated with a fleur-de-lis plaque in the pavement near the New Orleans Riverwalk. By this time, she had also received keys to the city from the Louisiana cities of Ponchatoula, New Orleans, Gonzalez, and Baton Rouge.

In October, she headlined the Crescent City Blues and Barbeque Festival with the Professionals in support. She performed songs spanning the full range of her career: from "Don't Mess with My Man," to her Rounder years (Al Anderson and Craig Wiseman's "Love Don't Change," and Joe Brocato's "Let It Be Me," sung as a duet with her drummer, Larry "Choo" Campbell), to songs written by Allen Toussaint (an Irma Thomas set in New Orleans would be incomplete without "It's Raining"), to a reprise of "Sing It!" performed with Marcia Ball, who was the opening act that day. She ended with an emotional reading of David Egan's ballad "Even Now," and Galactic's funky "Heart of Steel." A highlight of the set for Irma was watching the joy on her son James's face as he played congas as part of her band.

The next weekend, she participated in the Women of Louisiana Blues Symposium at the NOLA Funk Fest, held at the New Orleans Jazz Museum, with fellow panelists Marcia Ball, journalist Gwen Thompkins, Scott Billington, and writer Ben Sandmel, interviewed by Jazz Museum curator

David Kunian. Irma told the audience, "Sometimes, young artists ask me about singing the blues. I tell them, 'You're not old enough yet to sing the blues!'" At the conclusion of the symposium, she performed "Wish Someone Would Care" and "Don't Mess with My Man" with a band led by bassist George Porter Jr., which included drummer Herlin Riley, guitarist John Fohl, saxophonist Eric Bernhardt, and keyboardist Michael Lemmler. Many in the audience were moved to tears by her performance.

On November 27, 2024, Tipitina's and promoter Sonny Schneidau presented *A Tribute to the Queen: Irma Thomas*, with a roster of all-women singers, including Anjelika "Jelly" Joseph, Ani DiFranco, Marcia Ball, Erica Falls, Leyla McCalla, Joy Clark, Susan Cowsill, Gabrielle Cavassa, Sierra Green, and Jolynda "Kiki" Chapman, backed by an all-star cast of New Orleans musicians that included several who had recorded with her over the years: musical director George Porter Jr., keyboardist David Torkanowsky, and keyboardist Kyle Roussel. Irma sat in the wings on a throne that Schneidau had obtained just for the event, with Emile by her side, so the singers could see her as they performed her songs. When Irma took the stage in the second part of the show, she was first backed by Galactic, with whom she performed two of the songs from their new album. As accomplished as many of the vocalists were, it was Irma who most engaged the audience, effectively stealing her own show.

Then, New Orleans City Councilperson Lesli Harris's Director of Community Engagement, Matt Schoenberger, presented Irma with a proclamation declaring that November 27 would forever be known as Irma Thomas Day. Several generations of her family were in attendance. Irma sat on a stool for most of the set that followed, as she had on many recent performances, but her voice was big and strong and clear. Looking out into the crowd, she could see the faces of mostly older fans who remembered her from the heyday of New Orleans rhythm and blues, or who had come to venerate New Orleans music as a touchstone in their lives. It was also apparent to many that it was a treat to be present for a rare show anchored by the classic R&B format of piano, Hammond B-3 organ, guitar, bass, drums, a horn section, and background vocalists. Irma may be the most vital living artist from that bygone era, but for every person who attended that night, she was the star of the show, commanding the stage with a presence that might truly have been described as regal.

The next day, she participated in the Orleans Parish sheriff's annual Thanksgiving meal event for economically insecure residents (hosted by current Sheriff Susan Hutson), held at the New Orleans Convention Center. She performed a set, and then helped to serve the food, as she had done for several years for the same event.

The Krewe of Freret debuted an Irma Thomas float during the 2025 Carnival season, in their parade on February 22. (Photograph by Meredith Ragucci)

Wooden artist medallion of Irma Thomas produced for the Krewe of Freret in 2025 by artist Joycelyn Boudreaux of Copperhead Studios. (Courtesy of the Krewe of Freret; photograph by Johnette Downing)

As of January 2025, her most recent recording was a duet performance with pianist Kyle Roussel of the Paul Gayten song "True." Recorded at Roussel's studio, and mixed and mastered at Esplanade Studios in New Orleans, the song had been a showpiece for New Orleans pianist James Booker, and both artists give it a deeply emotional reading. Upon its release as a single in January, it was immediately added to Tidal's Top Jazz Vocal playlist. A well sought-after recording artist and beloved performer, there was no sign of Irma slowing down.

DISCOGRAPHY

LPs

Love Is the Foundation (Newvelle Records NVN001), 2022.

Side A

1. My Love Is (Billy Myles) 2. I Don't Know (Bobby Stevenson-Brook Benton) 3. It's Too Late (Chuck Willis) 4. Picture on the Wall (Freddie McKay) 5. Perfidia (Alberto Domínguez)

Side B

1. So Long (Irving Melsher-Remus Harris-Russ Morgan) 2. Don't Go to Strangers (J.J. Cale) 3. Love Is the Foundation (Devon Russell Barrant)

4. Crying Eyes (J.J. Cale) 5. Second Chance (Ken Boothe) 6. Our Day Will Come (Mort Garson-Bob Hilliard)

Kyshona Armstrong, Paggy Prine, Sierra Green, backing vocals; Alfred "Uganda" Roberts, congas; Johnny Vidacovich, drums; Paul Defiglia, electric bass, acoustic bass; Stephen Daly, electric guitar, pedal steel guitar; Kyle Roussel, piano, organ; Roderick Paulin, saxophone; Terrance Taplin, trombone; Andrew Baham, trumpet

Produced by Ben Chace

Recorded by Misha Kachkachishvili at Esplanade Studio, New Orleans

Audience with the Queen (Tchoupzilla Records/Thirty Tigers), 2025.

1. How Glad I Am (Sean Carey-Galactic) 2. Where I Belong (Sean Carey-Galactic) 3. Love's Gonna Find Away Again (Sean Carey-Galactic) 4. Lady Liberty (Sean Carey-Galactic) 5. Puppet on Your String (Boyfriend-Princess Shaw-Galactic) 6. Peace in My Heart (Sean Carey-Galactic) 7. People (Sean Carey-Galactic) 8. Over You 9. Be Your Lady (Sean Carey-Galactic)

Anjelika "Jelly" Joseph, Boyfriend, Josh Kagler, Princess Shaw, Sean Carey, backing vocals; Jeff Raines, guitar; Rich Vogel, keyboards and organ; Robert Mercurio, bass; Stanton Moore, drums and percussion; Ivan Neville, organ; Mike Dillon and Pedro Segundo, percussion; Ben Ellman, saxophone and harmonica; Eric Gordon, trumpet; Rick G. Nelson, strings

Produced by Ben Ellman and Robert Mercurio

Recorded at Number C Studio, New Orleans

Engineers: Ben Ellman, Robert Mercurio, Aaron Boudreaux, and Mack Major

Horn arrangements by Nick Ellman

Mixed and mastered by Count

My Journey to the Sky (unreleased as of press time).

1. My Sweet Lord (with Lauren Daigle) 2. What Is This 3. Every Grain of Sand (with Cyril Neville) 4. Living in Vain (with Valerie June) 5. Chamber of Reflection 6. My Journey to the Sky (with Charlie Gabriel) 7. People Get Ready (with The Blind Boys of Alabama) 8. Victory 9. Brother (with Jorge Ben, Trombone Shorty, Ivan Neville) 10. Jesus 11. How I Got Over 12. Up Above My Head (with Little Freddie King) 13. Order My Steps 14. Because He Lives 15. Oh How Precious 16. I Am Redeemed

Nicolas Michaux, guitar and keyboards; Clement Nourry, lead guitar; Edgar C. Clark, bass; Yannick Dupont, drums; Kyle Roussel, piano; Diane T. Peterson, Valentine Williams, Hilda Grayson, Gwenette Williams, and Rev. Cornelius Tilton, backing vocals; Big Chief David Montana, Big Chief Shaka Zulu, percussion, backing vocals. Guests include The Blind Boys of Alabama, Jorge Ben, Trombone Shorty, Lauren Daigle, Valerie June, Cyril Neville, and Little Freddie King.

EP

For the Rest of My Life (Swamp Island Records), 2013.

1. For the Rest of My Life (Kurt Brunus) 2. Forever Young (Bob Dylan) 3. For the Rest of My Life (instrumental) (Kurt Brunus) 4. Forever Young (instrumental) (Bob Dylan), 2010.

Produced by Kurt Brunus, Warner Williams, Emile Hall, and Brennan Williams.

Tracks

May Ev'ry Day Be Christmas (Louis Jordan) with the Preservation Hall Jazz Band, from *Holidays Rule* (Hear Music HRM-34045-02). Produced by Chris Funk and Sara Matarazzo, 2012.

Even Now (David Egan) with Walter "Wolfman" Washington, from *My Future Is My Past* (Anti-7595-2). Produced by Ben Ellman, 2018.

Poor Worry Anna (Johnette Downing) with Johnette Downing, from *Swamp Romp* (Wiggle Worm Records 011). Produced by Johnette Downing and Scott Billington, 2019.

Ruler of My Heart (Naomi Neville), Old Rugged Cross (traditional) from *Jazz Fest: The New Orleans Jazz & Heritage Festival* (Smithsonian Folkways Recordings SFW40250). Live Jazz Fest recordings from the 2010s. Compilation produced by Jeff Place, Rachel Lyons, Dave Ankers, Michael Murphy, and Cilista Eberle, 2019.

True (Don Albert, Lloyd Glenn, Louis Cottrell) vocal with Kyle Roussel, piano, from *Church of New Orleans* (SS Records). Produced by Kyle Roussel, 2025.

Why You Wanna Do Me Like That (Joe Gelini-Shane Theriot) from *Rise Up* (UPT Music-Gallatin Records). Produced by Dave Trumfio, 2025.

Documentary Film

My Life in Music. Produced by Cilista Eberle, Michael Murphy, Jim Moriarty, and Rachel Lyons. Michael Murphy Productions, 2021.

CHAPTER FIFTEEN

Coda

At the age of eighty-four, Irma Thomas continues to perform with vigor and conviction. Along with just a few fellow artists who came up in the New Orleans rhythm and blues scene of the 1960s, including Aaron Neville and Deacon John Moore, she carries the torch for both a style of music and an approach to performance that continues to inspire others. The New Orleans–born, Grammy®-winning singer, actress, and author Ledisi commented, "I love her intention behind what she's singing, she doesn't just sing to sing. There's only a few singers that have that—it's an anointing."[1] Bonnie Raitt may have said it best: "Irma Thomas's voice today is just as beautiful and sultry and powerful as it was on her first records. She has been a talisman for me to watch how to go through this business with class and not lose your strength and your power. I mean, like Tina Turner, like Patti LaBelle, these are the divas that I look to. Irma has continued to prosper and thrill audiences in New Orleans, and handle her career really well. And she's a legend."[2]

It is increasingly clear that Irma's recording sessions represented a way of making records that is mostly fading into the past: a singer, a song, a group of musicians, a producer, an engineer, and perhaps an arranger whose collective goal was to capture an emotion on the fly—to conjure a record in the moment at hand. Irma was present at almost every tracking session throughout the years, singing live with the rhythm section, and she went for it every time, never holding back.

Irma's professional choices have always involved family, stability, and control of her own destiny, even if some of those choices might have curtailed greater commercial success. She made her decisions with integrity, and with no regrets, learning the music business as her career evolved, and almost always making the choice not to delegate too much control to business

Irma Thomas at home in New Orleans, February 2025. (Photograph by Thom Bennett)

partners that she did not know or trust. In doing so, she maintained a level of professional longevity and prosperity that many of her contemporaries did not. Indeed, few of them have prospered and survived for as long.

She philosophized, "You know, I had to work off of my gut feeling, and my gut feeling was to take care of my kids. If it didn't feel right to me, I just didn't do it. So you look at the ups and downs of the career. Some opportunities came through. You know, when you're naïve, sometimes it's better to be naïve than it is to know it all. In life, the things that have always sustained me are my faith in God, my faith in doing the right thing, and faith in myself to make the best decisions that I can at the time. This faith has brought me to where I am today." She added wryly, "I didn't have the sense to give up."

More than any other motivating factor, Irma loves to sing, and she loves the interaction with her fans, whom she respects greatly. She also loves the validation that comes along with her power to transport each person in her audience to a state of connectedness with her and the feelings she evokes, each and every time she sings. As she straightforwardly told the audience at her 2024 tribute concert, "God gave me this voice to make people happy." Whether she was in a hit-making recording studio, or on a concert stage

Irma and Emile Jackson at home in New Orleans, February 2025. (Photograph by Thom Bennett)

shared with a pop star, her focus was the singing and the song itself, and usually not on the intrinsic prestige of the situation she was in, or with whom she was singing, at least with one exception. "If someone had told me when I was six years old, in the middle of the strawberry patch, dancing and singing 'Boogie Chillen,' that I'd ever be on the same stage with John Lee Hooker! I'm not in awe of very many people, but I was in awe of him."[3] Still, her overriding concern was how she could get the song's story across to her audience, and in giving herself over to the heart and empathy to do so. If that meant singing a song *a cappella* to please just one audience member, that's what she would do.

She was also practical about her career. Her experience in working at jobs other than music made her appreciate how her gift and her voice could provide her with an income that otherwise would have been out of the reach of a high school dropout, albeit one who would later graduate from college. She took her job and her business seriously, especially after Emile began negotiating her performance fees. Perhaps a manager with a broader vision and perspective could have taken her business farther, but it is difficult to second-guess the decisions they made together, as she sustained a sixty-year career with her integrity and health intact, and with a secure "retirement."

She continues to work, although she is selective about the jobs she takes, and is ever reluctant to accept gigs without her band. "They have always been loyal to me," she said, "and we're loyal to them." She admitted that the travel, especially overseas, is difficult for her now, and that having a regular local club gig might be nice.

While Irma Thomas may be the embodiment of a star to her fans, and a glamorous presence on stage, she has always been as forthright, unpretentious, and straightforward in performance as she is in person—the humblest of divas. Her ability to convey both vulnerability and toughness as she sings, without embellishment and without second-guessing her emotional response to the stories in the lyrics she sings, are perhaps the qualities that have drawn such a diverse and talented cast of musicians, songwriters, and producers into her orbit. Even as her voice has become an iconic part of the American popular music landscape, she does not consider herself special. "I'm just Irma, and you either like what you see or you don't like what you see. Everyday I wake up and I'm still alive, thank God."[4]

"I have always lived by the thought: can't nobody block your blessings but you. It's the choices you make in life that matter. God knew better than I knew what was right for me. He gave me a voice, and I use it."[5]

Irma Thomas's Red Beans Recipe

Ingredients

1 lb. red beans

Use your favorite meat. I use smoked ham hocks sometimes or pickled riblets, but boil first to get rid of most of the salt. Smoked sausage is also good.

1 cup onions

1 cup bell pepper

1/2 cup celery

1/4 cup parsley

Directions:

1.) In a 5-quart pot, wash beans, and add all of the seasoning including the meat.

2.) In the pot, add at least 6 cups of water to cover all, and bring to a boil.

3.) Lower the fire to a low boil, stirring often until creamy.

4.) When almost done, add a large spoon of brown sugar.

I think that should make a great pot of beans.

Acknowledgments

Research for this book was partially funded by a fellowship grant from the New Orleans Jazz and Heritage Foundation.

Unless otherwise credited, Irma Thomas's quotations are from a series of interviews conducted by Johnette Downing and Scott Billington between 2022 and 2025, and from excerpts of several reminiscences of her early life transcribed by her friend and fan club president Linda Boudreaux in the late 1990s. These are included without citations.

The authors are indebted to the following people, without whom this book would have been incomplete:

Charlene Bonnette, M.L.I.S., C.A., Manager, Louisiana Collection, State Library of Louisiana, for articles and photographic research.

John Broven, for his help, kindness, and pioneering work in documenting New Orleans rhythm and blues.

Tony Burke, editor of *Blues and Rhythm* Magazine, who made many connections for us.

Cilista Eberle and Michael Murphy for graciously giving us access to interviews conducted for *Make It Funky* and *My Life in Music*.

David Kunian at the New Orleans Jazz Museum.

Roger Lewis, for his recollections and for his diligence in photographic research.

Rachel Lyons at the New Orleans Jazz and Heritage Foundation.

Lisa Moore at the Amistad Collection, for showing us the way to *Louisiana Weekly*.

Tina Thomas for her photographic research and support.

Thank you also to Lynda Barry, Thom Bennett, Jonas Bernholm, Ben Chace, Jeff DeLia, Mildred and Donald Dix, Charles Dreibe, Ben Ellman, David Farrell, Isaiah Gibbs, Craig Gill, Chris Goldsmith, Jeff Hannusch, Warren Hildebrand, Paul Kahn, Peggy Scott Laborde, Darell Stokes Jackson,

Emile Jackson, Danny Jones, Bob McGrath, Robert Mercurio, Rick Olivier, Erin Patterson, Brad Paul, Diane T. Peterson, Kim Phillips, Jack Randall, Steve Reynolds, Barbara Roberds, Kia Robinson, Ben Sandmel, Andrea Thomas, James Thomas, Jean Marie Thomas, Katie Turner, Graziano Uliani, and Cyril E. Vetter.

A note on photographs: Unfortunately, in the days just before digitization, Irma Thomas's personal collection of photographs and memorabilia, as well as many of Rick Olivier's photographs documenting the early Rounder Records years, were lost to Hurricane Katrina.

Notes

FOREWORD

1. "The Fabulous Irma Thomas!" NOLA Family, nolafamily.com, November 7, 2018.

2. "True Believer," by Daryl Burgess, is the title song of the album *True Believer*, Rounder Records, 1992.

3. Melissa Block, "Irma Thomas: The Soul Queen of New Orleans," NPR 50 Great Voices, *All Things Considered*, NPR, August 23, 2010. https://www.npr.org/2010/08/23/129345910/irma-thomas-the-soul-queen-of-new-orleans.

INTRODUCTION

1. Eric Seiferth interviewed by David Walker, for the exhibition *New Orleans Medley: Sounds of the City*, at the Historic New Orleans Collection, June 5, 2020. https://www.hnoc.org/virtual-tour/new-orleans-medley/.

CHAPTER ONE: COUNTRY GIRL (1941–1946)

1. *A Short History of How Jukeboxes Changed the World*, Rock-Ola, August 12, 2009. https://www.rock-ola.com/blogs/news/a-short-history-of-how-jukeboxes-changed-the-world?srsltid=AfmBOorprgWy-HIPs7Y68gSOl-KgKsbvto-qCE9t4RjWoiluuSfS39li.

2. Keith Spera, "Irma Thomas, Soul Queen of New Orleans, at 80: 'I'm living fine, as far as I'm concerned,'" Nola.com, February 18, 2021.

3. Interview with Cilista Eberle for *My Life in Music*, WYES, New Orleans, 2021.

4. Grace Liechtenstein and Laura Dankner, *Musical Gumbo: The Music of New Orleans* (New York and London: W. W. Norton, 1993), 172.

5. Meg Pier, *Irma Thomas, Soul Queen Of New Orleans, Shares Wisdom*, People Are Culture, November 15, 2024. https://www.peopleareculture.com/irma-thomas/.

6. Elsa Hahne, *The Gravy: In the Kitchen with New Orleans Musicians* (New Orleans: High ISO Music, 2013), 133.

CHAPTER TWO: SURROUNDED BY MUSIC (1947–1953)

1. Eric Seiferth interviewed by David Walker.

2. Jeff Hannusch, *I Hear You Knockin': The Sound of New Orleans Rhythm and Blues* (Ville Platte, LA: Swallow Books, 1986), 119.

3. Vernon "Dr. Daddy-O" Winslow Broadcast Recordings, Tulane University Digital Library, https://digitallibrary.tulane.edu/islandora/object/tulane:vernonwinslow.

4. Melissa A. Weber, Jivin' with Dr. Daddy-O: Race, Radio and Representing Black in Jim Crow New Orleans, lecture at Tulane University, October 2, 2023. https://www.youtube.com/watch?v=UgXOFkpIia4.

5. Interview with Cilista Eberle for *My Life in Music.*

6. *Legends Who Lunch*, with Tricia "Sista Teedy" Boutte, *Offbeat*, March 2004, 56.

7. Hahne, *The Gravy: In the Kitchen with New Orleans Musicians.*

8. *Legends Who Lunch*, 56.

9. Liechtenstein and Dankner, *Musical Gumbo: The Music of New Orleans*, 173.

10. Danny Barker, *A Life in Jazz*, edited by Alyn Shipton (New Orleans: The New Orleans Historic Collection, 2016), 53.

11. "'Soul Queen' Irma Thomas: 'I Can't Choose a Song That Doesn't Make Sense to Me,'" LAist, July 19, 2016.

12. Mike Scott, "New Orleans 101: Why do we call it a 'neutral ground' instead of a median?" https://mikescottwrites.com/2019/06/13/new-orleans-101-why-do-we-call-it-a-neutral-ground-instead-of-a-median/.

13. Video interview with Irma Thomas, Music Rising at Tulane, Tulane University. https://musicrising.tulane.edu/watch/video/interview-irma-thomas/.

14. Shane Lief and John McCusker, *Jockomo: The Native Roots of Mardi Gras Indians* (Jackson: University Press of Mississippi, 2019), 136–37.

15. Matt Hoggart, "Behind the Song: Sugar Boy and His Canecutters / The Dixie Cups, 'Jockamo / Iko Iko,'" *American Songwriter*, August 2, 2021.

16. Lief and McCusker, *Jockomo: The Native Roots of Mardi Gras Indians*, 49–51.

17. Barker, *My Life in Music*, 179.

CHAPTER THREE: ALL GROWN UP (1947–1957)

1. Interview with Roger Lewis by Johnette Downing and Scott Billington, New Orleans, June 9, 2023.

2. Interview with Cilista Eberle.

3. Jeff Hannusch, "The Irrepressible Irma Thomas," New Orleans *Times-Picayune*, August 14, 1988, 180.

4. "The Fabulous Irma Thomas!"

5. "The Fabulous Irma Thomas!"

6. Interview with Roger Lewis by Johnette Downing and Scott Billington, New Orleans, June 8, 2023.

7. John Broven, *Rhythm and Blues in New Orleans* (New Orleans: Pelican Publishing, 1983), 198–99.

CHAPTER FOUR: DON'T MESS WITH MY MAN (1958–1960)

1. David Kunian, "Dew Drop Inn," 64 Parishes. https://64parishes.org/entry/dew-drop-inn.

2. Kenneth Jackson, interview for Library of Congress, December 18, 2018. https://tile.loc.gov/storage-services/service/afc/afc2018029/afc2018029_05400/afc2018029_05400_ms01.pdf.

3. Interview with Allen Toussaint, *The Legend of the Dew Drop Inn* Documentary Interviews by Julia Dorn, April 19, 2005, Tulane University Libraries. https://library.search.tulane.edu/discovery/fulldisplay?docid=alma9945514977306326&context=L&vid=01TUL_INST:Tulane&lang=en&adaptor=Local%20Search%20Engine.

4. *Louisiana Weekly*, advertisement, January 10, 1959.

5. *Louisiana Weekly*, advertisement, March 21, 1959, 15.

6. The History of Rock and Roll, Song by Song, https://www.spontaneouslunacy.net/artists-mr-google-eyes/.

7. Interview with Roger Lewis by Johnette Downing and Scott Billington.

8. Interview with Cilista Eberle.

9. Interview with Irma Thomas, *The Legend of the Dew Drop Inn* Documentary Interviews by Julia Dorn, February 14, 2005, Tulane University Libraries. https://library.search.tulane.edu/discovery/fulldisplay?docid=alma9945514161606326&context=L&vid=01TUL_INST:Tulane&lang=en&adaptor=Local%20Search%20Engine.

10. Jeff Hannusch, "Thibodaux's Sugar Bowl," *Offbeat* Magazine, May 1, 1999. https://www.offbeat.com/articles/thibodauxs-sugar-bowl/.

11. Interview with Kim Bledsoe for *Make It Funky*, The Lion's Den, New Orleans, 2003.

12. *Legends Who Lunch* with Tricia "Sista Teedy" Boutte, *Offbeat*, March 2004, 56.

13. "Irma Thomas, Soul Queen of New Orleans," Music Rising at Tulane: Gender, Archives, and Musical Culture, Chapter 12, Tulane University. https://musicrising.tulane.edu/learn/courses/gender-archives-and-musical-culture/.

14. Mahalia Jackson, *Louisiana Music Trail*. https://www.explorelouisiana.com/music/mahalia-jackson.

15. "Pearl Bailey, American Entertainer," Britannica.com. https://www.britannica.com/biography/Pearl-Bailey.

CHAPTER FIVE: IRMA AND ALLEN (1961–1963)

1. Neil Slaven, "The Instant and Minit Labels." https://web.archive.org/web/20110820051328/http://lm-mail.com/mailouts/web16_web.html.

2. "The All-Black Airstaff at WMRY," Arcane Radio Trivia, September 20, 2013. https://tenwatts.blogspot.com/2013/09/the-all-black-airstaff-at-wmry.html.

3. Ben Sandmel, *Ernie K-Doe: The R&B Emperor of New Orleans* (New Orleans: The Historic New Orleans Collection, 2012), 57.

4. Sandmel, *Ernie K-Doe, The R&B Emperor of New Orleans*, 57.

5. John Swenson, "Best of the Beat Lifetime Achievement in Music: Irma Thomas," *Offbeat Magazine*, January 1, 2006.

6. "'Soul Queen' Irma Thomas: 'I Can't Choose a Song That Doesn't Make Sense to Me.'"

7. Interview with Cilista Eberle.

8. Interview with Cilista Eberle.

9. Interview with Roger Lewis by Johnette Downing and Scott Billington.

10. Jeff Hannusch, "Percy Stovall, 'Rural Bandit,' Dies at 77," *Wavelength*, April 1984, 7.

11. Hannusch, "Percy Stovall, 'Rural Bandit,' Dies at 77."

12. Interview with Roger Lewis by Johnette Downing and Scott Billington.

13. Interview with Cilista Eberle.

14. Interview with Ben Sandmel, New Orleans Jazz and Heritage Festival Allison Miner Heritage Stage, April 29, 2016.

15. Recalled from a conversation between Scott Billington and Cosimo Matassa, late 1990s.

16. "Kid Ory and the tailgate style of playing trombone," *Musicology for Everyone*, 2012. https://music.allpurposeguru.com/2015/08/kid-ory-trombonist-businessman/.

17. Block, *Irma Thomas: The Soul Queen of New Orleans.*

18. Interview with Kim Bledsoe for *Make It Funky*, The Lion's Den, New Orleans, 2003.

19. Interview with Cilista Eberle.

20. Interview with Cilista Eberle.

21. John Broven, *Rhythm and Blues in New Orleans, Revised and Updated* (Gretna, LA: Pelican Publishing, 2016), 210.

22. Interview with Kim Bledsoe for *Make It Funky*, The Lion's Den, New Orleans, 2003.

23. Block, "Irma Thomas: The Soul Queen of New Orleans."

24. Interview with Alison LeBeaux Toussaint for *My Life in Music.*

25. Giovanni Russonello, "Irma Thomas, A Soul Queen Far Beyond New Orleans," *New York Times*, February 16, 2022.

26. Conversation with Johnny Vidacovich, Maple Leaf Bar, New Orleans, July 4, 2024.

27. "Germania Hall," *A Closer Walk*, WWOZ. https://acloserwalknola.com/places/germania-hall/.

28. Interview with Ben Chace by Johnette Downing and Scott Billington, October 15, 2024.

29. Interview with Kim Bledsoe for *Make It Funky.*

30. Interview with Robert Fontenot for "Backtalk: Irma Thomas," *Offbeat Magazine*, May 1, 2003.

31. Email interview with Warren Hildebrand by Scott Billington, July 5, 2023.

32. Jeff Hannusch, "Irrepressible Irma Thomas," New Orleans *Times-Picayune*, August 14, 1988, 180.

33. "Flashbacks," New Orleans *Times-Picayune*, November 21, 1993, D-11.

34. Interview with Kim Bledsoe for *Make It Funky.*

35. Mike Scott, "New Orleans' bowling craze: A visual history," *NOLA.com/The Times-Picayune*, March 13, 2019, updated July 22, 2019.

36. "Kegler's Kix," *Louisiana Weekly*, November 9, 1963, 15.

37. Angus Lind, "Irma's Rolling Along for a New Generation," *New Orleans States-Item*, March 10, 1978.

38. "Kegler's Kix," *Louisiana Weekly*, June 16, 1962, 10.

39. Mildred and Donald Dix, interview with Johnette Downing and Scott Billington, June 5, 2024, New Orleans, LA.

40. Broven, *Rhythm and Blues in New Orleans, Revised and Updated*, 211.

CHAPTER SIX: THE FIRST CALIFORNIA SESSIONS (1964)

1. Edward Ray, with Barbara Hall, *Against All Odds* (self-published, 2012), 118–19.

2. Excerpt from an unpublished interview with Eddie Ray by John Broven, Arlington, VA, December 18, 2015.

3. Interview with Cilista Eberle.

4. Dan Philips, "Wishing Well," Home of the Groove, September 11, 2005. https://homeofthegroove.blogspot.com/2005/09/wishing-well.html.

5. Correspondence between Carol Kaye and Scott Billington, March 30, 2025.

6. Alison Fensterstock, "Shocking Omissions: Irma Thomas, 'Wish Someone Would Care,'" NPR, November 13, 2017. https://www.npr.org/2017/11/13/563381359/shocking-omissions-irma-thomas-wish-someone-would-care.

7. Art Schuna, Art, "Irma Thomas, The Soul Queen of New Orleans," Broadcasting the Blues: The Art Schuna Interviews, *Blues & Rhythm The Gospel Truth*, no. 385, August/September 2024, 4–9.

8. From John Broven's email correspondence with Russ Wapensky, January 2025.

9. Fred Bronson, "'Anyone Who Knows What Love Is': Why an Obscure '60s Song Is Bigger Than Ever In 2018," *Billboard*, August 18, 2018.

10. "'Soul Queen' Irma Thomas: 'I Can't Choose a Song That Doesn't Make Sense to Me.'"

11. Jeff Hannusch (writing as Almost Slim), "Irma Thomas: The Soul Queen of New Orleans," *Goldmine*, June 1983.

12. Jennifer Maas, "Here's Why You Hear That One Song Over and Over in 'Black Mirror,'" *The Wrap*, February 11, 2018. Archived from the original on October 23, 2019. Retrieved February 15, 2022.

13. "Desert Island Discs: Black Mirror's Charlie Brooker on his 'goofy' persona." BBC News, January 7, 2018. Retrieved February 6, 2022.

14. Keith Spera, "Irma Thomas, Soul Queen of New Orleans, at 80: 'I'm living fine, as far as I'm concerned,'" Nola.com, February 18, 2021.

15. Bronson, "'Anyone Who Knows What Love Is': Why an Obscure '60s Song Is Bigger Than Ever in 2018."

16. Spera, "Irma Thomas, Soul Queen of New Orleans, at 80."

17. Spera, "Irma Thomas, Soul Queen of New Orleans, at 80."

18. Ken Ehrlich interview with Cilista Eberle for *My Life in Music*, 2021.

19. Interview with Kim Bledsoe for *Make It Funky*, The Lion's Den, New Orleans, 2003.

20. Caryn Rose, "Rolling Stones Perform 'Time Is on My Side' With New Orleans Legend Irma Thomas at Steamy Jazz Fest: Concert Review," *Variety*, May 3, 2024.

CHAPTER SEVEN: TIMES HAVE CHANGED (1965–1969)

1. Excerpt from an interview with Eddie Ray by John Broven, Arlington, Virginia, December 18, 2015.

2. "The Fabulous Irma Thomas!"

3. Interview with James Thomas by Scott Billington and Johnette Downing, August 15, 2024.

4. *Louisiana Weekly*, advertisement, June 6, 1959, 16.

5. Interview with James Thomas by Scott Billington and Johnette Downing, August 15, 2024.

6. "Irma Thomas: The Lady Got Soul!" The Krewe du Vieux presents *Le Monde de Merde*, February 7, 1998, 2.

7. John Marriott and Mick Maltby, list of Irma Thomas 1966 tour dates, *Blues and Rhythm* no. 385, August-September 2024, 5.

8. Marriott and Maltby, list of Irma Thomas 1966 tour dates, 5.

9. Email interview with Tony Burke by Scott Billington, March 2024.

10. Bill Millar, "A Rock n Roll Diary: 1966, Part One," *Now Dig This* magazine, issue 470, May 2022.

11. Dean Budnick, "Interview: Irma Thomas, Soul Queen of New Orleans," *Relix*, May 16, 2019.

12. Liechtenstein and Dankner, *Musical Gumbo: The Music of New Orleans*, 186–87.

13. Interview with James Thomas by Scott Billington and Johnette Downing, August 15, 2023.

14. Hannusch, "Irrepressible Irma Thomas," 180.

15. Jyrki Ilva, "Irma Thomas, the Soul Queen of New Orleans," https://www.mv.helsinki.fi/home/ilva/irma.html.

16. Liechtenstein and Dankner, *Musical Gumbo, The Music of New Orleans*, 186–87.

17. Art Schuna, "Irma Thomas, The Soul Queen of New Orleans," *Blues and Rhythm*, no. 385, September-October 2025, 8.

18. Hannusch, *I Hear You Knockin': The Sound of New Orleans Rhythm and Blues*, 234.

CHAPTER EIGHT: LOS ANGELES AND OAKLAND (1970–1975)

1. The Negro Motorist Green Book. https://negromotoristgreenbook.si.edu/virtual-exhibit/the-green-book/.

2. John McWhorter, "The Future of Black History Is Right Here," *The New York Times*, May 18, 2025, Sunday Opinion, 6.

3. Interview with Andrea Thomas Gibbs, James Thomas, Jean Marie Thomas, and Tina Thomas by Scott Billington and Johnette Downing, April 15, 2024.

4. Interview with Andrea Thomas Gibbs, James Thomas, Jean Marie Thomas, and Tina Thomas by Scott Billington and Johnette Downing, April 15, 2024.

5. Interview with Andrea Thomas Gibbs, James Thomas, Jean Marie Thomas, and Tina Thomas by Scott Billington and Johnette Downing, April 15, 2024.

6. Interview with David Kunian by Scott Billington and Johnette Downing at the New Orleans Jazz Museum on December 6, 2023.

7. Dan Phillips, "Irma and Swamp Dogg: The Canyon Sessions," Home of the Groove, May 4, 2013. https://homeofthegroove.blogspot.com/2013/05/irma-swamp-dogg-canyon-sessions.html.

8. Interview with Cilista Eberle.

9. Keith Spera, "Irma Thomas Has Mixed Feelings About the Rediscovery of her 1970s-era 'Lost Cotillion Album,'" NOLA.com, *The Times-Picayune*, May 17, 2014.

10. Interview with Cilista Eberle.

11. Interview with Cilista Eberle.

12. "Remembering Harold Battiste," *Offbeat* Magazine, June 15, 2015. https://www.offbeat.com/news/remembering-harold-battiste/.

13. "Rare '70s-Era Tracks by Irma Thomas Issued on Vinyl for the First Time," *Offbeat* Magazine, March 2022.

14. Spera, "Irma Thomas has mixed feelings."

15. Interview with Jean Marie Thomas by Scott Billington and Johnette Downing, August 15, 2024.

16. "Irma Thomas in New Orleanes" [*sic*], Echo Point Studio, Japan, circa mid-1990s, YouTube. https://www.youtube.com/watch?v=i70_YfZYZtQ.

17. Interview with Roger Lewis by Scott Billington and Johnette Downing, New Orleans, Louisiana, June 8, 2023.

18. Interview with James Thomas by Scott Billington and Johnette Downing, August 15, 2023.

19. Bill Mongelluzzo, "Prom Singer Irma Thomas Still 'Killing Them Softly,'" New Orleans *Times-Picayune*, December 13, 1974.

20. "A Brief History of the New Orleans Jazz & Heritage Festival," nojazzfest.com. https://www.nojazzfest.com/history/.

21. "Mason's Las Vegas Strip," A Closer Walk, WWOZ. https://acloserwalknola.com/places/masons-las-vegas-strip/#:~:text=Built%20in%20the%20early%201970s,coffee%20shop%2C%20and%20a%20motel.

22. Interview with Emile Jackson by Johnette Downing and Scott Billington, December 2, 2024.

23. Conversation with concert producer Sonny Schneidau by Johnette Downing and Scott Billington, New Orleans, January 9, 2026.

24. Interview with Cilista Eberle.

25. Interview with Emile Jackson by Johnette Downing and Scott Billington, December 2, 2024.

CHAPTER NINE: LOS ANGELES AND OAKLAND (1970–1975)

1. Interview with Kim Bledsoe for *Make It Funky*.

2. Hannusch, "Irrepressible Irma Thomas," 180.

3. Interview with Darell Stokes Jackson by Johnette Downing and Scott Billington, June 19, 2025.

4. Spera, "Irma Thomas, Soul Queen of New Orleans, at 80."

5. Irma Thomas interview with Music Rising at Tulane, https://musicrising.tulane.edu/watch/video/interview-irma-thomas/.

6. Doug MacCash, "Remembering the Riverboat President music club," *The Times-Picayune*, November 15, 2009.

7. Schuna, "Irma Thomas, The Soul Queen of New Orleans," 8.

8. Online interview with Cyril E. Vetter by Johnette Downing and Scott Billington, April 8, 2024.

9. Online interview with Danny Jones by Johnette Downing and Scott Billington, April 9, 2024.

10. Conversation with Danny Jones by Johnette Downing and Scott Billington in New Orleans, May 2, 2024.

11. Online interview with Cyril E. Vetter by Johnette Downing and Scott Billington, April 8, 2024.

12. Tom Aswell, "Irma Thomas," Louisiana Music Hall of Fame. https://louisianamusichalloffame.org/irma-thomas-2/.

13. Interview with Kim Phillips by Scott Billington and Johnette Downing, December 31, 2024.

14. Hannusch, "Irma Thomas: The Soul Queen of New Orleans."

15. Interview with Darell Stokes Jackson by Johnette Downing and Scott Billington, June 19, 2025.

16. Interview with Emile Jackson by Johnette Downing and Scott Billington, December 2, 2024.

17. Hannusch, "Irrepressible Irma Thomas," 180.

18. Betty Guillard, "A couple of gigs for Irma Thomas," *The Times-Picayune*, Lagniappe section, November 7, 1984, D-6.

CHAPTER TEN: THE NEW RULES (1985–1991)

1. John Pope, "Remembering when New Orleans' Blue Room was red hot," New Orleans *Times-Picayune*, June 11, 2017.

2. David Menconi, *Oh, Didn't They Ramble: Rounder Records and the Transformation of American Roots Music* (Chapel Hill: University of North Carolina Press, 2023), 43.

3. Interview with Kim Bledsoe for *Make It Funky.*

4. Interview with Cilista Eberle.

5. Ellis Taylor, "Irma Thomas returns with 'The New Rules,'" Biloxi *Sun Herald*, May 3, 1986.

6. Vincent Fumar, "Irma sings by the 'Rules,'" New Orleans *Times-Picayune*, March 21, 1986.

7. Hannusch, "Irrepressible Irma Thomas," 180.

8. Eve Troeh, "History of WWOZ," WWOZ. https://www.wwoz.org/history-wwoz.

9. Interview with Cilista Eberle.

10. John Swenson, "Best of the Beat Lifetime Achievement Award in Music: Irma Thomas," *Offbeat* Magazine, January 1, 2006.

11. Ben Sandmel, "Irma Thomas," Music Rising at Tulane, https://musicrising.tulane.edu/discover/people/irma-thomas/.

12. "Review, *The Way I Feel: Her Brilliant Career*," *New Musical Express*, London, March 26, 1988.

13. James Hopkins, review of *The Way I Feel*, *Option*, May/June 1988.

14. "And all that jazz fest," New Orleans *Times-Picayune*, May 3, 1987.

15. Conversation with Bill Bentley and Scott Billington, August 12, 2024.

16. Joe Levy, "Talent on Stage: Irma Thomas," *Cash Box*, vol. 11, no. 35, March 5, 1988.

17. Jon Pareles, "Jazz: Irma Thomas," *The New York Times*, February 21, 1988.

18. Jim Washburn, "Irma Thomas' Life Is Now a Brighter Blue," *Los Angeles Times*, June 7, 1990. https://www.latimes.com/archives/la-xpm-1990-06-07-ca-1851-story.html.

19. Interview with Kim Bledsoe for *Make It Funky.*

20. Event program courtesy of the New Orleans Jazz Museum, New Orleans.

21. Mary Foster, "Irma Thomas Continues a Two-Decade Tradition," New Orleans *Times-Picayune*, April 28, 1989.

22. Interview with Cilista Eberle.

23. Interview with Darell Stokes Jackson by Johnette Downing and Scott Billington, June 19, 2025.

CHAPTER ELEVEN: GOING TO SCHOOL (1992–2004)

1. Email correspondence between Rick Olivier and Johnette Downing, July 25, 2025.

2. Bill Forman, "Still Reigning, New Orleans Soul Queen Bares All," *Grammy®* Magazine, vol. 10, no. 2, 1992.

3. Interview with Cilista Eberle.

4. Interview with David Farrell by Johnette Downing and Scott Billington, January 7, 2025.

5. Mike Joyce, "Time & Soul Still on Thomas's Side," *The Washington Post*, October 9, 1992, N14.

6. Bill Dahl, "Recordings," Tempo, *Chicago Tribune*, December 10, 1992, 7.

7. Geoff Chapman, "Fine collection of jazz divas a primer on the era since '54," *Toronto Star*, February 13, 1993, K12.

8. "First African Baptist Church," New Orleans Churches. neworleanschurches.com.
9. Interview with Cilista Eberle.
10. Interview with Cilista Eberle.
11. Tony May, "Irma Thomas—Walk Around Heaven: New Orleans Gospel Soul," *Cross Rhythms*, June 1, 1994. https://www.crossrhythms.co.uk/products/Irma_Thomas/Walk_Around_Heaven_New_Orleans_Gospel_Soul/19946/.
12. Interview with Cilista Eberle.
13. Conversation with National Park Ranger Matt Hampsey by Johnette Downing, October 4, 2024.
14. H.Con.Res.57, "A concurrent resolution expressing the sense of Congress respecting the designation of jazz as a rare and valuable national American treasure," US Congress. https://www.congress.gov/bill/100th-congress/house-concurrent-resolution/57.
15. Bill Milkowski, "Irma Thomas: The Story of My Life," *Jazz Times*, May 1, 1997.
16. Joseph Blake, "Sound Advice," *Times Colonist*, March 15, 1997, 1.
17. Interview with Darell Stokes Jackson by Johnette Downing and Scott Billington, June 19, 2025.
18. Interview with Brad Paul by Scott Billington and Johnette Downing, August 16, 2024.
19. Mike Joyce, "Marcia Ball, Irma Thomas and Tracy Nelson: 'Sing It!'" *The Washington Post*, June 26, 1998.
20. Interview with Brad Paul by Scott Billington and Johnette Downing, August 16, 2024.
21. Interview with Jack Randall by Johnette Downing and Scott Billington, August 12, 2024.
22. Interview with Kim Bledsoe for *Make It Funky*.
23. Correspondence by Scott Billington with Graziano Uliani, May 31, 2025.
24. Robert Gordon, liner notes to *My Heart's in Memphis*, Rounder Records 2163, 2000.
25. Roger Hahn, "Irma Thomas, My Heart's in Memphis: The Songs of Dan Penn," *Offbeat*, New Orleans, August 1, 2000.
26. Aswell, "Irma Thomas," Louisiana Music Hall of Fame.
27. "Legendary N.O. blues singer Tommy Ridgley dead at 73," Obituaries, *The Town Talk*, Alexandria, LA, August 13, 1999.
28. "'Soul Queen' Irma Thomas: 'I Can't Choose a Song That Doesn't Make Sense to Me.'"
29. Interview with Paul Kahn by Johnette Downing and Scott Billington, October 22, 2024.
30. Interview with Paul Kahn by Johnette Downing and Scott Billington, October 22, 2024.
31. Interview with Michael Murphy by Johnette Downing and Scott Billington, August 8, 2024.
32. Interview with Kim Bledsoe for *Make It Funky*.
33. "About the Irma Thomas Center for W.I.S.E. Women," Delgado Community College. https://www.dcc.edu/student-services/wise/about.aspx.
34. Interview with Kim Bledsoe for *Make It Funky*.

CHAPTER TWELVE: AFTER THE STORM (2005–2006)

1. Scott Billington, *Making Tracks: A Record Producer's Southern Roots Music Journey* (Jackson: University Press of Mississippi, 2022), 125.
2. "A Visit with the Soul Queen of New Orleans," *Weekend Edition*, NPR, July 1, 2006. https://www.npr.org/2006/07/01/5526014/a-visit-with-the-soul-queen-of-new-orleans.
3. Interview with Cilista Eberle.
4. Interview with Cilista Eberle.

5. Aswell, "Irma Thomas," Louisiana Music Hall of Fame.

6. Budnick, "Interview: Irma Thomas, Soul Queen of New Orleans."

7. A. O. Scott, "A Tribute to the Music of New Orleans," *The New York Times*, September 9, 2005, E16.

8. Interview with Cilista Eberle.

9. Errol Laborde, "The Greatest Mardi Gras Ever," *New Orleans Magazine*, February 2016.

10. Interview with Cilista Eberle.

11. Jim Caligiuri, *After the Rain* album review in the *Austin Chronicle*, May 26, 2006.

12. Interview with Cilista Eberle.

13. Ashley Kahn, liner notes to Allen Toussaint, *Songbook*, Rounder Records, 2013.

14. Correspondence by Scott Billington with Graziano Uliani, May 31, 2025.

15. Interview with Ken Ehrlich by Cilista Eberle for *My Life in Music*, WYES, New Orleans, 2021.

16. "About Music Rising," Music Rising National Disaster Relief Fund. https://musicrising.com/about.

17. Interview with Cilista Eberle.

CHAPTER THIRTEEN: SOUL SURVIVOR (2007–2010)

1. Kalamu ya Salaam, "Irma Thomas, Musical Queen of New Orleans," *New Orleans Tribune*, February 1989.

2. Interview with Cilista Eberle.

3. Meg Pier, "Irma Thomas, Soul Queen of New Orleans, Shares Wisdom," *People Are Culture*, December 4, 2023. https://www.peopleareculture.com/irma-thomas/.

4. Interview with Erica Falls by Cilista Eberle for *My Life in Music*, WYES, New Orleans, 2021.

5. Interview with Ken Erhlich by Cilista Eberle for *My Life in Music*, WYES, New Orleans, 2021.

6. Interview with Erica Falls by Cilista Eberle for *My Life in Music*.

7. Keith I. Marszalek, "2008 Jazzfest poster released," New Orleans *Times-Picayune*, March 1, 2008.

8. Interview with Robert Mercurio and Ben Ellman by Scott Billington and Johnette Downing, August 27, 2024.

9. "Byron Bay Bluesfest 2011," Consequence.net. December 1, 2010, Retrieved August 23, 2017.

10. Block, "Irma Thomas: The Soul Queen of New Orleans."

CHAPTER FOURTEEN: THE LEGACY YEARS (2011–2025)

1. Sandmel, "Irma Thomas," Music Rising at Tulane.

2. *Simply Irma, A Musical Play*, Anthony Bean Theater. https://anthonybeantheater.com/ProductionHistory-Simply%20Irma.htm.

3. Interview with Cilista Eberle.

4. Sue Strachan, "Irma Thomas' 75th birthday bash celebrates the 'Soul Queen of New Orleans,'" *The Times Picayune*, February 14, 2015.

5. Email interview with Chris Goldsmith by Scott Billington, August 19, 2024.

6. Eve Abrams, "Soul Queen of New Orleans Becomes a Doctor," *Morning Edition*, National Public Radio, May 29, 2018.

7. Barri Bronston, "Netscape co-founder, Saints hero, Grammy® winner, healthcare advocate to be honored at Tulane commencement," Tulane University News Releases, May 7, 2018.

8. Interview with Isaiah Gibbs by Johnette Downing and Scott Billington, New Orleans, 2024.

9. Spera, "Irma Thomas, Soul Queen of New Orleans, at 80."

10. Irma Thomas, liner notes, *Love Is the Foundation*, Newvelle Records, https://www.newvelle-records.com/collections/shop-newvelle/products/nvn001-irma-thomas#liner-notes-top.

11. John Swenson, review of Irma Thomas, *Love Is the Foundation*, *Offbeat* Magazine, New Orleans, January 28, 2021. https://www.offbeat.com/music/irma-thomas-love-is-the-foundation-newvelle-records/#:~:text=The%20whole%20package%20is%20a,shot%20portrait%20in%20meticulous%20detail.

12. Spera, "Irma Thomas, Soul Queen of New Orleans, at 80."

13. Interview with Michael Murphy by Johnette Downing and Scott Billington, August 8, 2024.

14. Interview with Michael Murphy by Johnette Downing and Scott Billington, August 8, 2024.

15. Keith Brannon, "Irma Thomas gets animated about the importance of clinical trials," Tulane University School of Medicine, April 15, 2022. https://medicine.tulane.edu/news/irma-thomas-gets-animated-about-importance-clinical-trials.

16. Katherine Hart, "After 50 years, Dew Drop Inn gets ready to open its doors," New Orleans *Uptown Messenger*, August 28, 2023.

17. Interview with Robert Mercurio and Ben Ellman by Scott Billington and Johnette Downing, August 27, 2024.

18. All Ben Chace quotes are from an interview with Johnette Downing and Scott Billington, October 15, 2024.

CHAPTER FIFTEEN: CODA

1. Interview with Ledisi by Cilista Eberle for *My Life in Music*, WYES-TV, New Orleans, 2021.

2. Interview with Bonnie Raitt by Cilista Eberle for *My Life in Music*, WYES-TV, New Orleans, 2021.

3. Aswell, "Irma Thomas," Louisiana Music Hall of Fame.

4. Aswell, "Irma Thomas," Louisiana Music Hall of Fame.

5. "The Fabulous Irma Thomas!"

Index

About the Authors

Photograph by Thom Bennett

Johnette Downing

Recipient of the 2017 Louisiana Writer Award, Johnette Downing is a musician, author, illustrator, and haiku poet who has performed on five continents, and has received numerous awards for her thirty-two books and thirteen albums. Her latest book *New England Animals A to Z* was published by Arcadia Children's Books in 2026, and her latest album is *My Little Snap Bean: Zydeco for Children*, a collaboration with Nathan Williams and the Zydeco Cha Chas. *Just Irma* is her second biography, following *The Spanish Tinge: Louisiana Music Pioneers of Canary Islands Descent* (Ediciones Idea, 2018).

Scott Billington

Multi-Grammy Award® winner Scott Billington is a musician, author, and record producer whose recordings by artists such as Solomon Burke, Johnny Adams, Charlie Rich, Ruth Brown, Buckwheat Zydeco, and The Dirty Dozen Brass Band have garnered thirteen Grammy® nominations. He has produced ten albums with Irma Thomas, including the Grammy®-winning *After the Rain*. Scott worked for many years as a staff producer for Rounder Records, a career recounted in his memoir *Making Tracks: A Record Producer's Southern Roots Music Journey* (University Press of Mississippi, 2022).

www.ingramcontent.com/pod-product-compliance
Lightning Source LLC
LaVergne TN
LVHW101604151026
850117LV00028B/177